IMAGES
of America

LOS ALAMOS
1944–1947

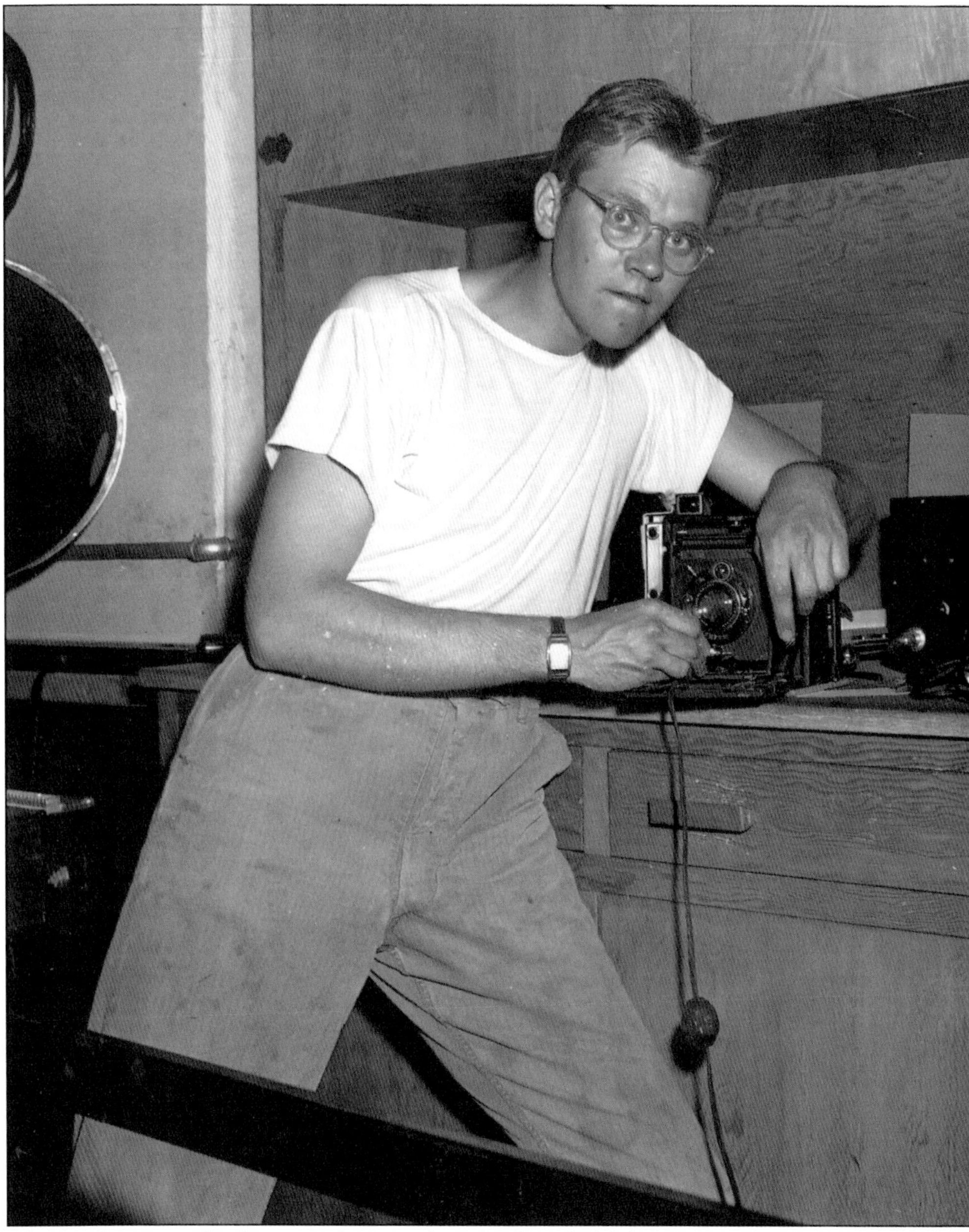

John Michnovicz takes his own photograph with a handheld shutter switch. As a young member of the Los Alamos photo group (he arrived at the Hill at age 20), he and his colleagues used whatever tricks they could improvise to document both the scientific progress and the social scene in Los Alamos during the exciting years between 1944 and 1947.

IMAGES
of America

LOS ALAMOS 1944–1947

Toni Michnovicz Gibson
and Jon Michnovicz

ARCADIA
PUBLISHING

ISBN 978-0-7385-2973-8

Published by Arcadia Publishing
Charleston, South Carolina

Printed in the United States of America

Library of Congress Catalog Card Number: 2004116966

For all general information contact Arcadia Publishing at:
Telephone 843-853-2070
Fax 843-853-0044
E-mail sales@arcadiapublishing.com
For customer service and orders:
Toll-Free 1-888-313-2665

Visit us on the Internet at www.arcadiapublishing.com

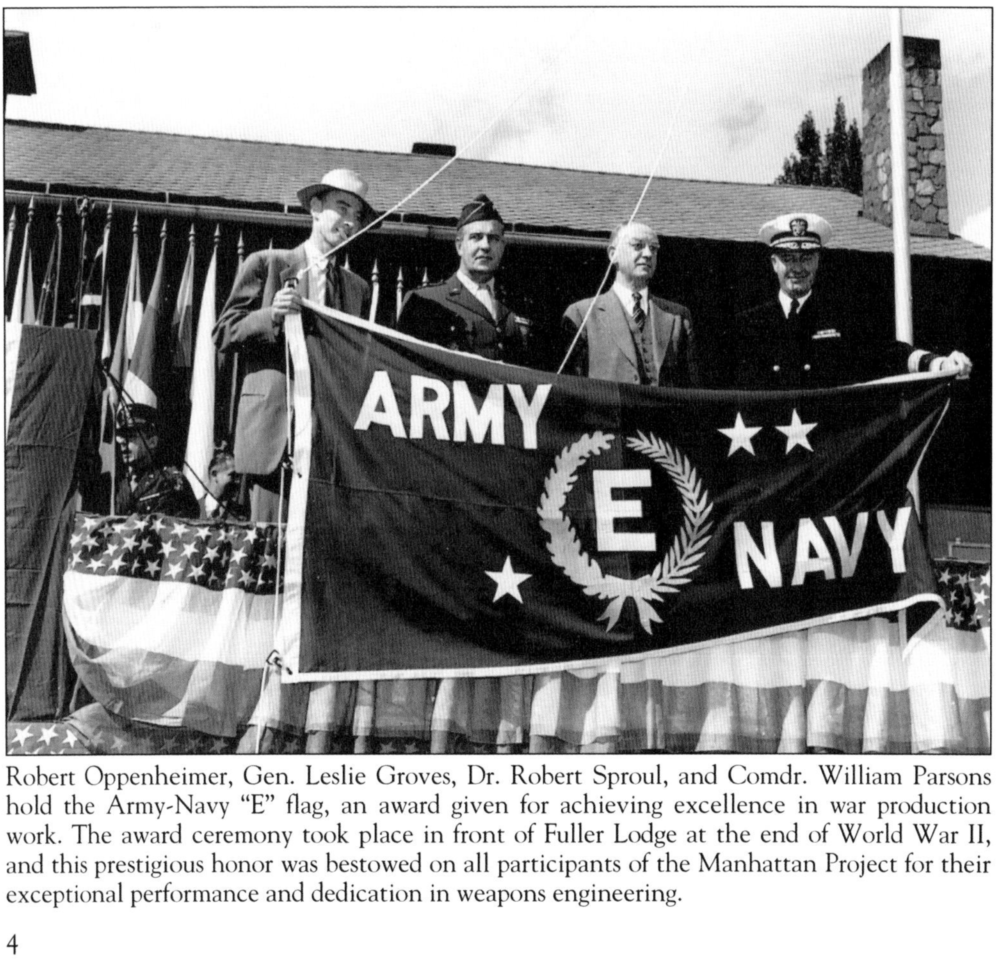

Robert Oppenheimer, Gen. Leslie Groves, Dr. Robert Sproul, and Comdr. William Parsons hold the Army-Navy "E" flag, an award given for achieving excellence in war production work. The award ceremony took place in front of Fuller Lodge at the end of World War II, and this prestigious honor was bestowed on all participants of the Manhattan Project for their exceptional performance and dedication in weapons engineering.

CONTENTS

Acknowledgments

This project is based almost entirely on the extensive collection of wartime photographs created by our father, John (Mike) Michnovicz, during his years in Los Alamos. Dad spent countless hours with us reviewing hundreds of photos. This oral history brought life to these photos and joy to our hearts as we traveled back in time, remembering friends and places from New Mexico's atomic beginning. Marylou Michnovicz, our wonderful mom, encouraged Dad, generously shared him for long stretches of time, and gave us pictures from her scrapbook. Many, many thanks to Sharon Snyder and the publications committee of the Los Alamos Historical Society who generously agreed to partner with us and added valuable research and caption information. Hedy Dunn, Rebecca Collinsworth, and Marianne Mortenson from the Los Alamos Historical Society were so gracious to locate photos, identify people, and review captions. Roger Meade and the Los Alamos Laboratory Archives researched the dates for several photos. Our appreciation extends to Joe Gluth and Elmer Donor who worked with our dad in Los Alamos and who gave us permission to include their photos. And we are very grateful for our families. Jon's family supported his frequent trips to New Mexico and long hours in the darkroom, and Toni's husband, John, faithfully encouraged both of us to press on until the project was done.

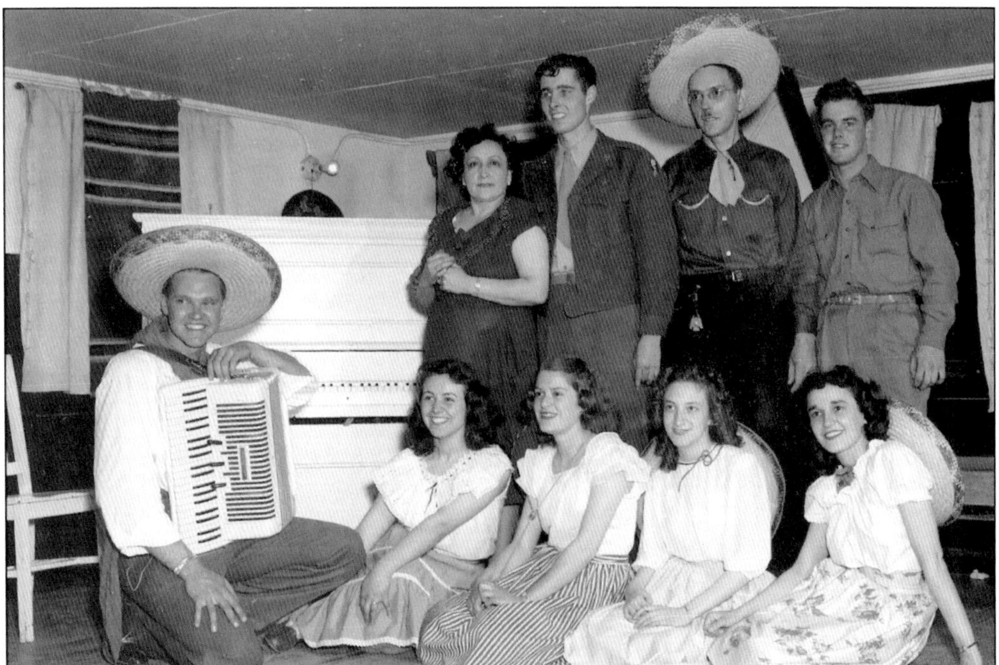

A 1947 fiesta for Los Alamos employees showcased John Michnovicz on accordion and the harmonies of Alice Gutierrez, Mary Louise Maloney, Marie Frank, and Connie Meyer. Social gatherings like these were organized by the Army chaplain and the Catholic pastor when military clubs were closing and Los Alamos was becoming a civilian town. Theresa Martinez, coordinator, stands next to Pvt. Les Bethel, singer; Pfc. George Hillhouse, square dance caller; and Pfc. Walter Sweeney, pianist. (Photo by Elmer Donor.)

INTRODUCTION

It is October 1944, and the whole world is at war. Men and women from towns and cities across America are being sent to far-flung regions of the globe. Pfc. John Michnovicz sits quietly on a train racing westward from Oak Ridge, Tennessee. He wonders why his orders say Manhattan Engineer District, yet he is traveling farther and farther from the East Coast.

Like so many others, he had been scooped up in the draft in 1943. Because of flat feet, he was disqualified from infantry service and, instead, given the opportunity to undergo testing for advanced technical training. He qualified for the elite Army Specialized Training Program (ASTP) and was sent on an accelerated course of engineering and physics studies at such colleges as the University of Michigan and the University of Maryland. Altogether, the Army placed almost 200,000 men in advanced training during the war.

His train eventually stopped in the tiny hamlet of Lamy, New Mexico, a few miles south of Santa Fe. The final destination still required an arduous trip up a winding road, full of switchbacks and cliffs. He was approaching "the Hill," the top-secret Army town of Los Alamos hidden in the Jemez Mountains. He and his fellow soldier-students were assigned as technical support staff for this project. Because Michnovicz's service record listed photographic activities during college, it seemed his Army career would involve shooting pictures, not bullets.

Before the war, northern New Mexico was dotted with numerous small ranching communities and about a dozen Indian villages. The Jemez Mountains also included a small private boys' school called the Los Alamos Ranch School. It was established in 1917 to provide a unique, outdoor education for teenage boys. Robert Oppenheimer, the scientific director of the Manhattan Project, owned a ranch east of the area, and knew firsthand about its isolation and obscurity. Los Alamos was ultimately selected in late 1942 to house this new community of scientists, soldiers, and local workers in an unprecedented effort to harness the atom.

Over the next few years, John Michnovicz would work on the Hill as part of the photo-documentation group that helped record this enormous undertaking. Everywhere he looked, he saw scenery, people, and activities that filled his imagination and would soon fill his camera lens. Michnovicz was inseparable from his camera during these years. He amassed a collection of more than 1,000 photographs of scientists, technical workers and laborers, award ceremonies, scientific conferences, buildings and barracks, and many other activities that took place on the Hill. Michnovicz was also an accomplished accordion player, and occasionally he would serve as both musician and photographer at the same event. For example, when a group from the Hill gathered at the San Ildefonso Pueblo for a dance, he snapped photos of scientists dancing with Indians and took pictures of well-known residents of the pueblo, such as the famous potter Maria Martinez. Then he would put his camera down long enough to strap on the accordion and play a few rounds for the square dancers.

A comprehensive view of the social and scientific world of Los Alamos between 1944 and 1947 was captured on film by this young man. This is a photographic journal of a time unique in American history, a time when disparate groups of people—who ordinarily would never even meet each other—would find themselves thrown together for a brief period in a small mountain town in northern New Mexico.

After the war ended, scientists and workers were released from the secret project, free to re-establish their lives elsewhere. However, many chose to stay in the Los Alamos area, thereby creating a new county for the state, host to the new Los Alamos Scientific Laboratory. For Michnovicz, the war's end meant transferring to Albuquerque to marry his new bride and begin what would eventually be a family of 13 children. His large collection of photos and negatives was safely tucked away in a back room of the house and forgotten.

Fifty years later, one of us (Toni) was perusing a memoir of women who had lived in Los Alamos during the war. One particular photograph was oddly familiar: it showed a wide panorama of mountains, mesas, and canyons, with a long winding road coursing slowly up the hillside. She knew this photo! It was hanging in a hallway of our Albuquerque home. Showing the book to Dad, he instantly recognized it and several other photos to be among the many he had taken on the Hill. He excused himself for a few moments, and soon returned with box after box of old photos, portraits, slides, and negatives from the period between 1944 and 1947. As a teacher, Toni instantly understood the unique value of this collection and the broad appeal it might have for Americans who were familiar with this important historic event.

But the task of presenting these photos would be a difficult one. There was a half-century of dusty memories to revive for Dad: long-forgotten associations and friends, famous scientists whose now-familiar faces were scarcely recognizable at a much younger age. Over a two-year period, each photo was sorted and identified and important details were recorded. A unique story emerged from the pictures. Individually, the photos captured the detail, and together they illuminated a simpler, yet very complex time, when a secret town of people from all over the world came together in New Mexico and the Atomic Age began.

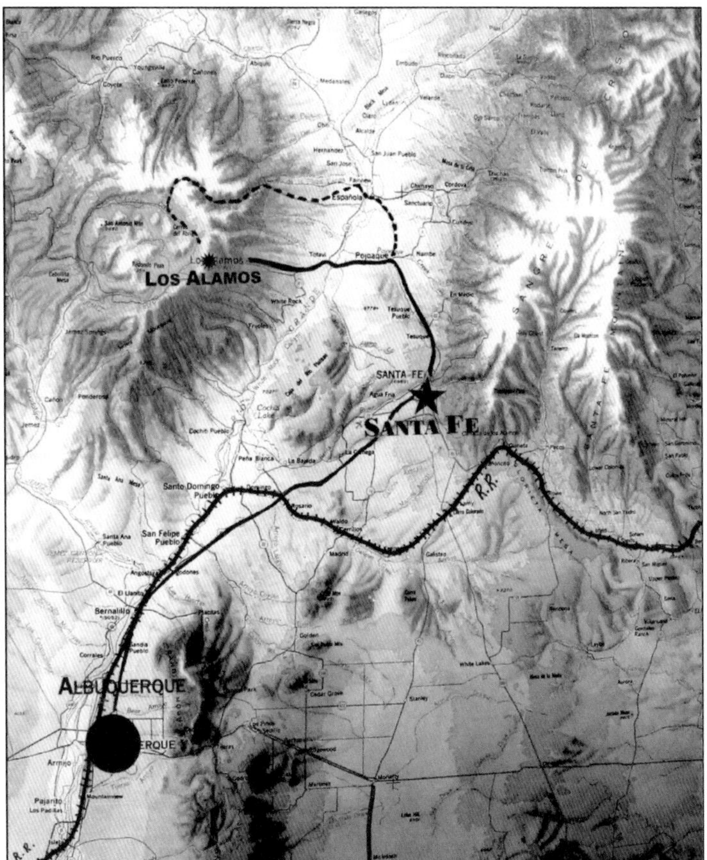

This topographical map indicates the locations of Los Alamos, Santa Fe, and Albuquerque. The circular outline of an ancient volcano, 15 miles across, is discernable just to the west of Los Alamos. The distance from Santa Fe to Albuquerque is about 60 miles. The two roads to Los Alamos are also indicated: the solid line shows the shorter, steeper route, and the dashed line shows a longer, but gentler route passing through Espanola. A branch of the AT&SF railroad can be seen south of Santa Fe (R.R.), with the Sangre de Cristo Mountains rising to the east.

One

Up the Hill to Los Alamos

Why was Los Alamos picked to complete the top-secret Manhattan Project? As with most endeavors, the choice was determined by three simple things: location, location, location.

By late 1942, it had become clear that a new Army facility was needed for the final phase in the development of an atomic weapon. Its tasks would include final processing of the fuel, assembly of the bomb, and successful testing of the device. Military planners knew that any potential site would have to meet a strict set of criteria. For example, a useful site would need to be kept secret for several years, and, therefore, would have to be fairly remote. Yet, if it was too remote, it might prove inaccessible to automobiles. Therefore, the following factors had to be carefully considered for any potential site:

- The population within 100 miles of the site had to be sparse, both for security purposes, and in case of an accident.
- Access by roads and railroads was necessary for bringing large amounts of personnel and material to the site.
- Housing facilities had to be immediately available to quarter the first personnel to arrive, and there needed to be room to grow quickly as the project proceeded.
- Some parts of the area had to be large enough to provide for adequate testing.
- The climate was to be mild enough to allow outdoor work to proceed throughout the winter.
- Water, electricity, and an adequate fuel supply had to be readily available.
- The ownership and/or easy acquisition of the land had to be considered.

Though other sites were still being considered, Los Alamos met each of the above criteria. For example, the area was largely government-owned forestland. A small ranch school located on-site could be purchased to meet the immediate housing needs. Space was available nearby for eventual growth of the Project. Northern New Mexico, while sparsely populated, did include a fair number of small ranching communities to help meet labor needs. Finally, some roads already existed, as did a branch of the Atchison, Topeka & Santa Fe (AT&SF) railroad passing just south of Santa Fe, about 30 miles away.

As we know, Los Alamos, nestled at 7,200 feet near the top of an ancient volcano, ultimately got the nod. Before long, new roads were being bulldozed and compacted, and soon hundreds of military people began to appear. The stage was set, and the race to build a secret bomb was under way.

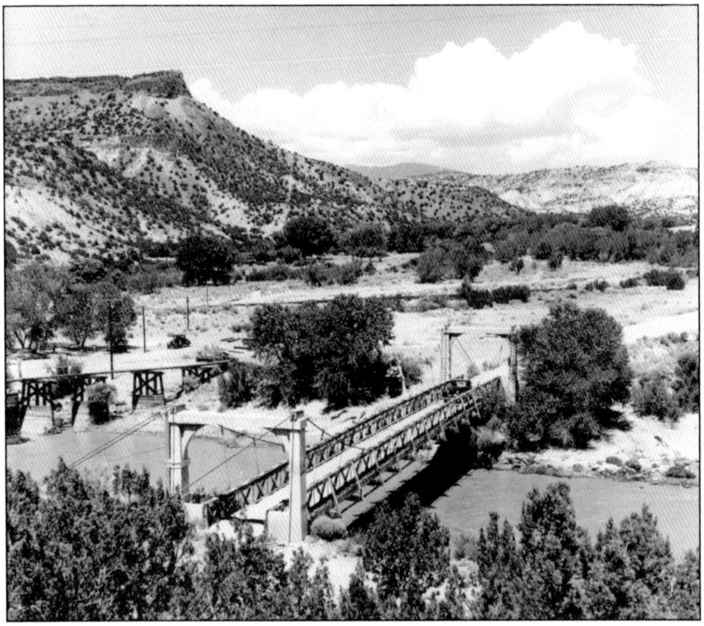

Approaching Los Alamos from Santa Fe, the shortest route crossed the Rio Grande over a bridge at Otowi, a Pueblo Indian word meaning "the place where the river makes a noise." This one-lane suspension bridge was built in 1924 with a 10-ton capacity, limiting its use to passenger vehicles. Entering the bridge required turning a sharp 90-degree angle from the adjoining road, an impossible task for some military vehicles.

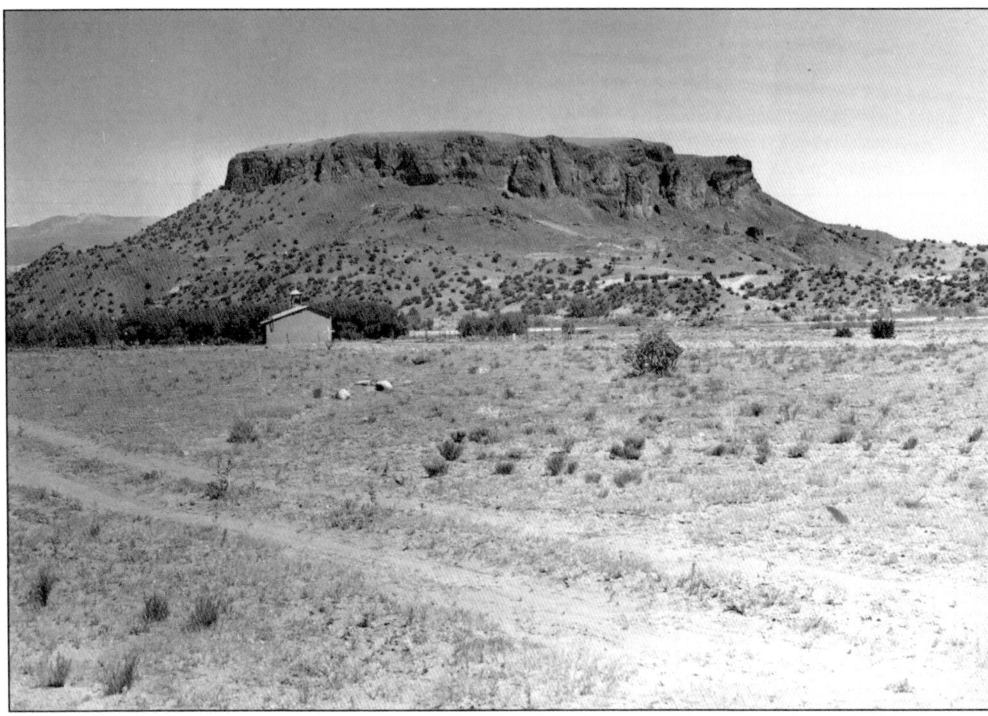

Los Alamos is situated near a huge extinct volcano, still evident in the volcanic plugs that dot the landscape near Black Mesa, shown here. Local Pueblo Indians consider this site sacred and used it as a refuge in the 1690s, when the Spaniards reentered the territory of New Mexico after the 1680 Pueblo Revolt. This photograph includes a small *capilla* built by the Vigil family. Originally a private chapel, it later became a community center and is now being restored as a local historic structure.

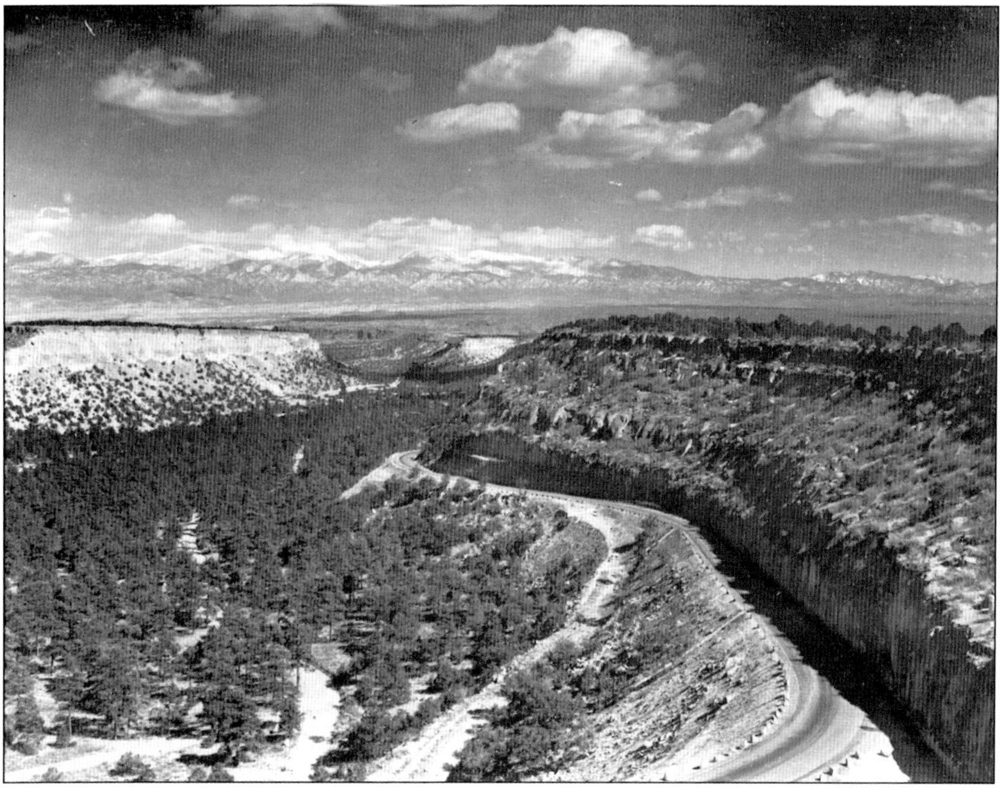

Looking east from Los Alamos, one sees the Sangre de Cristo range hugging the state capitol of Santa Fe. Construction of the newer road seen at right was begun in 1943, and asphalt was added mid-1944. It climbs upward toward the Pajarito Plateau—a mesa of fingerlike projections formed from ancient volcanic activity. Older dirt roads with dangerous switchbacks (center) originally granted access to the Los Alamos Ranch School, established in 1917. When the Manhattan Engineer District Project arrived in 1943, truck travel in these mountains was slow and laborious.

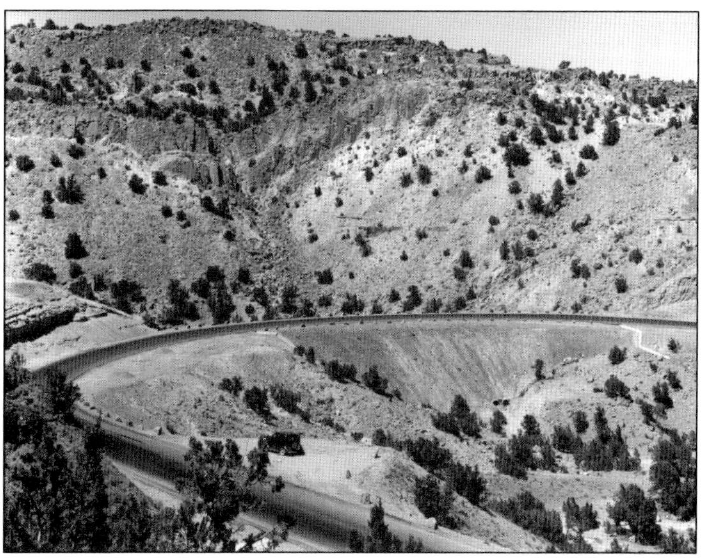

Arriving in Santa Fe at the end of their journey, military and scientific personnel were often surprised that the "Project" or "Site Y" was many miles farther up the road. Before the main road was surfaced with asphalt, travelers encountered fewer problems with mud and potholes by taking this alternative, though longer, northern route through Española.

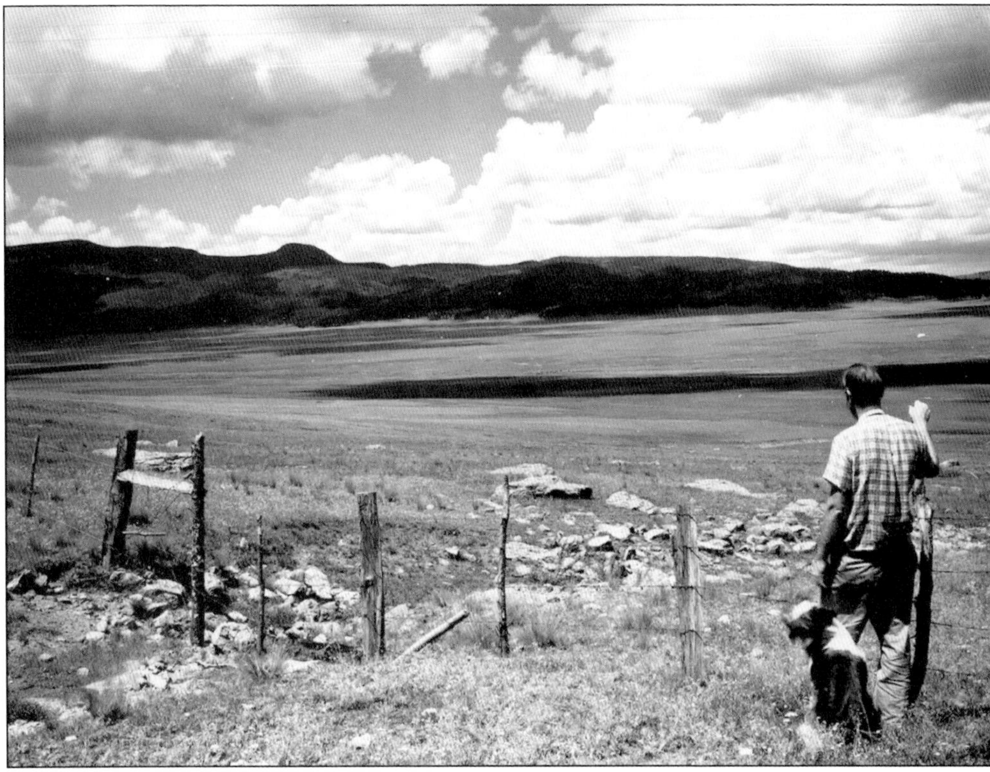

The Jemez Mountains west of Los Alamos contain four wide-open valleys in the crater of the ancient volcano. The largest of these is Valle Grande, being admired here by Gil Campbell, a native of Detroit hired in 1946 to be the tech librarian. Several eruptions about 1.4 million years ago made the recent Mount St. Helens explosion seem feeble by comparison. Together, the four sister valles comprise the Valles Caldera, a 15-mile-wide depression at the heart of the extinct volcano.

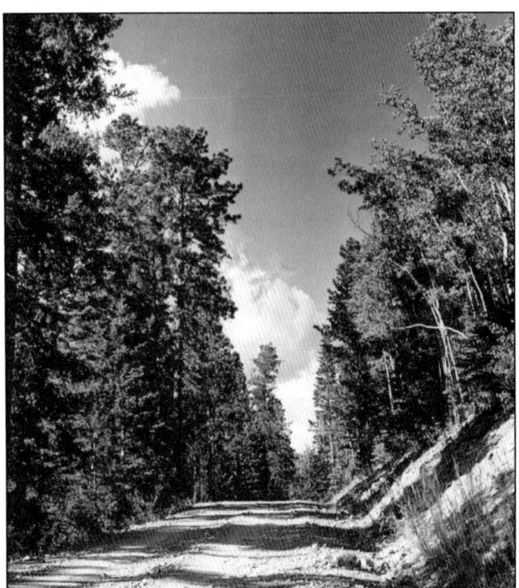

This is the road to Jemez Springs, a small town in the mountains west of Los Alamos. Forest peaks, ghost towns, waterfalls, old haciendas, lush meadows, pre-Columbian ruins, thriving Indian villages—it has all the elements that make northern New Mexico so distinct. The Jemez Mountains contain several active geothermal springs, hence the name Jemez Springs. This town was also considered as a possible site for the project but was rejected by Gen. Leslie Groves and by Robert Oppenheimer, who felt its canyon location too confining.

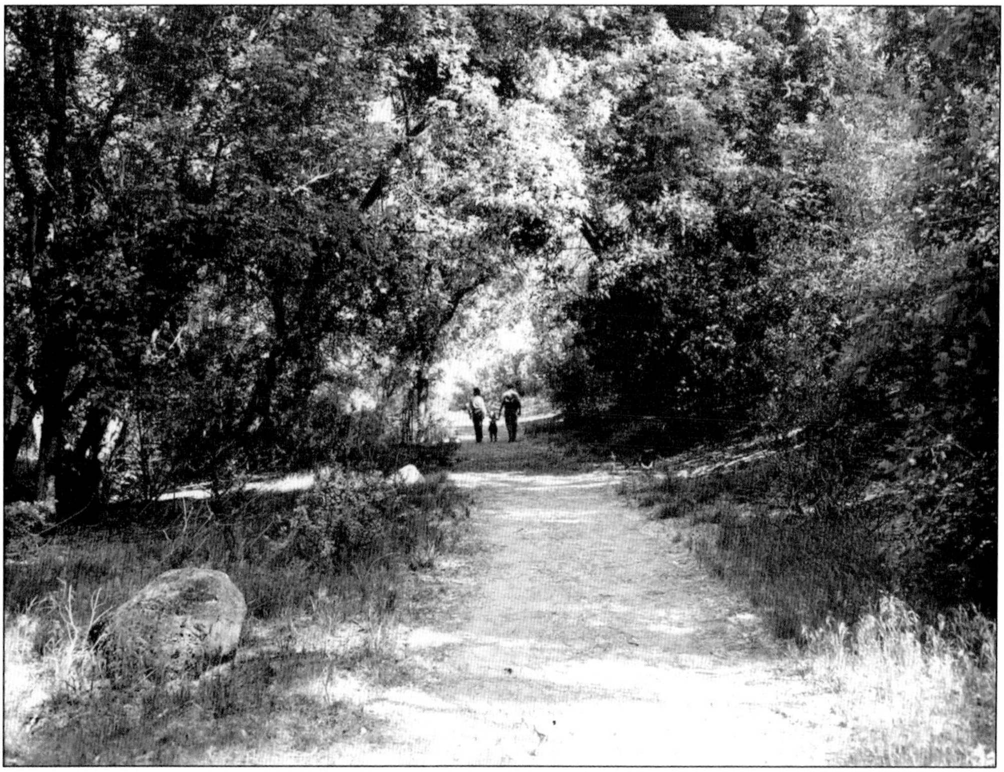

A family is shown hiking along one of the many roads and trails found in the Jemez Mountains. Scientists and civilians worked long hours throughout the week, and Sunday was often a day to rest, explore, hike, and picnic in the surrounding canyons and mountains. The rugged setting at Project Y was spectacular and scenic, more so than other Manhattan District sites, including Project X in Oak Ridge, Tennessee, and Project W in Hanford, Washington.

Los Alamos is nestled in mountains of 7,200 feet, making for many cold and snowy winters. The American Southwest, however, is nearly always sunny, and the cold doesn't linger. This point was essential to military planners, who knew that intense work must proceed briskly throughout the winter months as well. Stunning scenes, such as in this photo near Los Alamos, were always close at hand—bubbling creeks running through forests of pines and aspens.

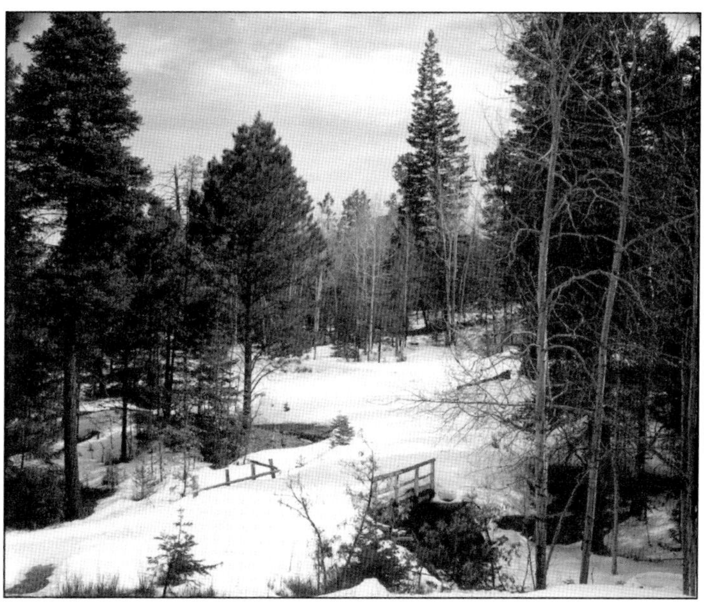

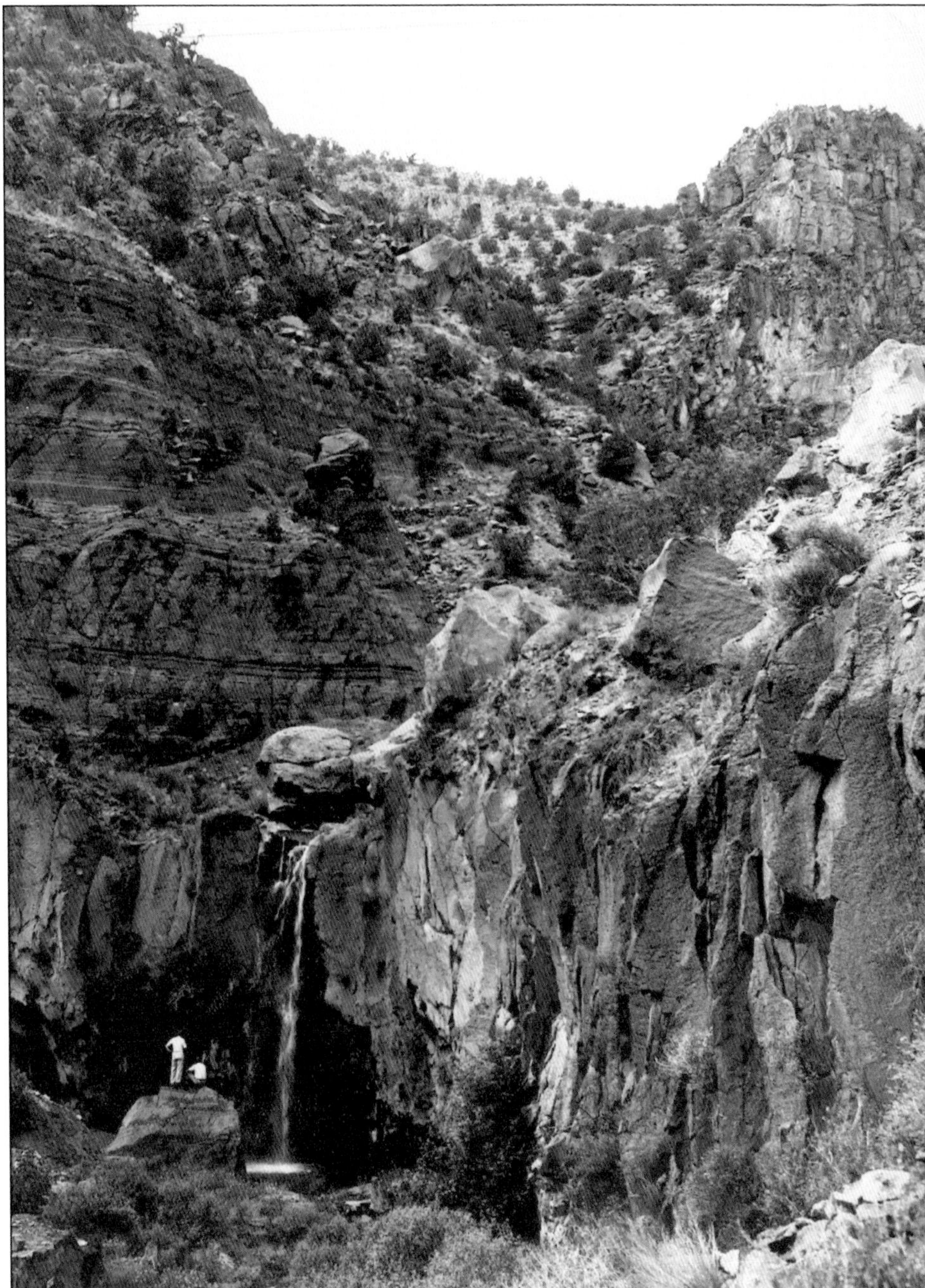

The Frijoles and Jemez are but two of the many creeks and rivers carrying snowmelt from the mountains down to the Rio Grande. Here we see the Upper Falls of the Frijoles River as it flows through Bandelier National Monument five miles south of Los Alamos. Filled with ancient Indian ruins, the site is named after Adolph Bandelier, an early explorer and ethnologist who studied the Pueblo Indians in the 1880s. Years of erosion through the layers of volcanic ash and basalt created these elaborate rock formations. Many residents and scientists from the nearby Project visited regularly, including Stanislaw Ulam, who remembers lively discussions with Enrico Fermi as they traversed the canyons.

Ancestors of the modern Pueblo Indian tribes, called the Anasazi or "ancient ones," occupied cliff dwellings in Frijoles Canyon as far back as A.D. 1200. Layers of volcanic ash deposited from huge explosions over a million years ago eventually created this soft rock known as tuff. The people carved their homes into the cracks and crevices of the tuff, creating rooms for storage and sleeping. This view shows the ruins of the Long House, complete with wooden ladders for entering and exiting the rooms.

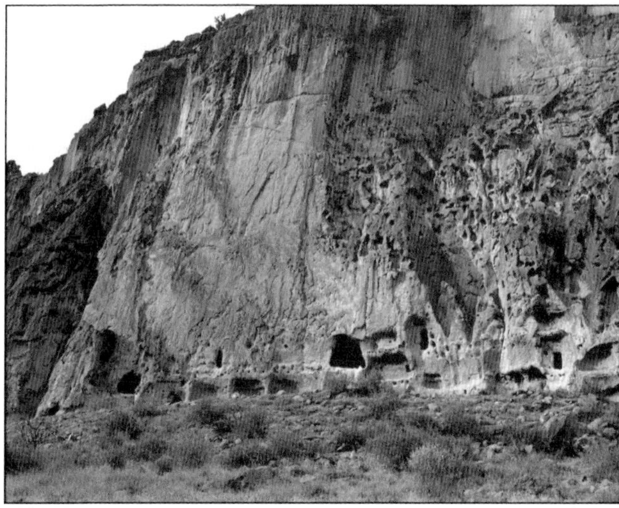

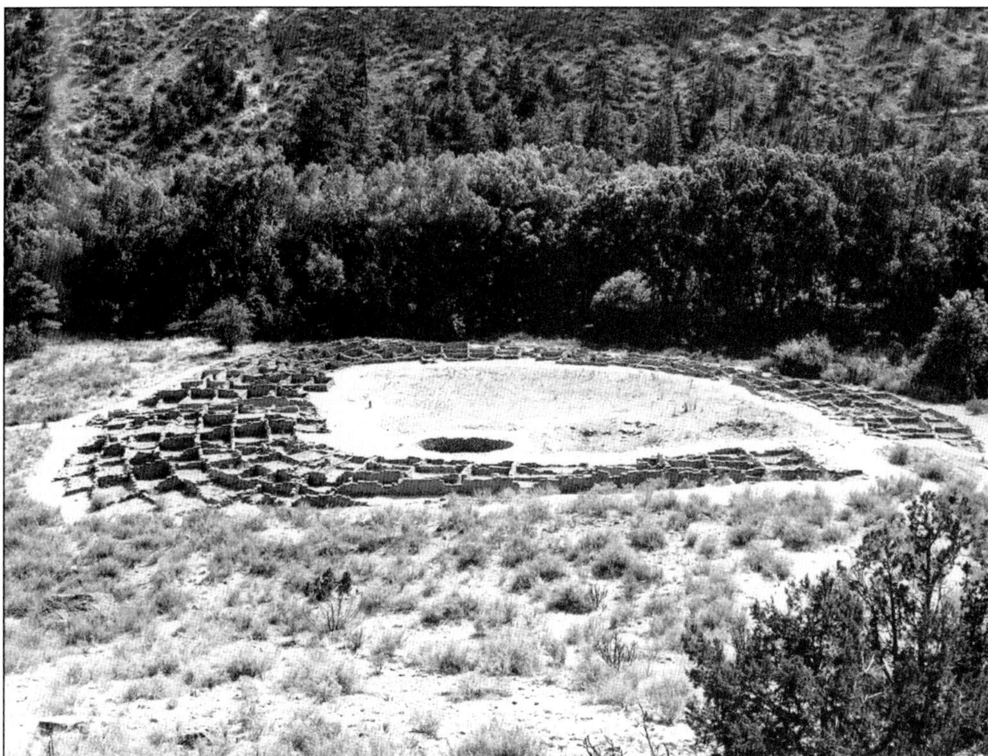

Frijoles Canyon contains the ruins of an ancient Pueblo settlement called Tyuonyi, first excavated in 1908 by Edgar Hewett. This photo shows some of the remaining ruins. The original pueblo was three stories high and included separate kivas, or ceremonial chambers, used by the men. Earlier, Hewett had proposed that the entire area become the Pajarito National Park, but he faced vigorous opposition from local homesteaders, ranchers, and lumbermen. The Bandelier National Monument was established under the U.S. Forest Service in 1916 and transferred to the National Park Service in 1932.

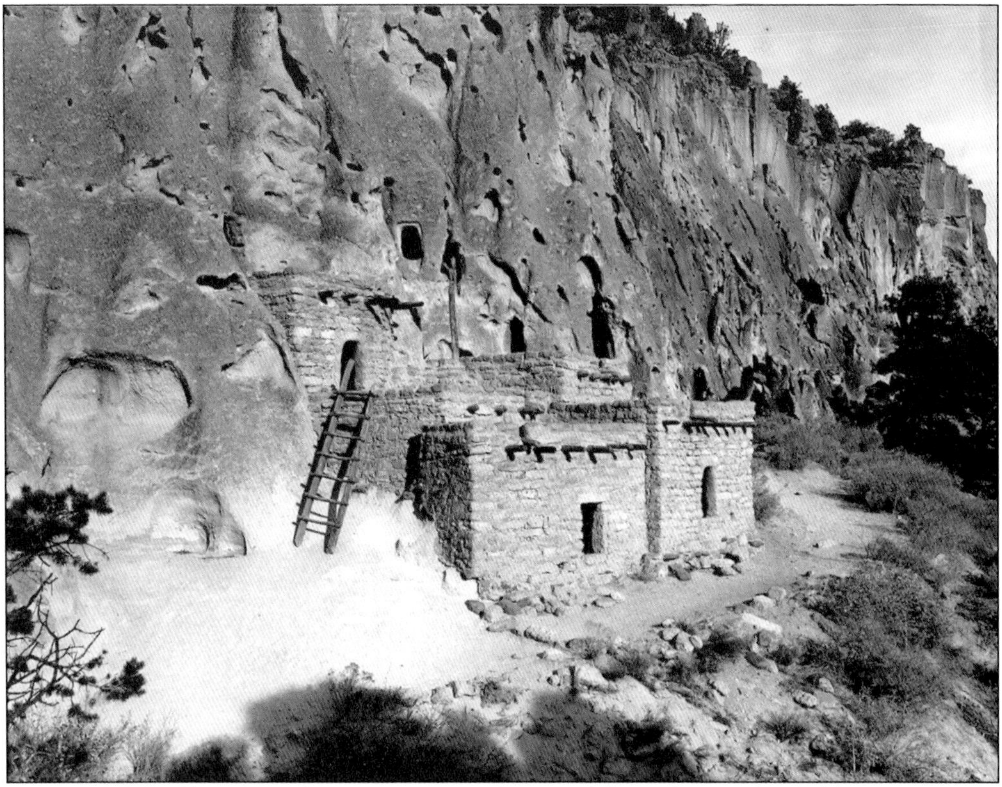

Several cliff dwellings have been reconstructed in Bandelier. The wooden ladders seen in this photo provided access to upper floors and were easily retracted for safety. Many dwellings were abandoned in the 1500s, probably due to prolonged drought. It is thought that populations from these and other abandoned ruins moved south to establish the present-day Pueblo cultures. These ruins provided evidence that the entire area had long been home to Indians prior to the arrival of the Manhattan Project.

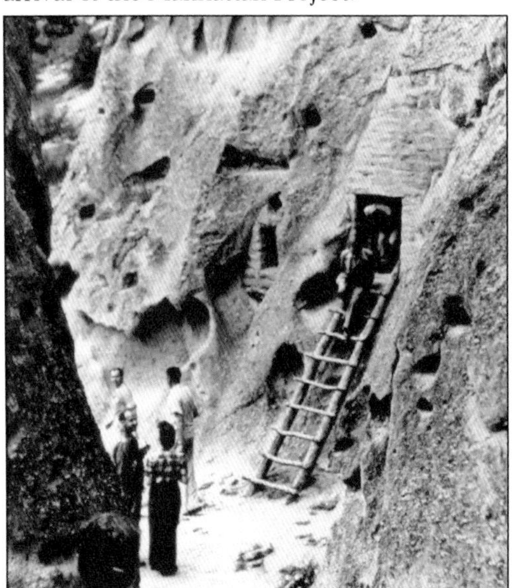

Several residents, including scientists and civilians, enjoyed climbing in and out of the ancient cave dwellings located a few miles from the Project. These recreational outings gave the visitors a chance to glimpse life as it would have been lived in these mountains hundreds of years before their arrival.

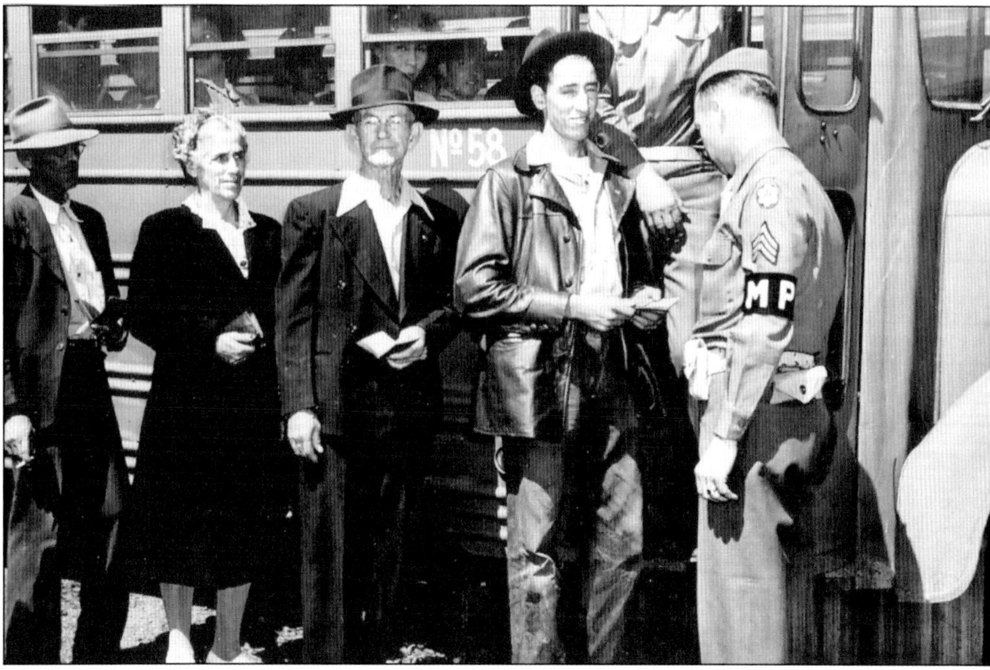

A group of employees prepares to board the bus to Los Alamos. Buses routinely traveled a circuit of over 50 miles through Española and Chimayo, as well as the San Ildefonso, Santa Clara, and Tesuque Pueblos. Free bus service for the maids, clerks, cooks, and mechanics working on the Hill was an important part of the solution to the perennial labor shortage.

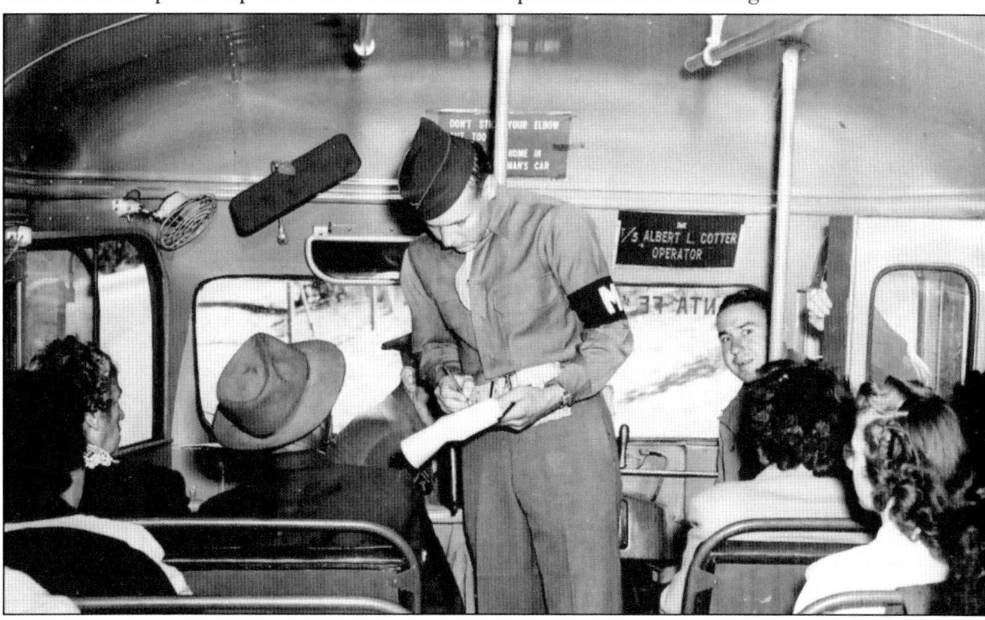

The Army bus also provided the occasional return trip to civilization in the form of a visit to Santa Fe. Everyone was instructed to mind his or her own business while in town. In this photo, an MP checks the identities and destinations of all travelers. In the earliest days of the Project, two seven-person station wagons were sufficient to transport residents to and from the site. By December 1946, however, about 500 passengers in 43 buses were making the daily round-trips.

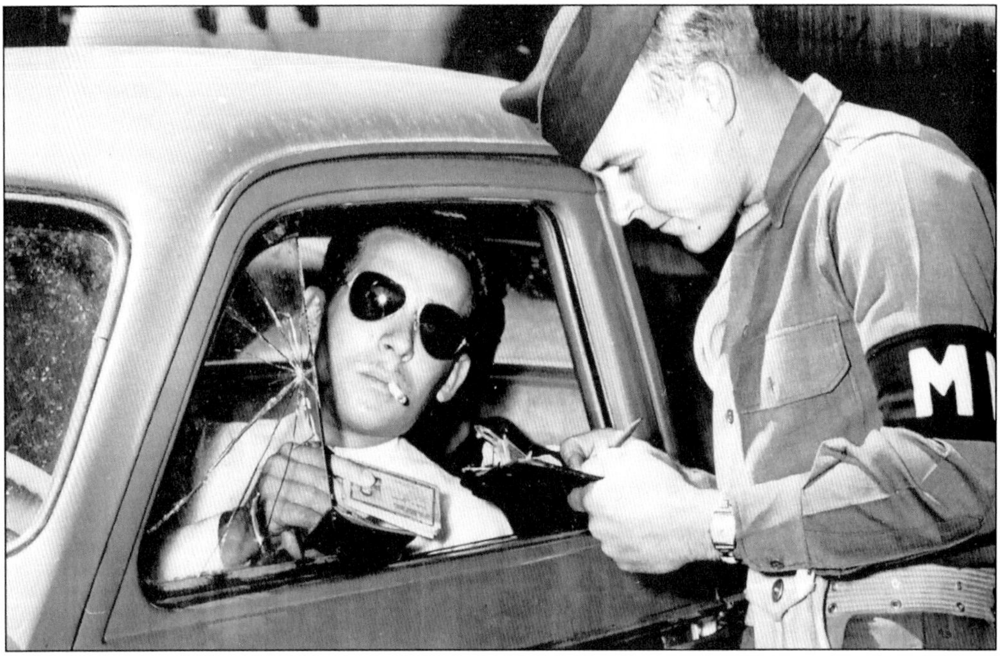

Anyone driving a car near the Project was expected to produce proper identification to the military police at any time. Automobiles were frequently subjected to ID checks. The *Daily Bulletin* from April 17, 1944, had this advice when stopped: "It cannot be overemphasized in the interest of preservation of life, limb and property that all individuals either afoot, mounted or in vehicles STOP whenever it appears that the guard indicates such a desire either by actions or by order."

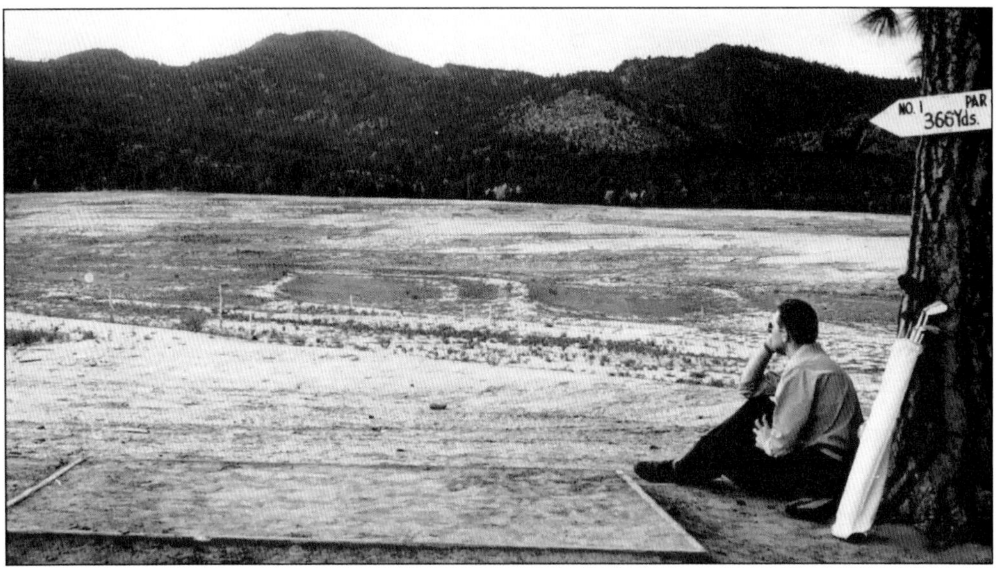

The ring of mountains surrounding the Pajarito Plateau, seen here, gave Los Alamos a snug sense of security. These were necessary ingredients to insure the completion of the secret Manhattan Project. Yet workers were often unhappy with the isolation of their mountain town, the absence of many of life's conveniences, and the mysterious nature of their work. The Jemez Mountains offered some relief from these struggles, as this dreamer quietly contemplates the future. (Photo by Joe Gluth.)

Two

Home, Home on the Hill

By late 1941, America was at war, and the nation knew that the next several years would bring sacrifice, privation, and even loss of life. As the team in Los Alamos settled in to do its job, nobody expected to live in luxury. As difficult as life seemed at this remote outpost, it was much worse elsewhere. After all, most soldiers had buddies overseas, struggling to keep alive in a jungle or desert.

One of the most complicated logistical tasks on "the Hill," as the Manhattan Project site came to be called, was housing. The population required for such a massive project was woefully underestimated and the housing construction never kept pace with the demand.

Housing-related issues were complicated by the fact that a schism of sorts existed between military and civilians. Many civilians on the site were university professors, and several had traveled there with their families. For the most part, these individuals had little interest in the military and no desire whatever to don a uniform. Several were Nobel laureates, who did not expect to be housed, bunk-bed style, around a smoky potbellied stove.

The scientists were assisted by a detachment of highly trained technicians recruited by the Army to meet several essential needs of the Project. This group was called the 9812th Special Engineer Detachment (SED) and numbered 1,823 men by late 1945. SED men worked all hours of the night and were ill suited for mandatory early morning drills. Bernice Brode, one of the wives writing years later, recalled "the SED boys were quite different from the regular post soldiers. They looked, in spite of the uniforms, like budding professors instead of combat troops . . . as they marched across the field, the newly arrived SED boys were terrible. They couldn't keep in step. Their lines were crooked. They didn't stand properly. They waved at friends and grinned."

Housing needs for all these people were initially met with buildings previously occupied by the Los Alamos Ranch School. These included 27 houses, dormitories, and other converted spaces. As a means of maintaining good will between the military brass and the scientific team, many of the top scientists' families were quartered in the stately ranch school buildings.

As the Project proceeded, however, there was always some sort of housing shortage. The population arriving on the Hill continued to grow throughout the war. By the end of the Project, many different types of housing arrangements were required. Possibilities ran the gamut from private trailer homes to government trailers, dormitories, hutments, and military-style barracks. As time went on, private homes were added as well. Many of the trailers and dormitories remained in place for several years after the war.

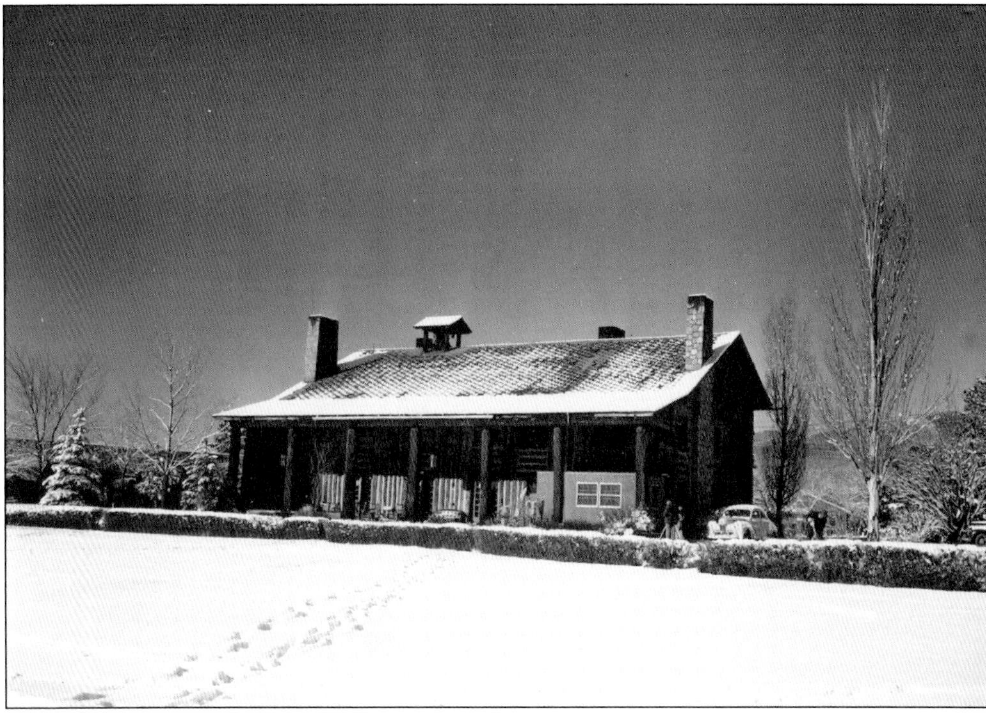

The Los Alamos Ranch School already occupied the future Site Y when the military arrived towards the end of 1942, and its main landmark was Fuller Lodge, shown here. Architect John Gaw Meem designed the lodge in 1928. It was named for Edward Fuller, an early staff member, whose father financed the construction of the building. The lovely log building had French doors that opened onto an expansive porch and a large stone fireplace that graced the end of the main room. Upper levels had single rooms available for housing. Fuller Lodge became a focal point for the Los Alamos community as well.

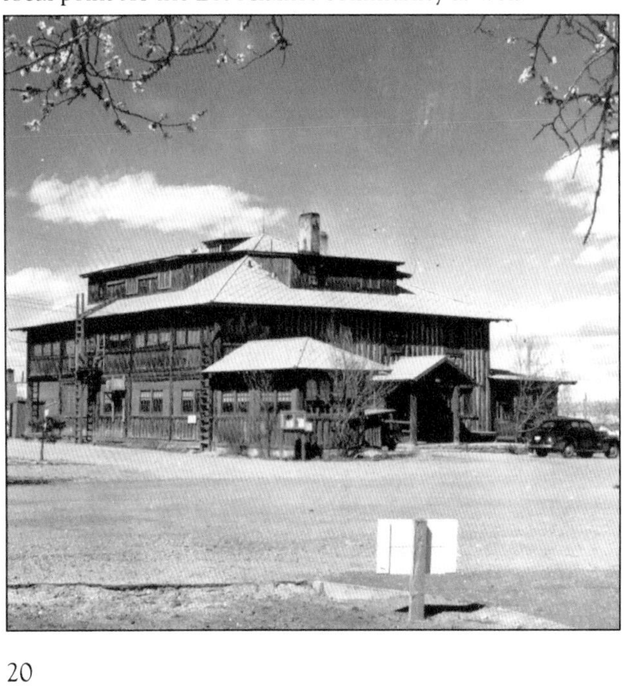

This Ranch School building was called the Big House and was the dormitory for the boys' school. The school's goal was to provide city boys with training in the rugged outdoors. Students slept on the porch summer and winter, with only canvas window coverings to provide protection against rain and snow. The Big House dominated the landscape during the Manhattan Project and was used as housing for single men, as a library, radio station, chaplain's office, and Red Cross Headquarters.

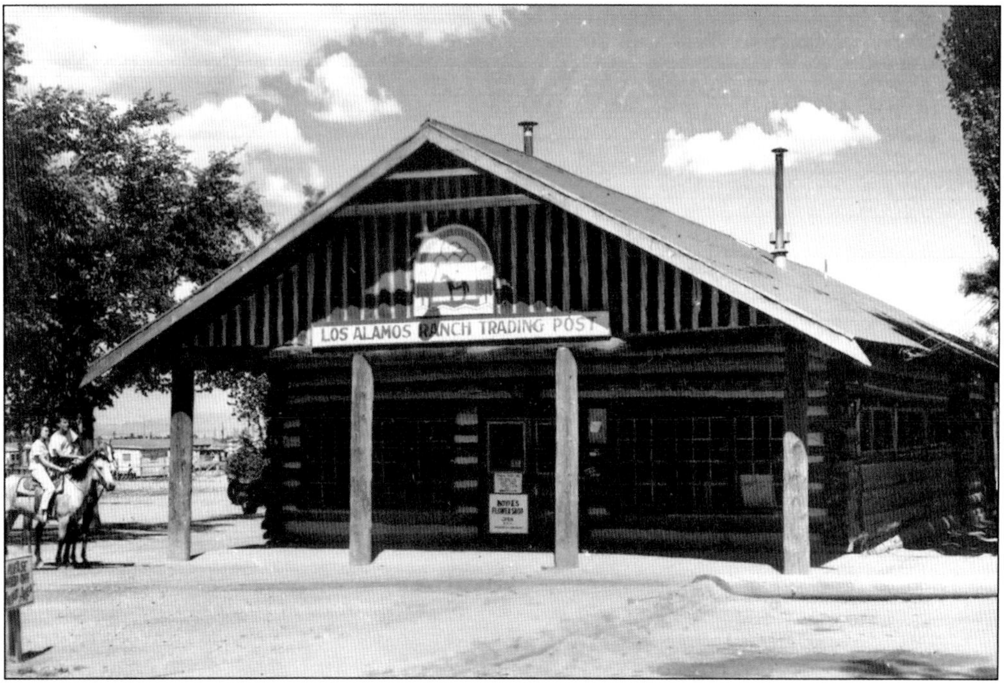

The Los Alamos Trading Post carried staples and supplies for the Ranch School. Many logs were used for this building, and the schoolboys contributed by stripping the bark before they were set in place. The structure initially served as the post exchange (PX) during the Manhattan Project, a place where residents could purchase beer, ice cream, cigarettes, and lunch items. As the population grew, the PX was eventually moved to an adjacent building called T-7, and the Trading Post became a general store with gifts and drugstore items.

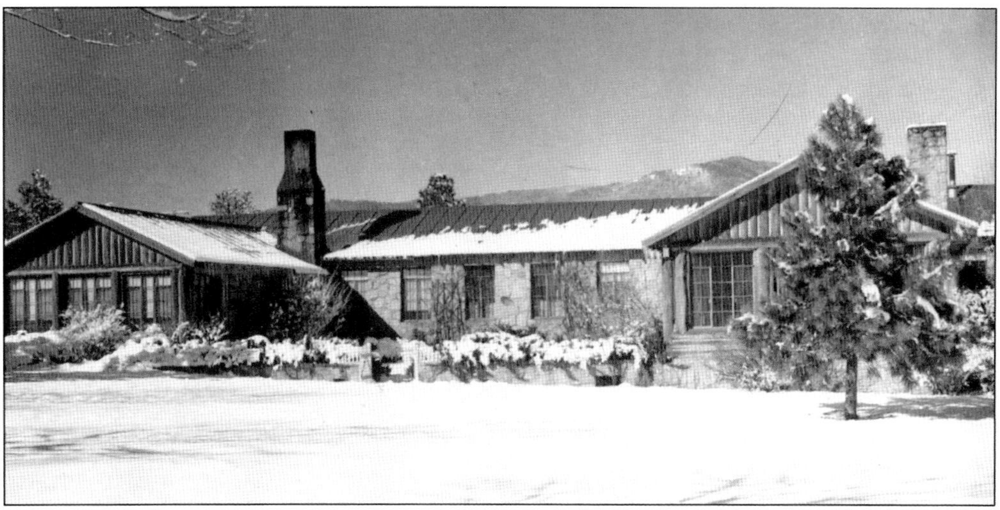

The original arts and crafts building shown here dates to 1934 and provided classrooms for woodworking, carpentry, and science for the Ranch School. Army engineers remodeled and renamed it T-114 in 1943. At first, it was divided into two apartments but later became a single-family home. This and other residences near Fuller Lodge were known as "Bathtub Row," as they were the only homes at the Project with that amenity. The families of both Enrico Fermi and Norris Bradbury lived in T-114 at various times.

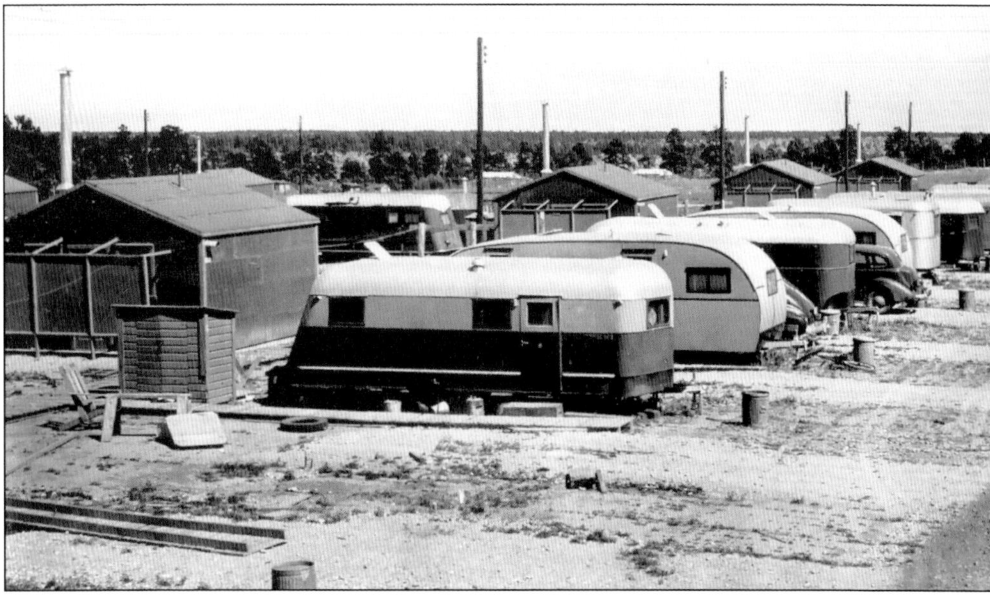

The rustic scenery of the Ranch School soon gave way to long rows of private and government-owned trailers seen in this photo. They were situated on the eastern edge of Los Alamos. Many employees brought trailers with them, and soon there were 250 of them in a five-block area. Community latrines and showers were erected between the trailers. Trailer life continued long after the war. As late as January 1947, Lt. Col. William Penly, deputy chief of operations, continued to advocate for improvements in heating and locking the latrines.

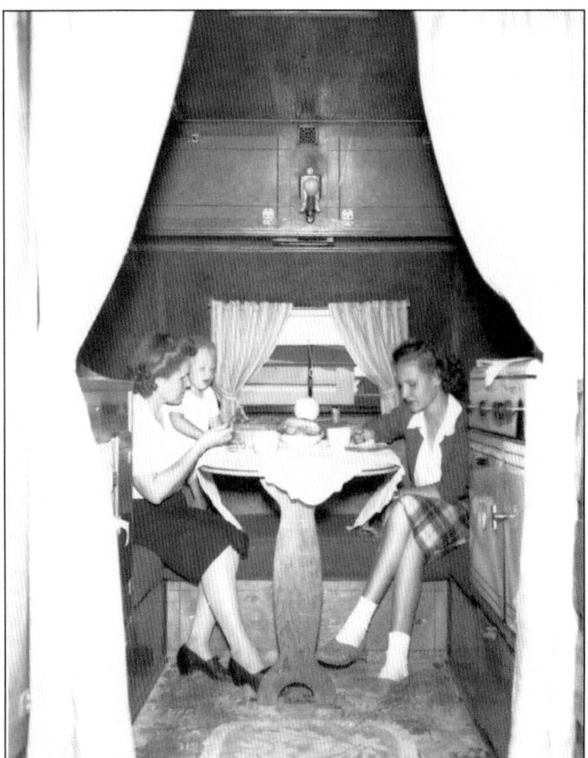

Private trailers could be rented for only $5 a month, but space was tight for families such as Melba Morris and her children, shown here. Morris worked in the photo lab making dry duplicates of engineering drawings. Wives were strongly encouraged to work at the site to keep the number of outside employees to a minimum. The population grew rapidly, however, nearly quadrupling from 1,500 in early 1943 to almost 5,700 by the end of 1944.

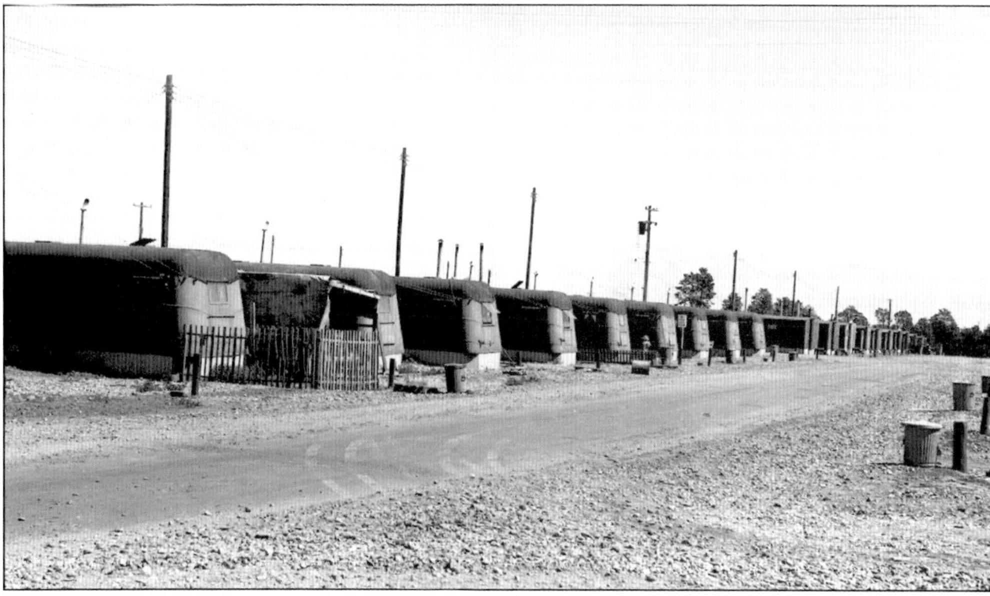

As many as 47 government-owned trailers were also available at the site. These structures rented for $28 a month, a price that included all utilities. The trailers were considered temporary housing. Though Los Alamos gradually evolved into a permanent town after the war, critical housing shortages persisted well into 1947. Government trailers, therefore, remained occupied throughout this period.

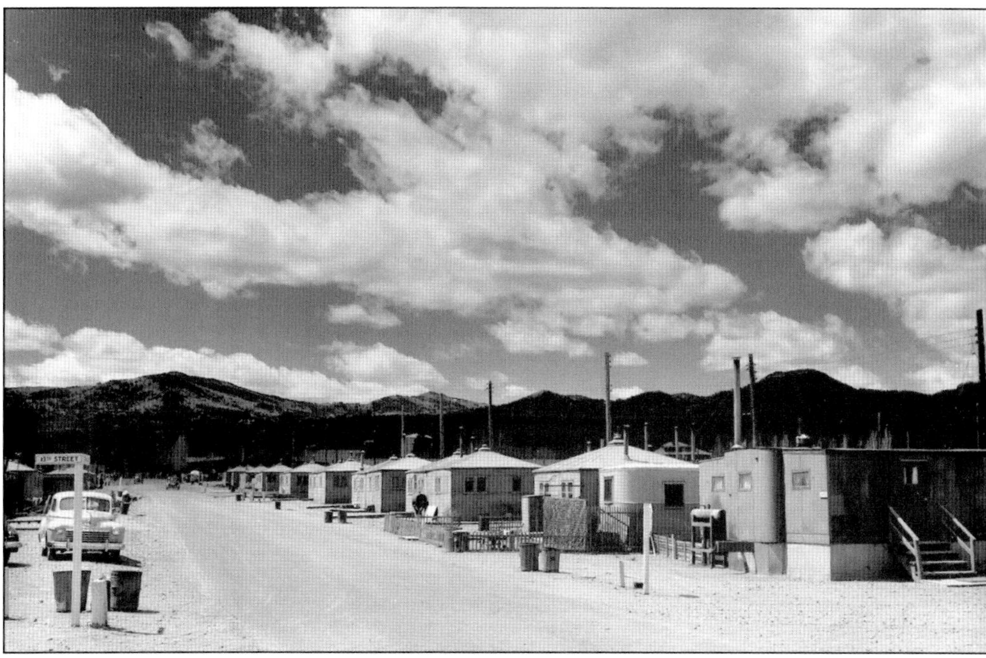

The building on the far right was one of 25 "expansible trailers." These were erected upon concrete foundations, with the side walls folding out and the floors folding down. Lined up neatly alongside this trailer were small square residences called "hutments." Hutments were considered a step below apartments, and rental rates were reduced by 15 percent. While some occupants added picket fences and landscaping, the tenement look remained.

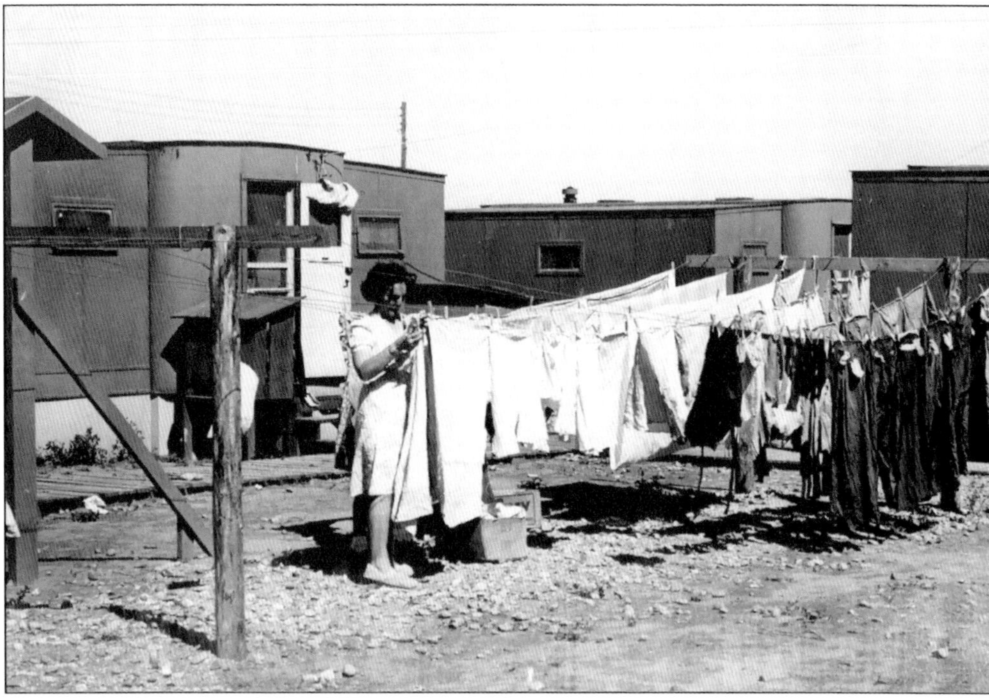

Tucked in between and behind the trailers and hutments, one could usually find a clothesline. Clothes dried quickly in the dry, sunny New Mexican climate. The local practice of hanging laundry out to dry in rain or shine, summer or winter, was not to the liking of many scientists' wives. Eleanor Jette commented in her memoir, *Inside Box 1663*, that "her basket of clothing was safe on a newspaper, but her feet were firmly stuck in the mud."

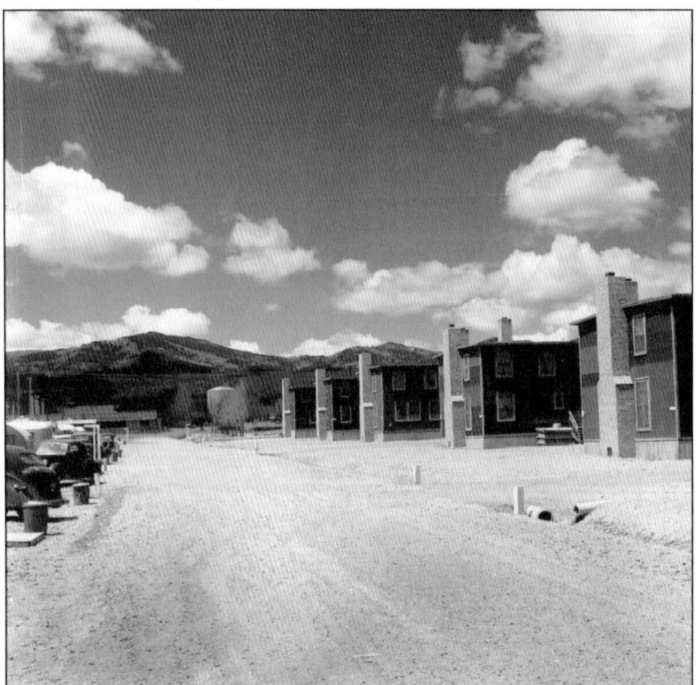

There was a huge population of single men and women at work on the Project. The most efficient way to provide them with housing was to build dormitories, many of which are visible in this photo. The dormitory buildings were situated near the trailers. Dorm rooms were also available for some married couples without children. Monthly rents ranged between $6 and $13. By the end of 1946, there were 36 dorms housing over 1,200 people.

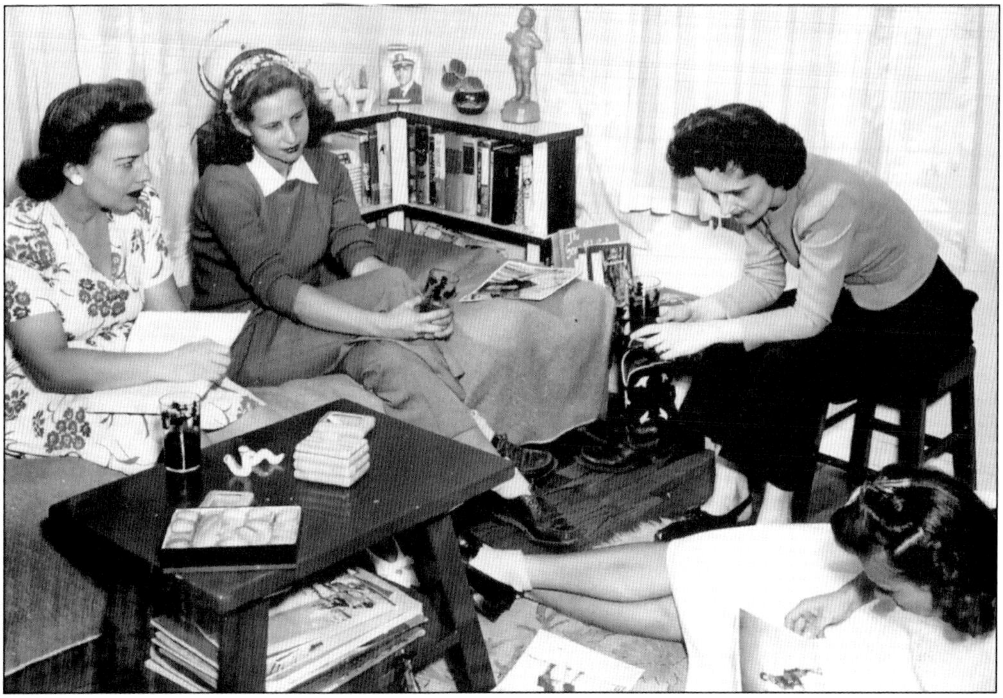

Dormitories might have seemed stark and dreary from the outside, but the rooms became comfortable and cheery once the young women and men moved in. This photo was taken to document the living conditions in Los Alamos. There seemed to be a constant housing shortage on the Hill during these years, and construction of new housing was never-ending.

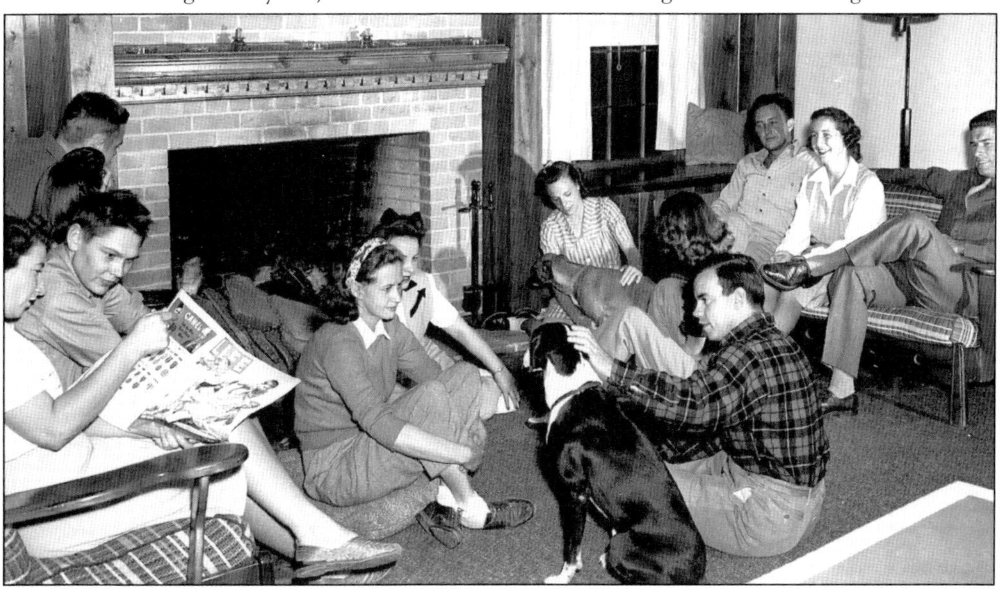

Each dormitory building had a large common room with a working fireplace, where men and women gathered to socialize and dance. Dorm residents were allowed to have pets, so that on quiet evenings friends and their animals could visit and relax. Veterinary care for the animals was supplied by the government at a small cost. Prescriptions cost 25¢, and the hospital rate for pets was 25¢ per day.

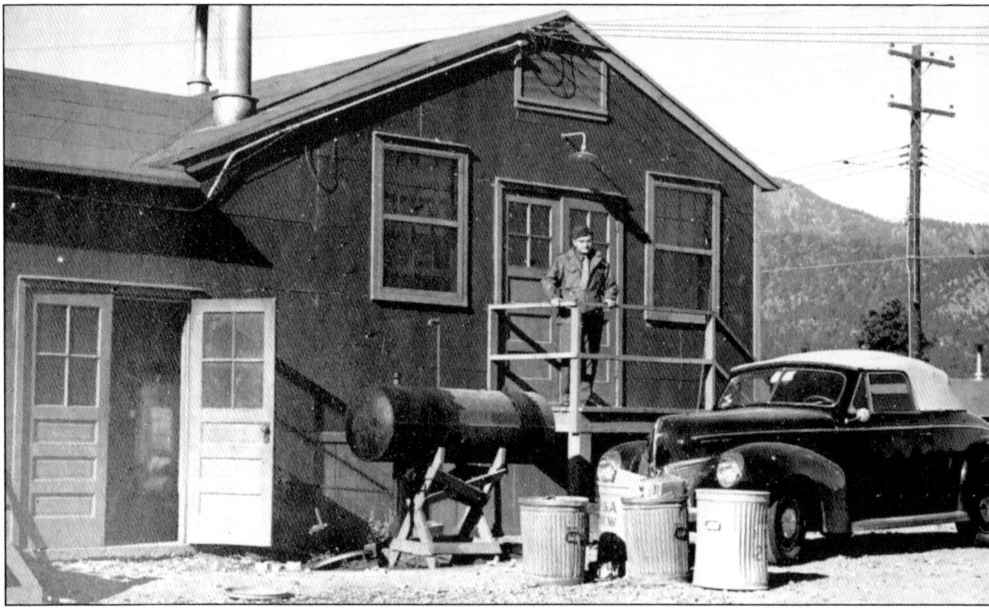

In addition to dormitories, traditional military barracks were also built. These buildings were typically overcrowded, with bunks packed around a propane or coal-burning stove in the center of the room. Here we see Stan Zembaty stepping outdoors for some fresh air. The car is a 1940 Mercury Convertible Coupe, packing a 95-horsepower V-8 engine. Cars went out of production in 1942, as factories converted to wartime production.

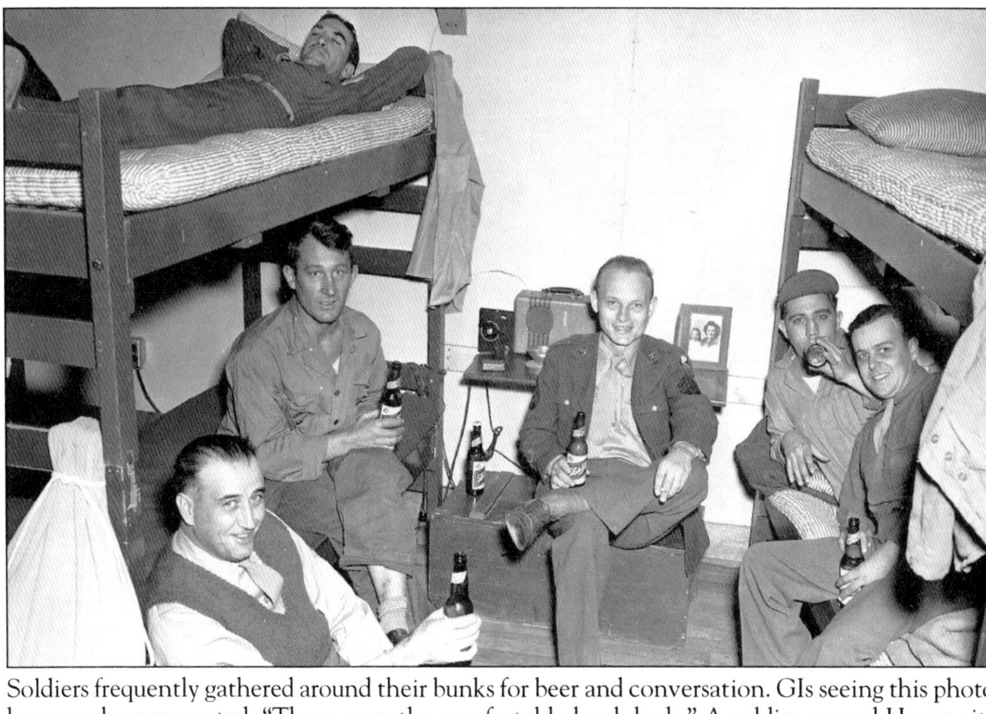

Soldiers frequently gathered around their bunks for beer and conversation. GIs seeing this photo have wryly commented, "Those were the comfortable bunk beds." A soldier named Harms sits on the footlocker at center. Joe Klein is visible on the left top bunk, and Jim Cavelli is taking a sip on the lower right bunk. The others are not identified.

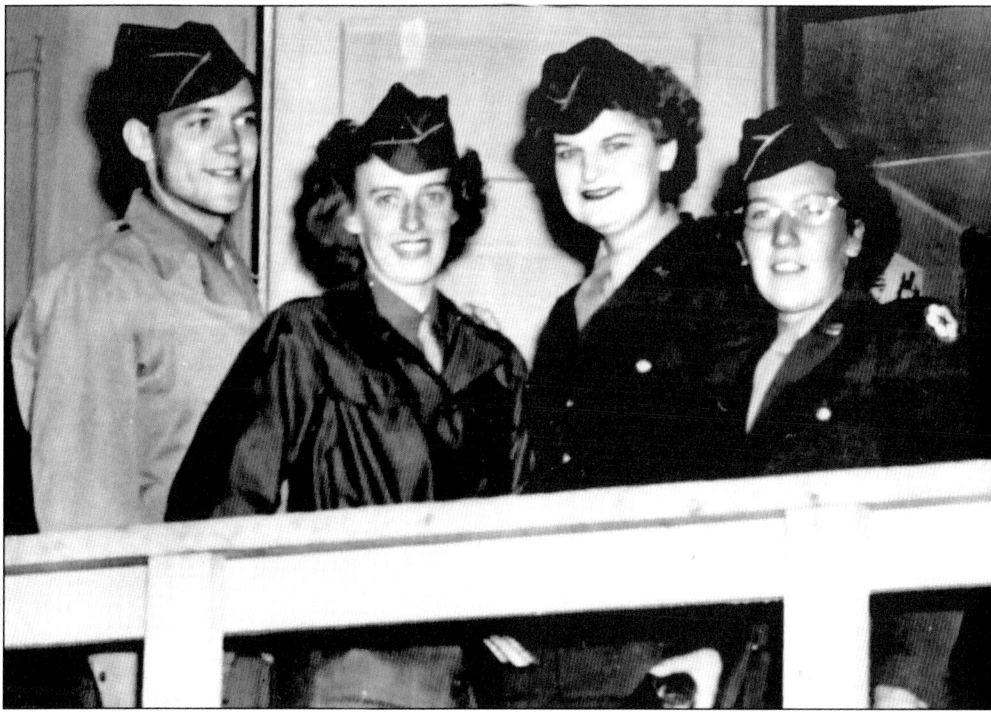

Roger Rasmussen (left) stands next to Jane Keller at the Women's Army Corps (WAC) barracks, along with two unidentified friends. Roger and Jane were married while in the Army. By 1945, there were so many married soldiers and WACs that suitable housing was simply unavailable. A rotating schedule was developed whereby couples could enjoy the use of an apartment for two weeks. The Rasmussens continued to work in Los Alamos as civilians for 30 years following the war.

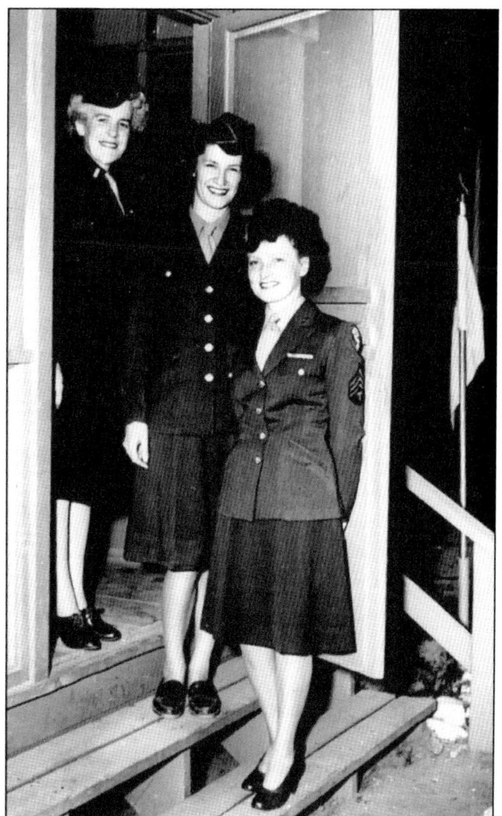

Lack of privacy was a concern for many WACs in their barracks. These units were placed so close together that some women complained the men could see directly into their rooms. Pictured here are Nellie Wallen (left), Lillian Roach (right), and an unidentified friend. Such inconveniences did not stop the WACs from doing their jobs as telephone operators, drivers, clerks, hospital technicians, and librarians. WACs also worked in chemistry, drafting, and experimentation divisions in the Tech Area. At its peak, their detachment numbered around 260.

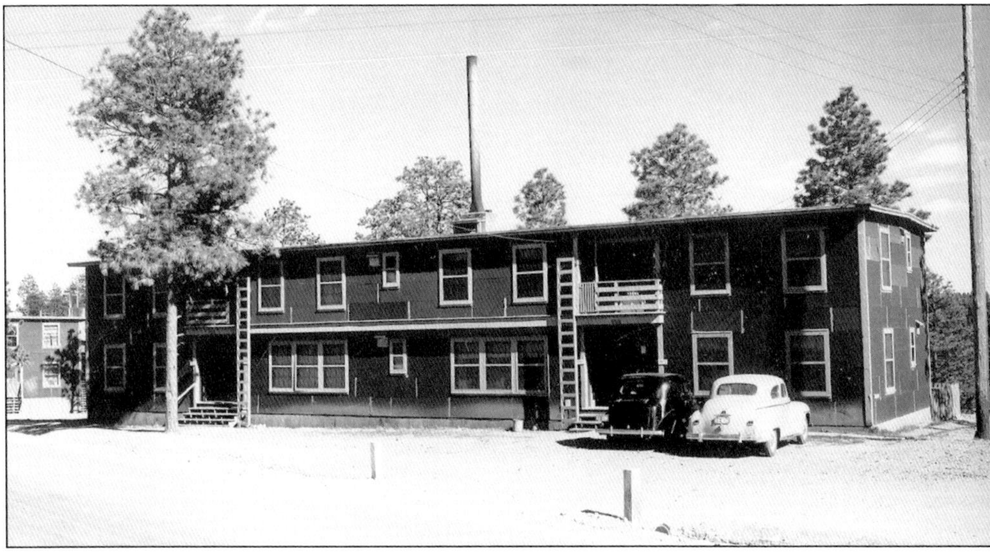

The Sundt Construction Company became the first contractor to build apartments for families arriving on the Hill. Initial estimates of 300 people needed for the Project were so inadequate that housing construction barely kept pace with demand. Row after row of apartment buildings sprang up and were immediately filled. The efficiency apartments pictured here were actually very small one-bedroom units. Bathrooms had showers only, since bathtub manufacturing had ceased due to the unavailability of cast iron.

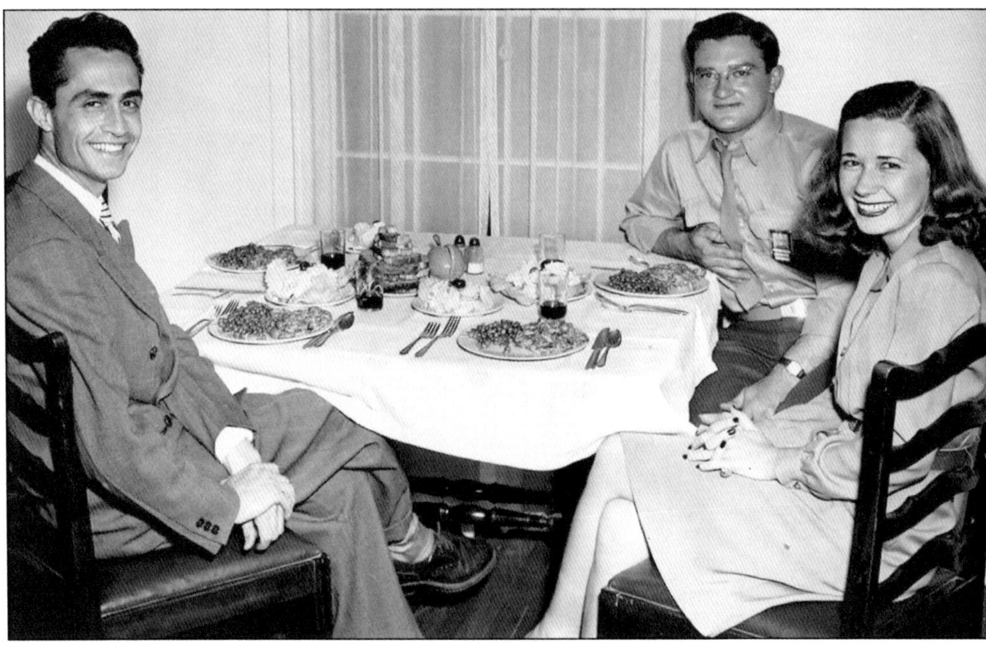

A group of friends gathered for a private Thanksgiving dinner celebration in 1945. Wright Langham sat opposite his wife, Ruby, at the feast, with Stan Zembaty in between. Both Mrs. Langham and Zembaty were photo lab employees. Civilian couples kindly extended hospitality to marooned soldiers on the Hill, often including them in holiday celebrations. The final place at the table was set for John Michnovicz, who was busy taking the picture.

These Sundt apartments had hardwood floors, fireplaces, and built-in bookshelves. Ruth Haley and her two children were photographed here to document housing arrangements in Los Alamos. Many apartments were overheated, with windows propped open even in winter. A large coal furnace typically supplied heat for four units within one building. Kitchen cooking stoves that used wood or kerosene were fondly called Black Beauties, and their inefficiency caused a near black market in electric roasters and hot plates.

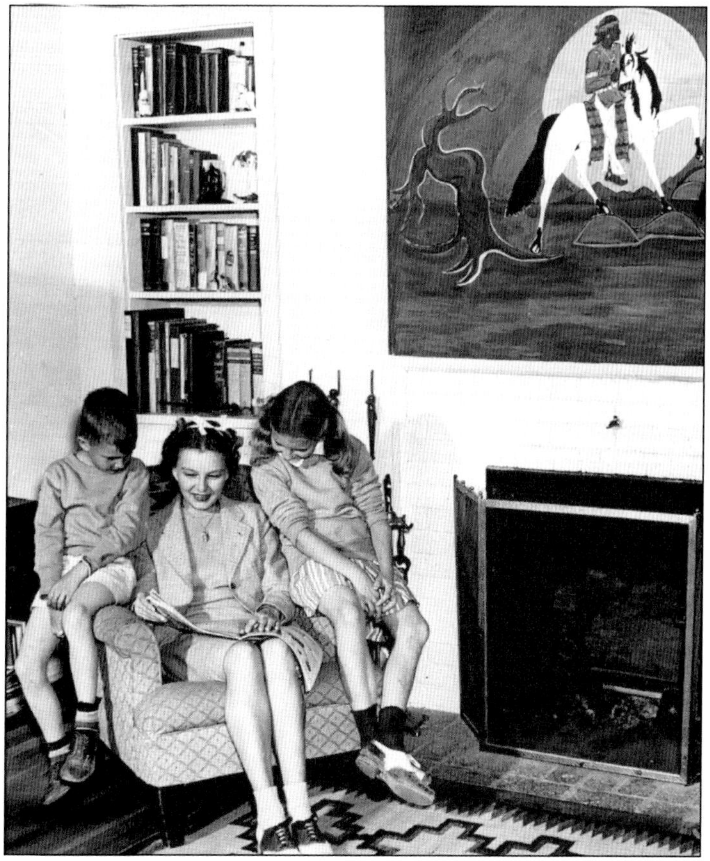

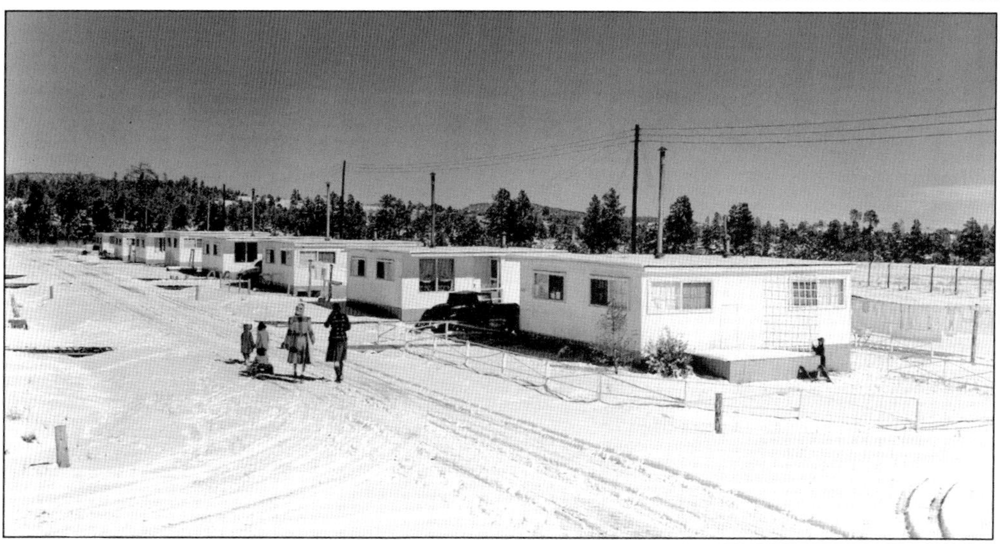

As the population increased throughout 1944, junipers and piñons were uprooted to make room for housing. The area shown here was affectionately called McKeeville and consisted of small prefabricated houses. Homes looked alike and were lined up military-style. They were built by the Robert McKee Construction Company and were the first single-family homes erected on the Project. Even in winter, clothes could be seen hanging out to dry.

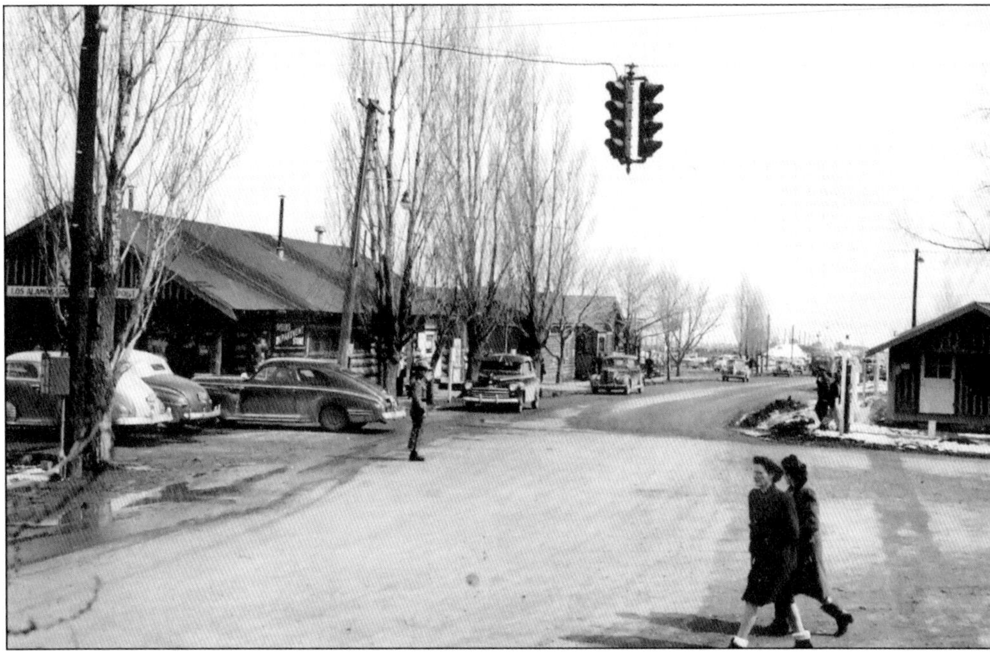

For a town that would change the course of history, the busiest street intersection in Los Alamos in 1946 still had a small town feeling. The MP seen in the center was assigned after the town council received suggestions "that one be stationed at the intersection near the Trading Post (left) to direct the large flow of traffic at that point." The local newspaper sponsored a contest to name the three main streets in Los Alamos. This street was one that gained a new name—Central Avenue.

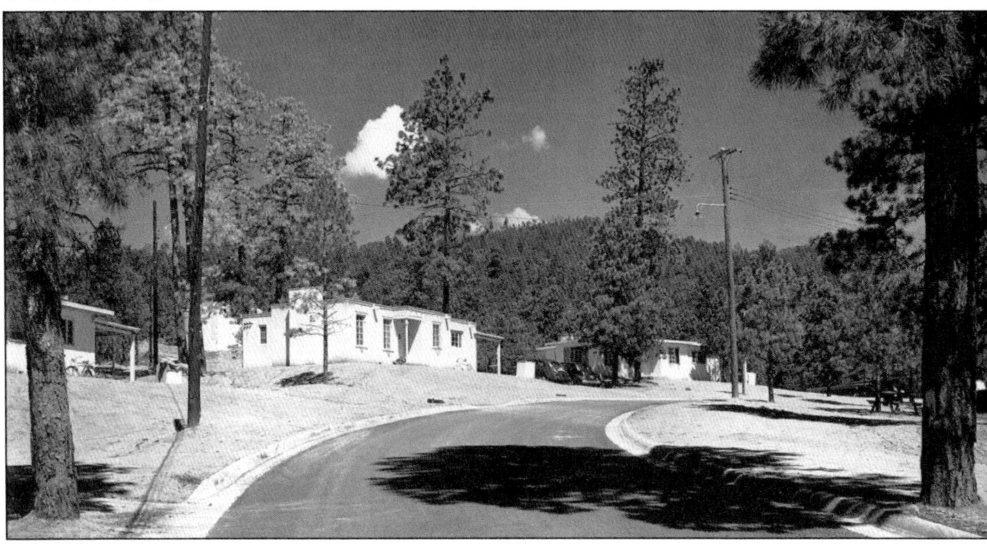

The Western Area, shown here, had been a golf course and horse pasture prior to the summer of 1946. As permanent housing was being constructed, Project engineers cooperated with the town council to preserve the natural contours of the land and save all trees over 12 inches in diameter. Traffic flow was reduced using curved roads and cul-de-sacs. Each unit had a bathtub, and for the first time, homes did not all look alike. Builders sought to please contemporary tastes, and before long, families were eager to move in.

Three

Life in the Secret Town

John Michnovicz was once asked how he felt when he first arrived in the desert southwest so many years ago. "Miserable, at first," he replied. "Why?" the questioner continued. "It was so sunny, so hot, and so quiet." Of course, these became the very reasons why he would never leave.

Life in this secret town was disorienting and disconcerting for many other residents of the Hill as well. First of all, there was the altitude to consider. Los Alamos was a vertical town of dizzying heights and precipitous cliffs. It took one's body weeks or months to acclimate to less oxygen and less moisture. Steep box canyons had been carved into the hillsides by eons of erosion. The thin air seemed scented, and the winds whispered rhymes through the Ponderosa pines. Most people on the site had never lived on the edge of a volcano.

This rapidly growing community was a military installation and that alone created certain difficulties for the civilian scientists. For example, George Kistiakowsky, the physicist in charge of explosives, once complained to General Groves about how badly he thought the technical teams (SEDs) were being treated. The SEDs were actually part of the military, but just like their professorial mentors, they were not eager to dress and act the part of soldiers. Kistiakowsky recalled, "Of course Groves immediately told me that as a civilian I had no business to tell him anything about Army matters."

Finally, this little town was just full of young women and men. As the population soared toward 6,000 in 1944–1945, small groups of GIs, WACs, and civilians were visible everywhere, heading out together for one social event or another. As soon as the work shift ended, there were romances to pursue, hair to be trimmed, shoes to be polished, and nails to be manicured. It is safe to say that a large percentage of people in Los Alamos were more concerned about learning a new dance step than speculating about the true nature of their secret project.

In the end, life was not so different than life at any other stateside military facility during the Second World War. Some people married, some had babies, and some learned physics. Children played in the hills, learned to ride horses, and hunted for arrowheads and lizards. People may not have known the true purpose of their secret community, but that was not about to stop them from living!

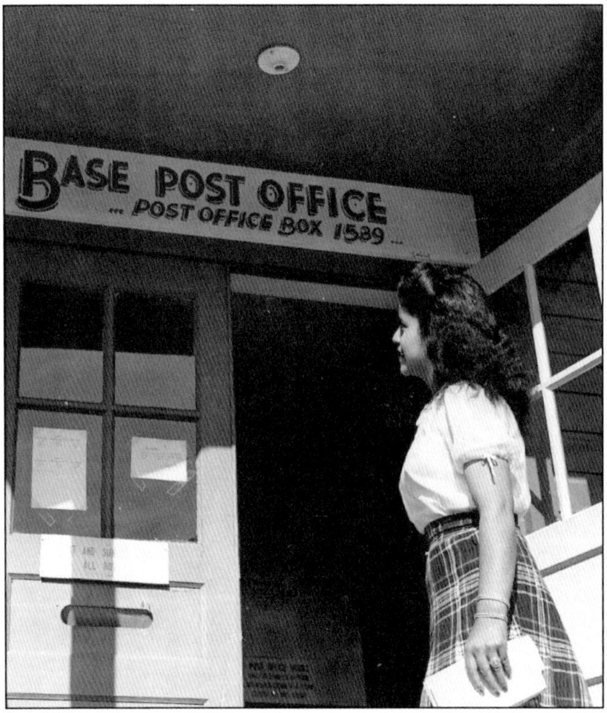

Marie Esquibel approaches the post office. Providing regular mail service for the thousands of individuals on the Hill posed a unique challenge. Official censorship was in force during the Project, and the security handbook stated specifically that personnel, professions, numbers of people, size and scope of the Project, and opinions or rumors could not be revealed. All mail was routed through Post Office Box 1663, Santa Fe, New Mexico, but as population increased, Box 1539 and Box 180 were added.

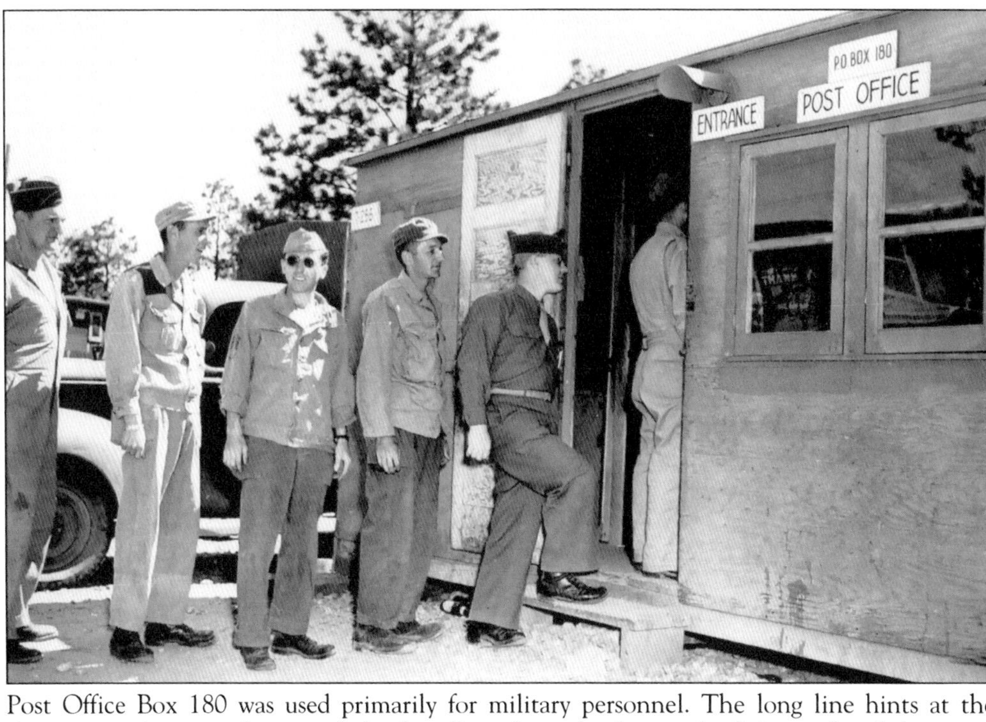

Post Office Box 180 was used primarily for military personnel. The long line hints at the time-consuming procedures needed to handle and sort the thousands of pieces of mail that came through the three P.O. boxes. In 1946 Project Director Norris Bradbury and Col. Herbert Gee requested that Los Alamos residents hand deliver Christmas cards to fellow residents, allowing postal clerks to devote their time to the heavy volume of outgoing and incoming mail.

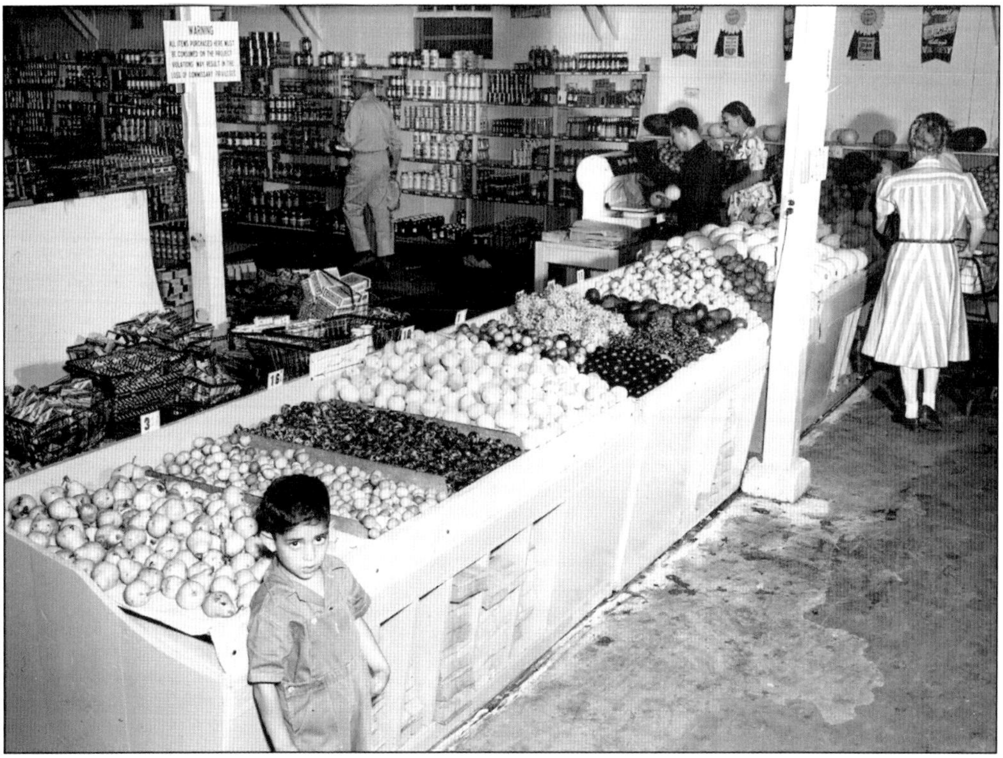

When the commissary first opened, fresh fruit and vegetables of inferior quality were supplied through the Army distribution center in El Paso. Project needs were made a priority and soon the quality and quantity improved. Civilian employees who traveled to the Hill had limited shopping opportunities when they returned home late, so they were given commissary privileges during wartime. The sign above the bins stating "all purchases must be consumed on site" was posted after the war.

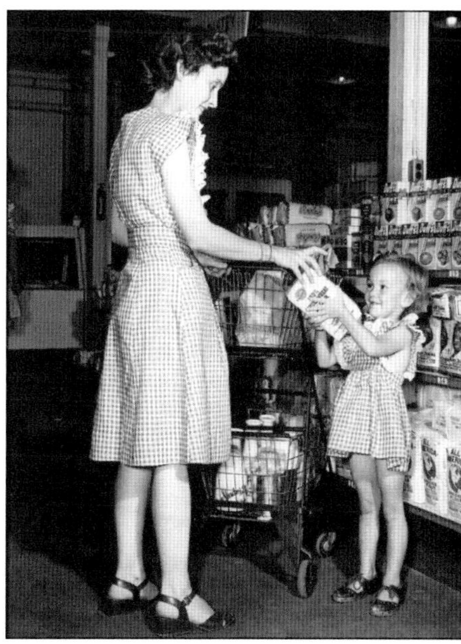

In the early days of the commissary, the likes of Army-issue gallon jugs of lemon flavoring or two gallon cans of tomatoes were shelved alongside family size items. The Project progressed, and the Army items disappeared. Although wartime rationing was in effect, a memo dated August 1944 instructed the commissary to procure a wider variety of goods than would ordinarily be allowed by Army regulations. It was felt that these additional supplies would help personnel put forth their best efforts while working on this all-important secret project. Betty Brixner and daughter Annette encountered fully stocked shelves, as they loaded up on milk, Jell-O, and other necessities.

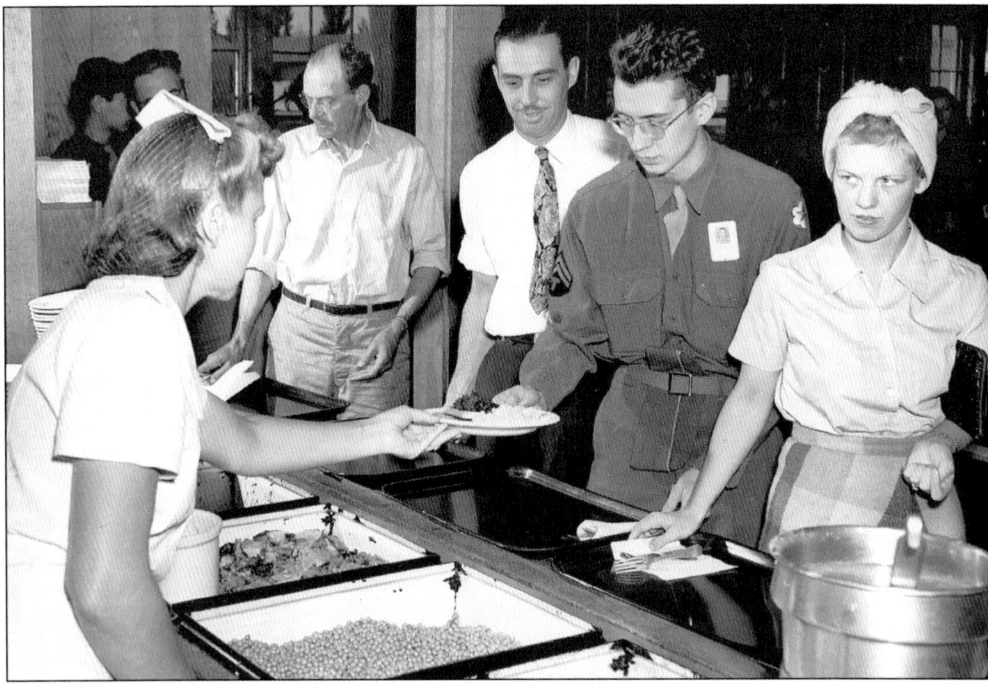

Providing meals was a constant challenge, so cafeterias like this one served a large portion of the civilian and military population. This one, called the North Mess, served 675 meals on the first day it opened in April 1943. The meals were cheap and unfortunately looked the part, but nothing else was available. Almost immediately changes were made to the building to accommodate more diners and the approximately 6,300 meals that were served weekly.

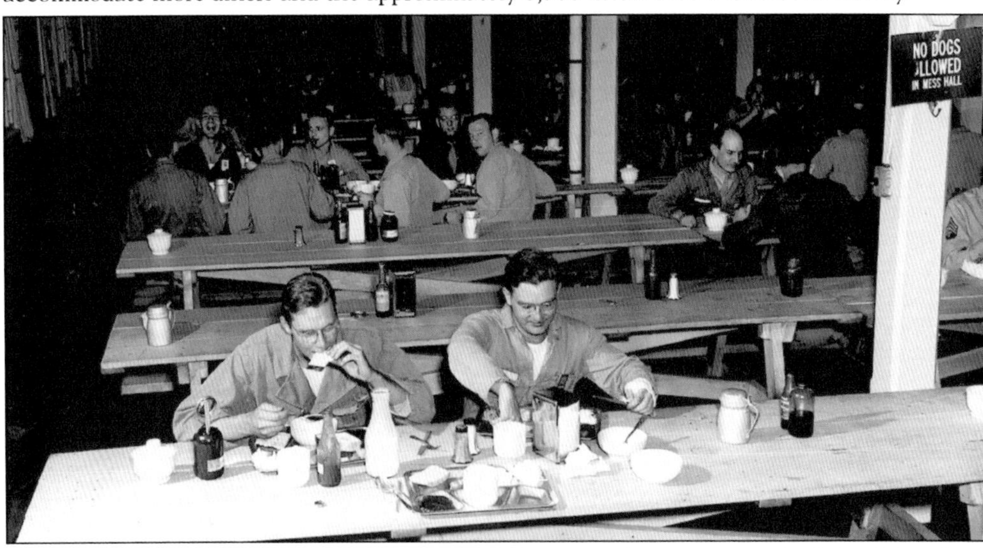

John Michnovicz (left) and Stan Zembaty (right) pose at dinnertime at the West Mess. Both were staff photographers in the photo group, and this shot was set up to document the military dining facilities at Project Y. WAC Jerry Roensch wrote, "I preferred to join my special soldier at West Mess, even though the cockroaches and silverfish scared me and the benches were a challenge for someone wearing a skirt." Note the sign: NO DOGS ALLOWED IN THE MESS HALL! (Photo by Joe Gluth.)

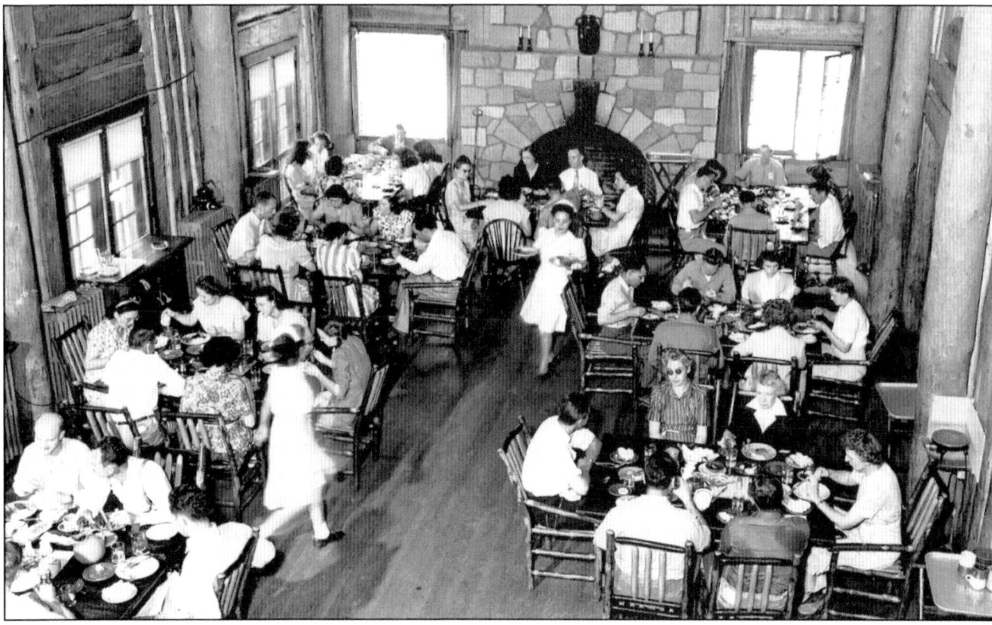

The main dining room of Fuller Lodge was used with few changes from when the room served the boys during the Ranch School years, even retaining the rustic dining chairs. This photo was taken from the balcony that overlooked the dining area that seated 70 people. More than one observation was made that mealtimes in Fuller Lodge resembled a scientific "Who's Who" with such men as Enrico Fermi, James Chadwick, Robert Oppenheimer, Ernest Lawrence, and Isador Rabi eating there.

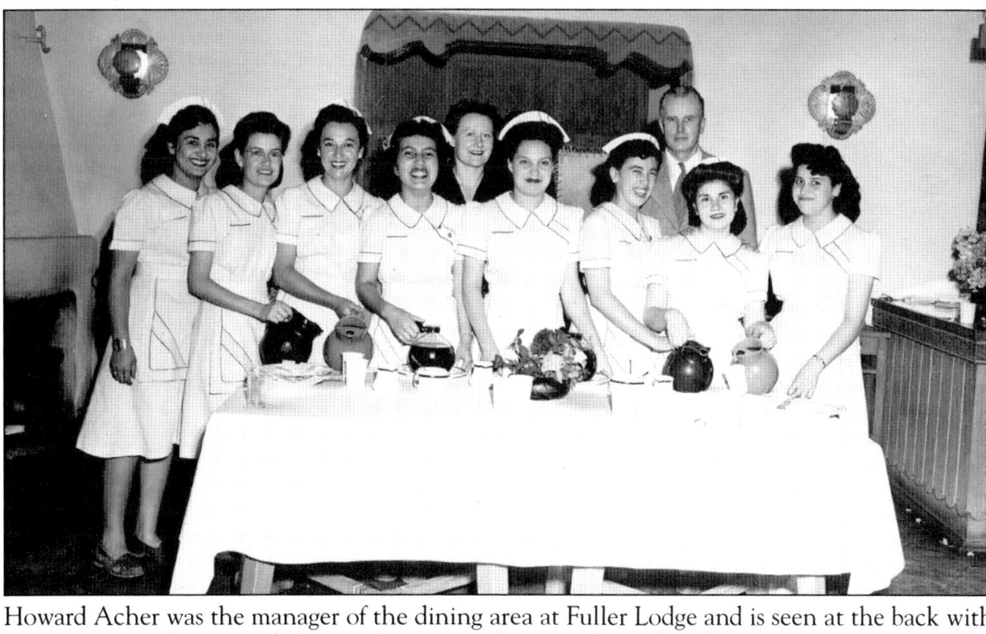

Howard Acher was the manager of the dining area at Fuller Lodge and is seen at the back with the waitresses that served the meals. Crisp, white uniformed staff and required reservations made this the finest dining on the Hill. Hours were limited: the Monday–Saturday schedule included a 7:30–8 a.m. breakfast, 12–12:30 p.m. lunch, and 6–6:30 p.m. dinner, with prices ranging from 50¢ for breakfast to $1.15 for dinner.

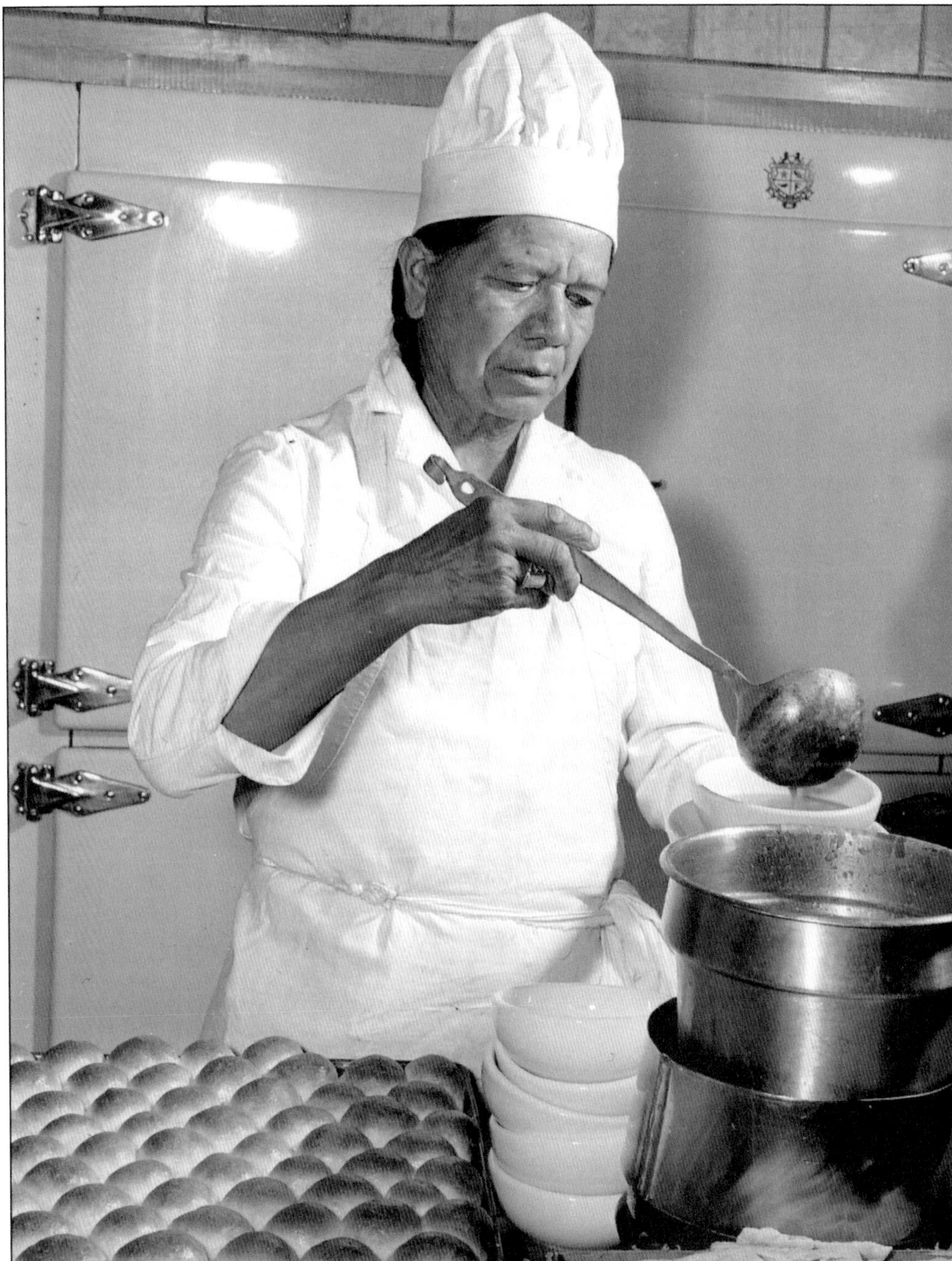

There was a marked improvement in dining when East Cafeteria opened in March of 1945. The overall appearance of the building and the wider variety of foods were purposely designed to improve morale of the residents. Here is Cleto Tafoya, a former governor of Santa Clara Pueblo, ladling soup alongside a tray of freshly baked rolls. Tafoya's culinary skills evidently impressed Eleanor Jette as she recalled in her memoir *Inside Box 1663* that he "presided behind the best hunk of roast beef I ever put a tooth on and it cost all of one buck twenty-five cents."

Framed nicely in the entrance to the beauty shop is T5 Dorothy Johnson. Building T-7 was the Service Club, and it housed a beauty shop, barbershop, restaurant, and post exchange. Four operators were employed here in 1946 and worked late until 10 p.m. on Wednesday and Thursday evenings to accommodate the ladies' hair and nail needs.

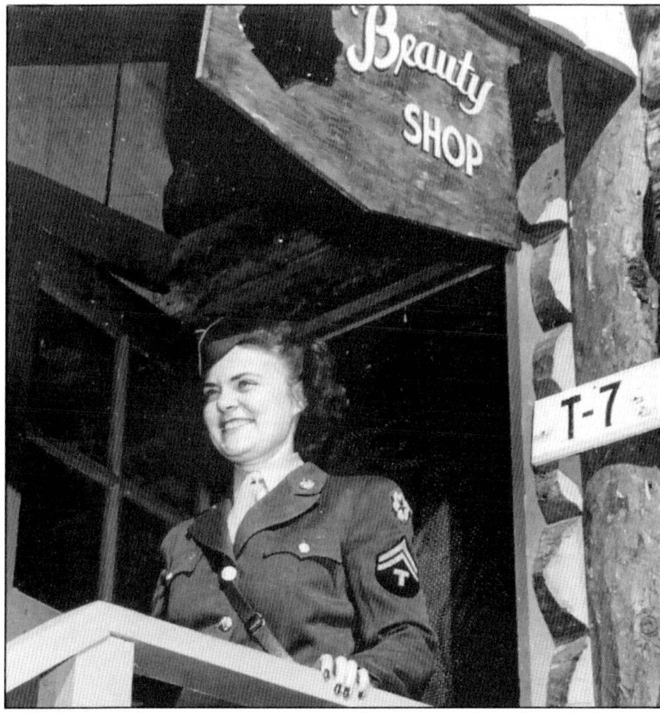

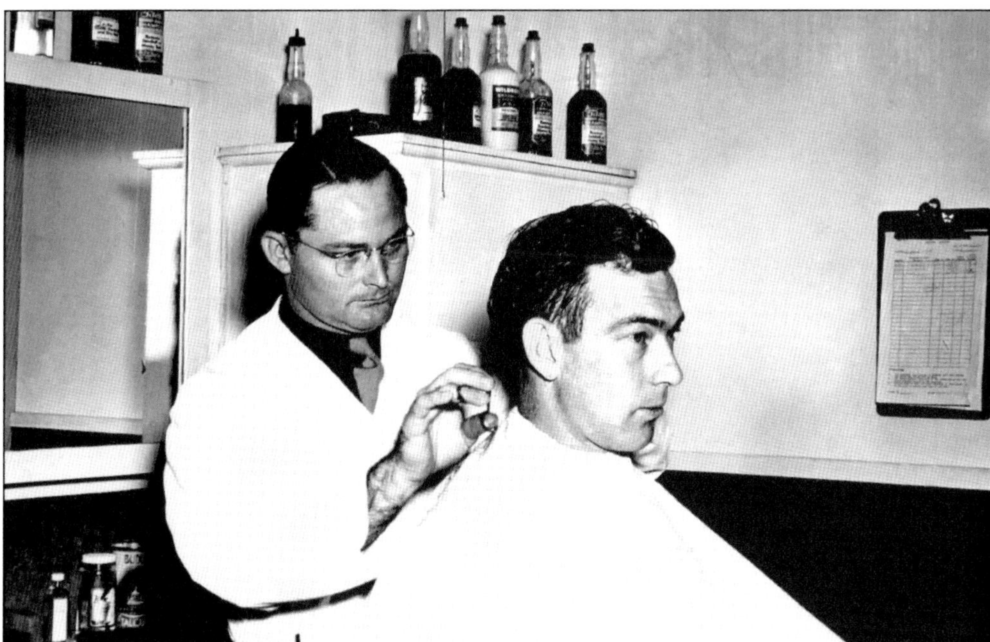

At first there were so few barbers available that the Tech Area men obtained a barber chair from supply and went to work on each other's hair. In time, barbershops were set up in the Service Club, the Military Police (MP) exchange, and the Special Engineering Detachment (SED) exchange. The SEDs had a colorful barber who bragged that he could complete 12 haircuts, as ordered, in one hour. One acquaintance questioned his ability, so a $50 bet was made, and the barber efficiently collected.

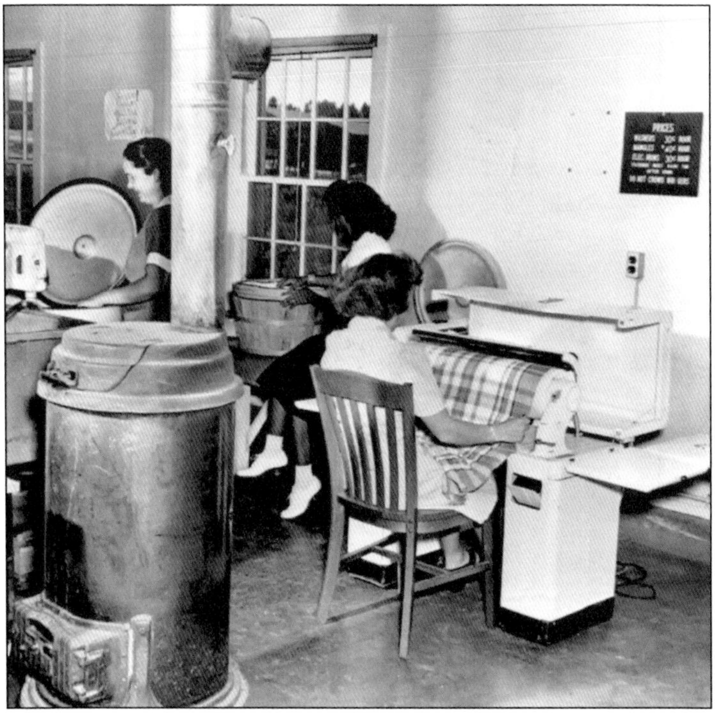

Laundries were available and equipped with washing machines and electric irons that cost 30¢ an hour and mangles that ironed materials between heated rollers for 40¢ an hour. In spite of that, there never seemed to be enough laundry areas or machines, so in the summer of 1946, the laundries were updated and a grand total of 36 community washing machines were available for the population of more than 6,000!

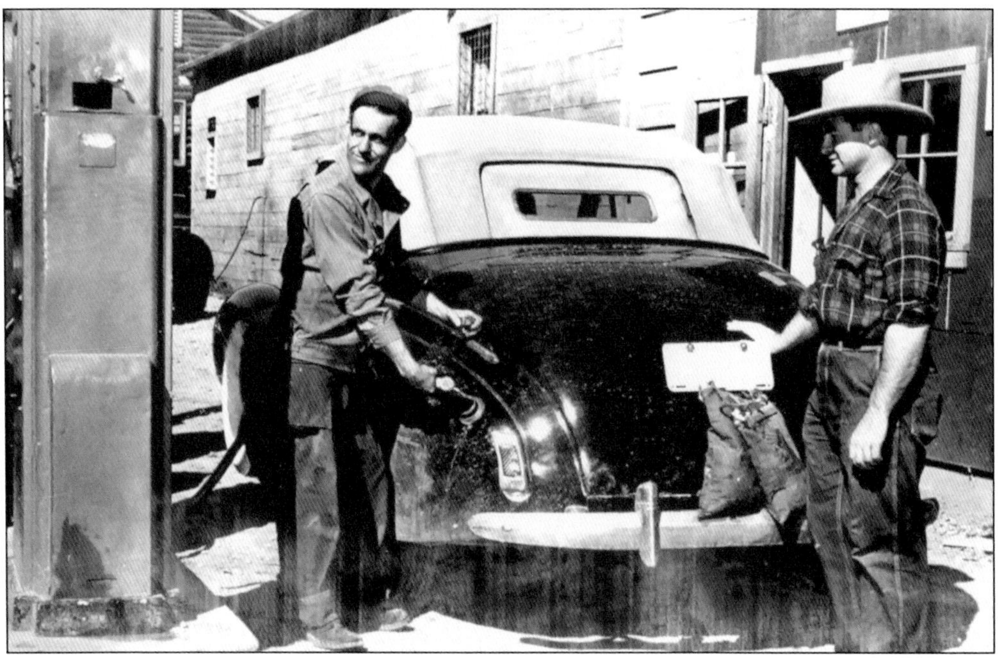

At the filling station, Pvt. Evern Sawyer and Pvt. Edwin Creutz could not only get gas but also have tires and engines repaired and get a good greasing. Note the two bags hanging from the license plate. This keen little Mercury Coupe carried its own water bags just in case the radiator went dry. Civilians were encouraged to bring their cars as long as they were in good condition and the owners did not mind "their being weathered." Car problems from mud, ruts, and snow kept the repair shop busy.

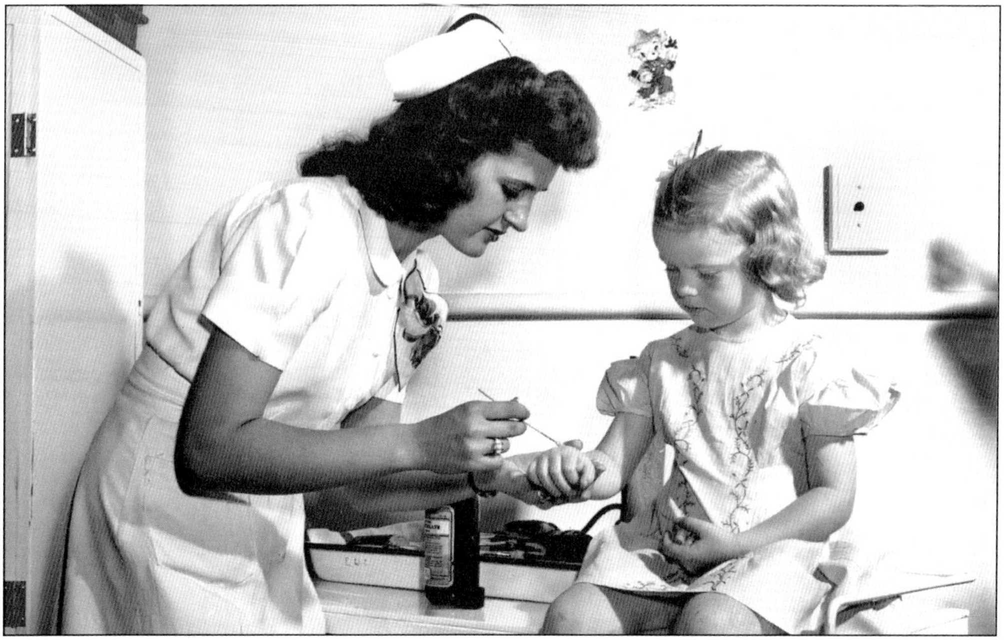

The nurse tenderly applied Merthiolate to even the littlest resident's scrape. During the years of the Project, the Army provided free medical care with Jim Nolan, obstetrician-gynecologist; Henry Barnett, pediatrician; and Louis Hempelmann, radiologist, and the aid of a few nurses and hospital orderlies.

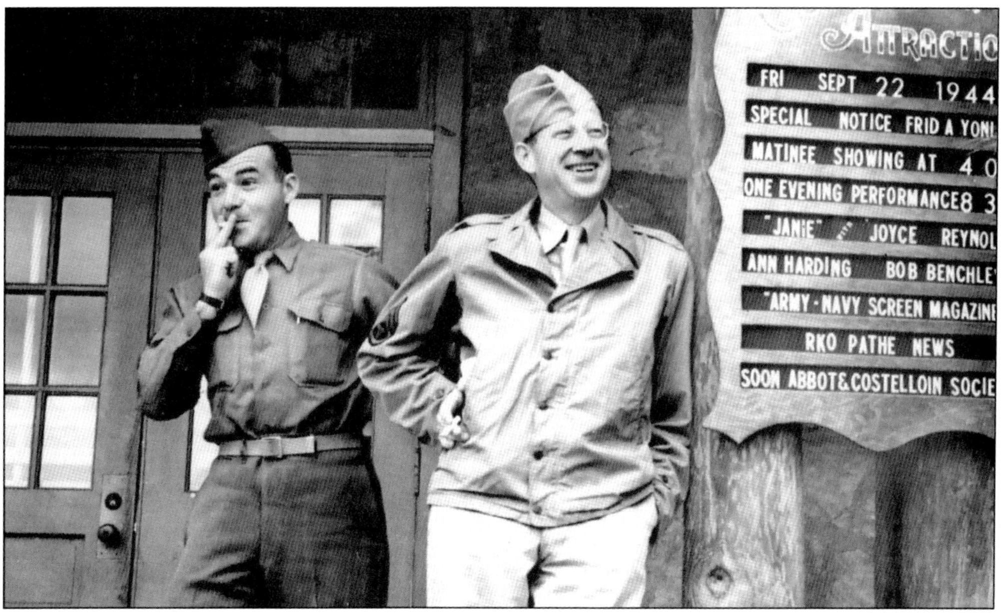

The men of the Special Engineering Detachment (SED) were a lively and well-educated group of enlisted Army guys. About a third of them had college and advanced degrees, and some had many years of work experience. Here are SEDs Herb Miller (left), a patent lawyer for the technical area, and Louis Jacot (right), a patent draftsman and claim writer. They are exiting one of the two theaters on the Hill. Nightly movies were popular diversions as reflected in the list of attractions on the marquee.

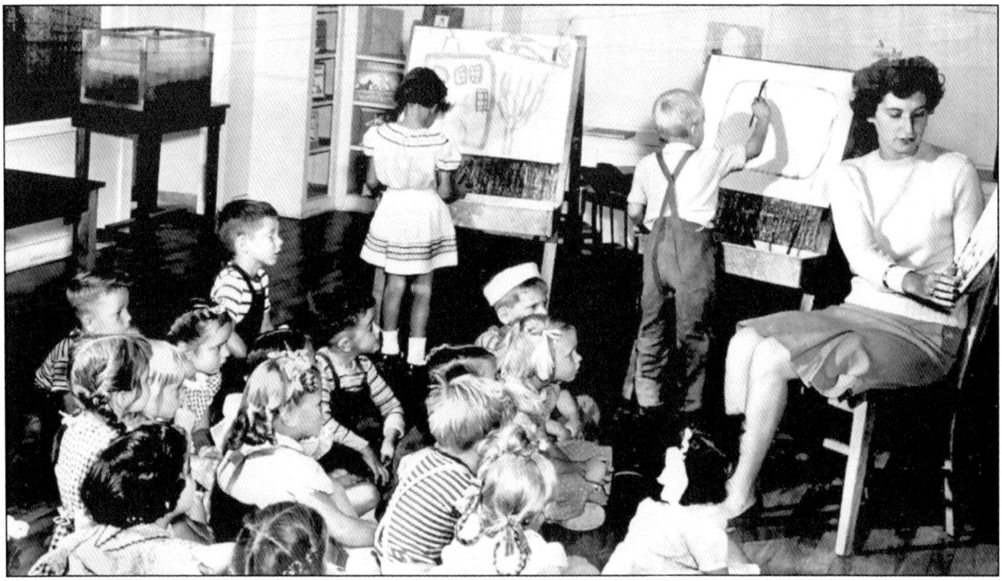

Young children were plentiful in Los Alamos during the war. In the first year of the Project, 80 children were born. Gen. Leslie Groves, the top military officer, was known to have complained about the prolific quality of his scientific colleagues. However, this complaint had no immediate effect. These children are in a kindergarten class being taught by June Labovitz. Nursery and kindergarten classes were set up primarily so that there would be adequate care while mothers worked on the Project.

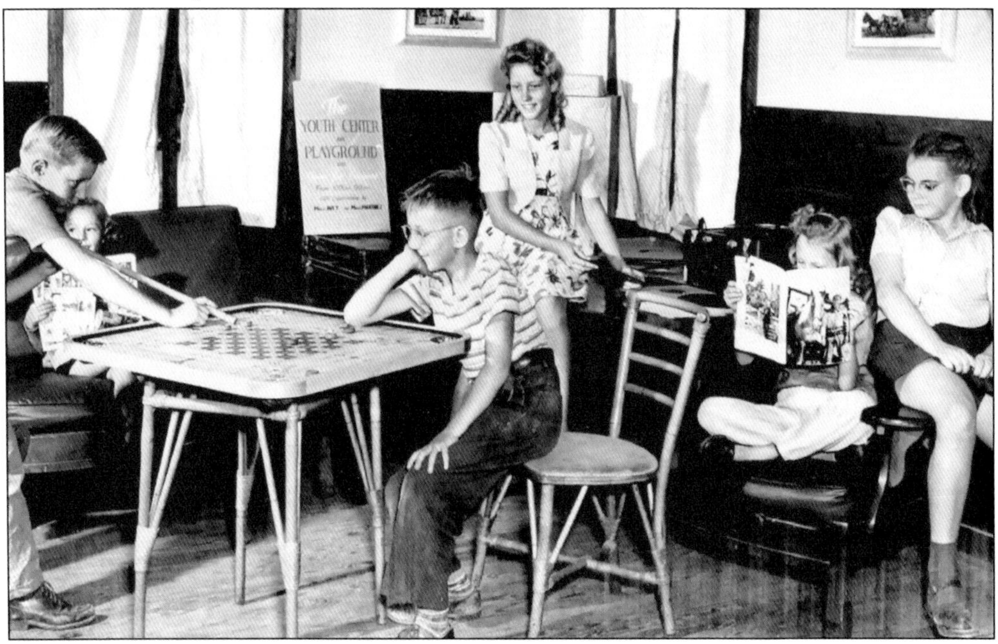

The isolation of the site and the undeveloped recreational facilities for the children laid the groundwork for the development of the youth center under the jurisdiction of Army chaplain Matthew Imrie. As Youth Council chairman, he and a group of seven community members managed the youth center and playground. Hours of operation were from 10 a.m. to 9 p.m., with supervision at all times. On this day, the kids played a game of Carom, a billiards-like table game.

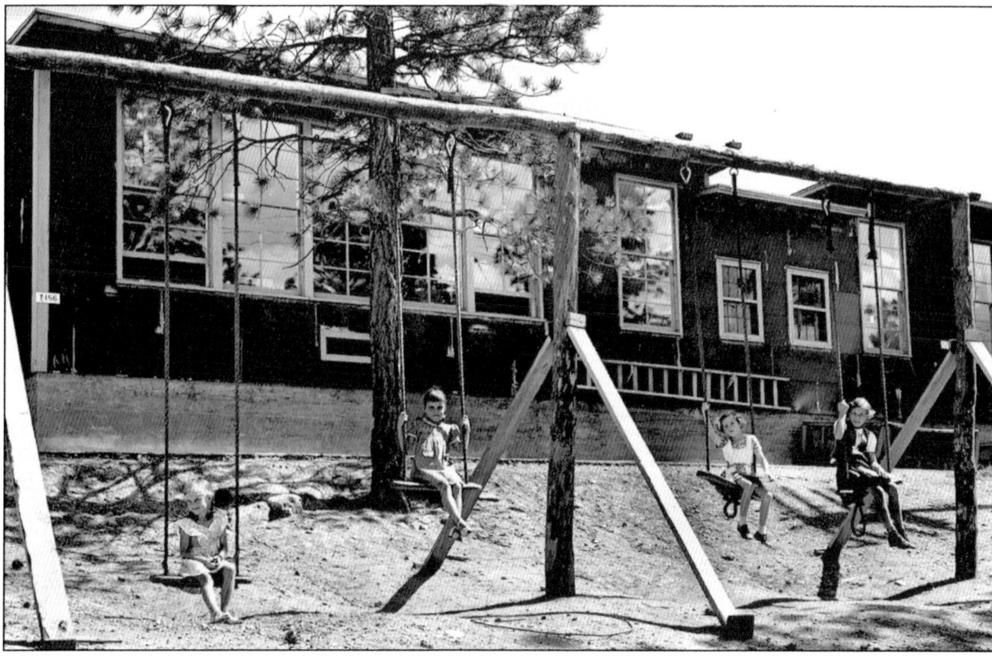

In this highly technical corner of the world, a mundane approach to swings—tree trunks and ropes—made playgrounds possible. This one was for the children at the elementary school. Constant construction and very crowded living conditions made life difficult for mothers of young children. The issue was brought before the town council, an elected advisory board, and eventually several swing sets and sandboxes were built.

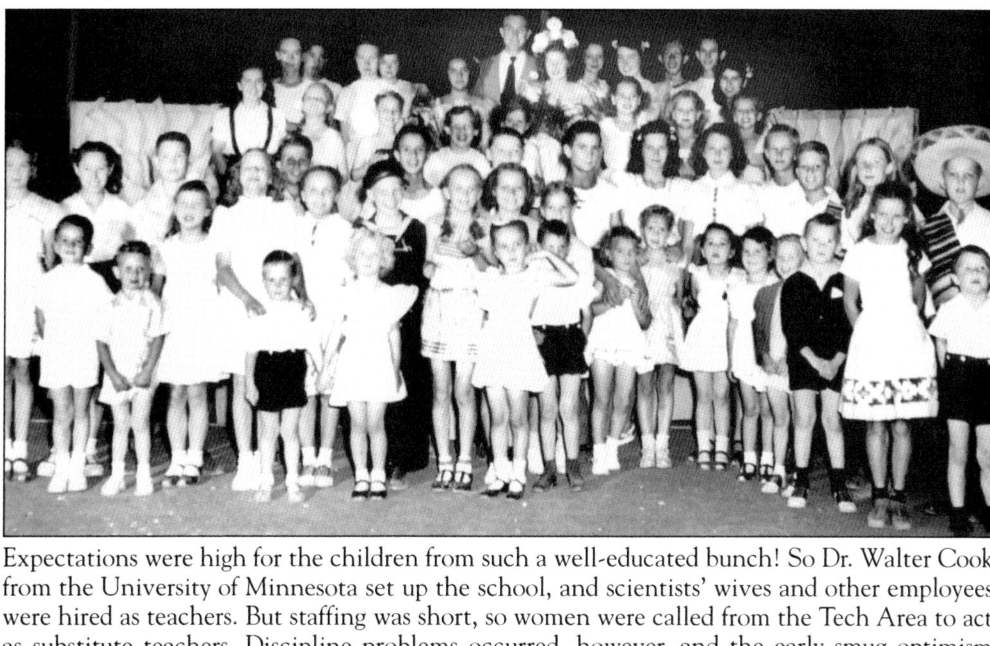

Expectations were high for the children from such a well-educated bunch! So Dr. Walter Cook from the University of Minnesota set up the school, and scientists' wives and other employees were hired as teachers. But staffing was short, so women were called from the Tech Area to act as substitute teachers. Discipline problems occurred, however, and the early smug optimism disappeared when it was obvious that the students knew how to capitalize on the lack of authority. This photo of the elementary school was taken when things were more settled, and permanent teachers and a superintendent were in place.

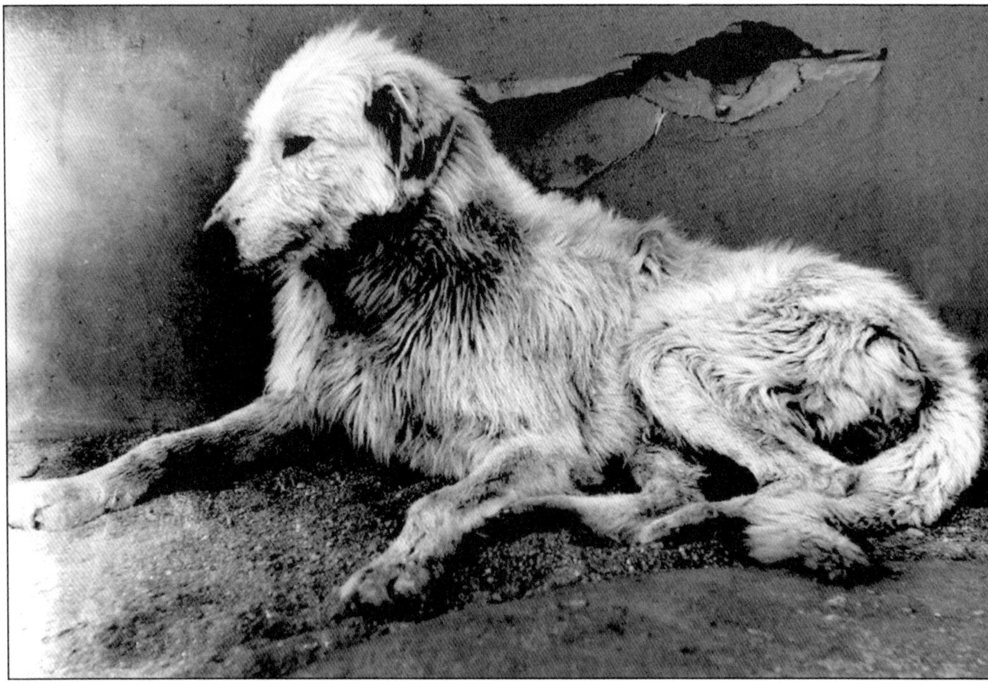

The story of the Manhattan Project wouldn't be complete without a portrait of Timoshenko, a cross between a Great Dane and a Russian wolfhound. He seemed to be a part of the site when the Army moved in, and he decided that life was good for a rangy dog that enjoyed handouts and the people who gave them. His namesake was a Russian general, but his reputation was more of a pacifist. This wise, old dog slept on the hospital steps, guarding them for as many as 10 hours a day.

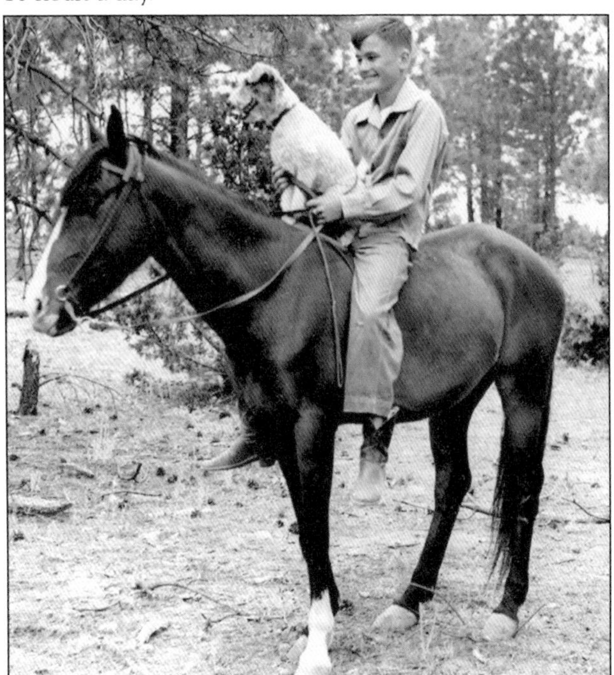

Kids, dogs, horses, and the outdoors made a perfect combination for Robbie Robinson, pictured here. Robbie, the teenage son of Charles Robinson, a site engineer, preferred to ride bareback and considered the use of a saddle as "sissified." A horse stable and pasture were in place when the Army took over, and the use of the horses was open to residents who wanted to ride the range and explore the mountains.

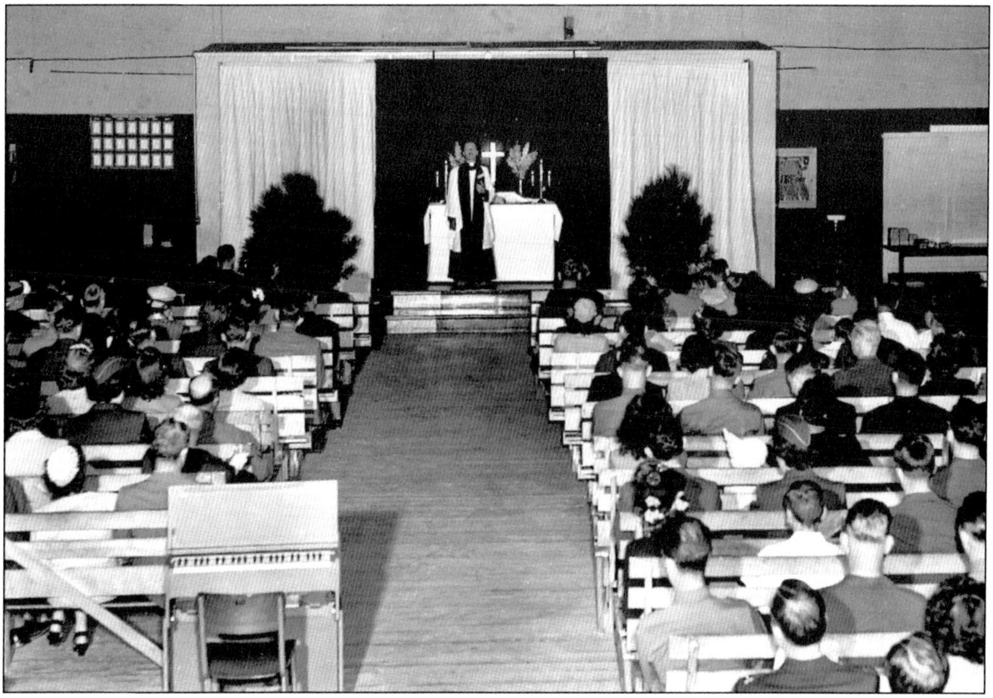

There were two multi-use buildings called Theater #1 and Theater #2 that were used for church services on Sunday mornings. Before the benches could be set up, the remnants of the previous night's dance had to be swept from the building. Still, there were times when the faint odor of beer could be detected while worshipping. This is Theater #2, which was the larger and more centrally located of the two theaters.

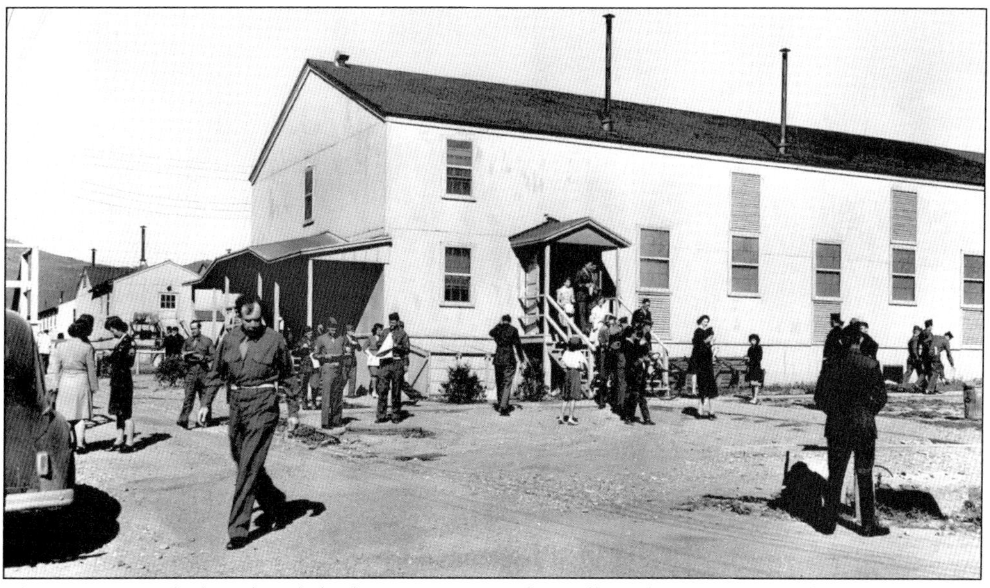

The Roman Catholic Church had a presence on the Hill, and a priest came from Santa Fe to conduct Sunday mass in Theater No. 1, from which these folks are emerging. Some Protestant groups met in homes, and not until the fall of 1944 was there a regular Army chaplain stationed in Los Alamos to enable regular worship for Catholics, Protestants, and Jews.

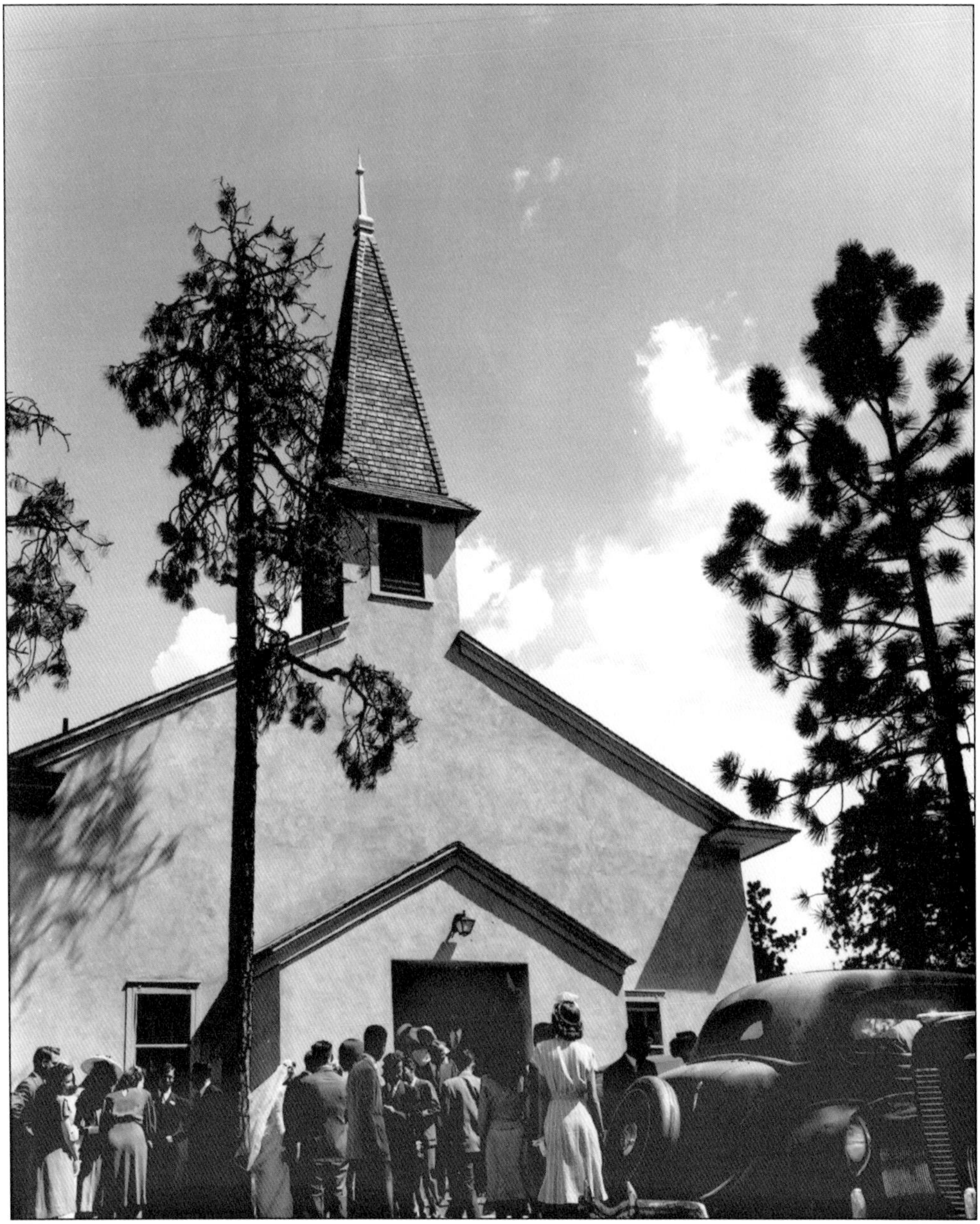

This wedding of Katherine Mahoney and Gustav Linenberger took place on August 9, 1947, in the new Los Alamos Chapel. Faith-based activities had been limited to theaters, schools, and homes until this multi-use, government-funded chapel was built and dedicated on Sunday, April 27, 1947. In the midst of its construction, a campaign was begun by Army chaplain Kenneth Ames to raise private funds for a chapel annex. The annex plans included a smaller chapel, church school classrooms, and space for denominational meetings and scouting activities. When the campaign fell short of its goal, the matter was brought before the town council, which referred the issue to the area manager of the Atomic Energy Commission (AEC). The AEC agreed to pay the remaining cost for the completion of the annex.

Four

The Photo Lab at Work

While much is made of the extreme secrecy surrounding "the Project," the fact is that many scientists and top military brass knew exactly what was going on, but they also knew that the final outcome of all this intense work was far from certain. Were they on the right path? Would the "device" work at all? Might something go wrong? Many restless nights were spent worrying about these matters.

The Army, to its great credit, knew that someone should be documenting everything that was going on within the gates of Site Y. It would be some story to tell, if they indeed achieved their goal. The task of recording it fell to the photographic division on the Hill.

The main tasks of the photography groups assembled on the Hill fell into two categories. First were the experimental procedures. One photo group was assigned the extremely difficult task of capturing high-speed events for further analysis and study. Early designs of the atomic weapon called for "uranium guns," or projectiles fired precisely at one another, with the goal to compact the fissionable material into a highly confined space. Since these events occurred at astonishing speed, it was essential to develop the means of creating a permanent photographic record of the procedure. That had to be captured on film. This same group was also responsible for safely capturing the light of a "thousand suns," as Dr. Oppenheimer characterized the result at the Trinity test site in July 1945. How could film capture the energy of 20,000 tons of TNT exploding in the desert? Experimenters had to think of the location of cameras, how to protect the film and photographer, and even what kinds of photographic chemicals would be necessary to make these images permanent.

A second, but different task of the other photo group was to document the living history of Los Alamos itself. Here was a town of nearly 6,000 people springing up right before everyone's eyes. Nearly every day more people arrived from around the world. How were these people living? What were they eating? What was it like on the Pajarito Plateau, living amidst pumice-filled canyons and ancient Indian ruins? This was an unprecedented program of research and development to be recorded for all time. Long before such national efforts as the race to the moon, the Hubble telescope, or the Human Genome Project, there was the Manhattan Engineer District—the precursor to all these national efforts.

What you see here is the work of John Michnovicz and his friends in the photo-documentation group. They carried their cameras everywhere they went, and the work helped bring the story of Los Alamos to future generations.

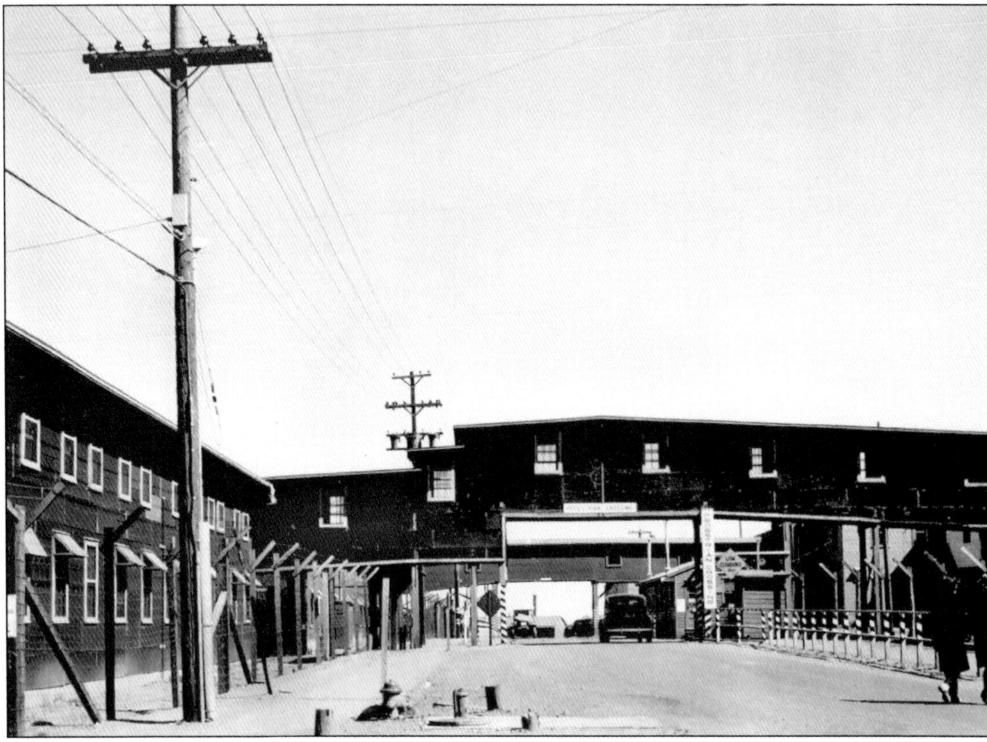

The Technical Area that housed the Project's secret work was built near Ashley Pond, and Building A, home of the photo lab, was within this fenced area. Expansion across the main road created the need for the elevated passageway shown here so all areas could be easily accessed. Barbed wire enclosed the area, and military police controlled security on the ground and from towers overhead. Buildings had English alphabet names A, B, C, D, F–K, and R–Z, and the Greek alphabet names of Gamma, Delta, and Sigma.

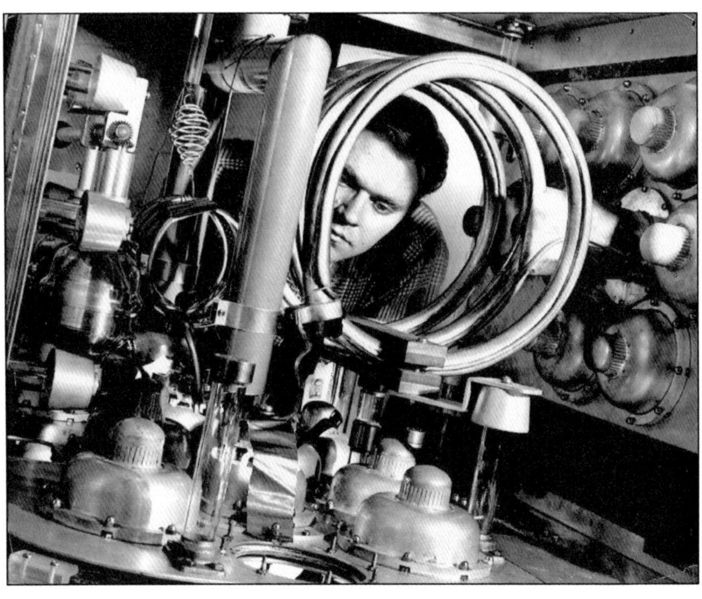

John Michnovicz was a youthful GI technician when he arrived in Los Alamos, but he soon took on the photographer's role. In an assignment to document machinery in the Tech Area he framed a person's head through a circular opening and created a science fiction look. Michnovicz worked with another photographer on this assignment, and his buddy snapped him in the pose. He probably did the same for his friend.

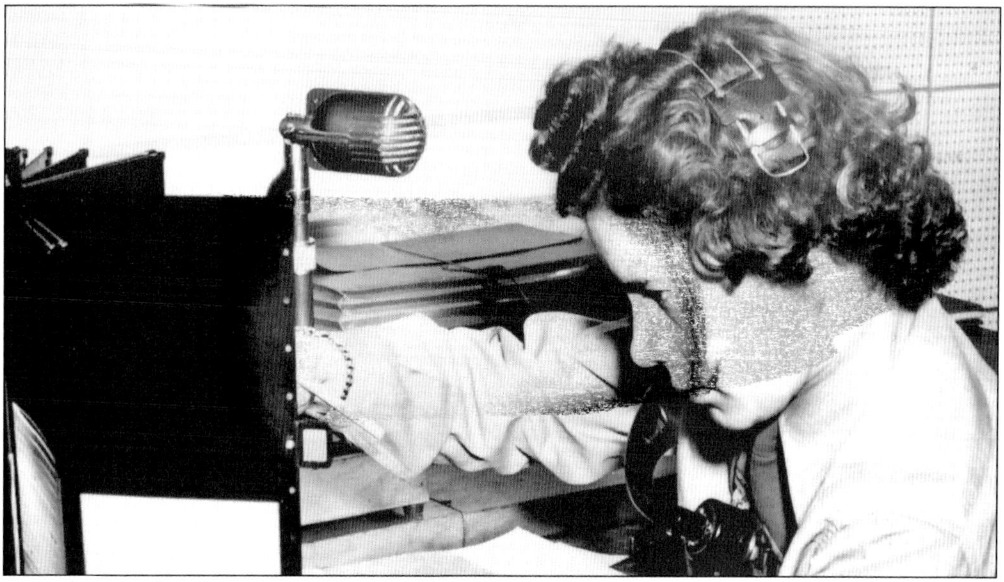

Sgt. Eleanor Blanchard operated the Tech Area paging switchboard as a WAC in Los Alamos, which meant answering as many as 1,500 calls daily. Her microphone stood ready to page any scientist or technician or the ever-popular J.J. Gutierrez, maintenance man. Callers occasionally tricked the operator into paging Shostakovich or Roger Wilcoe. Fellow soldiers would take pity to correct the information.

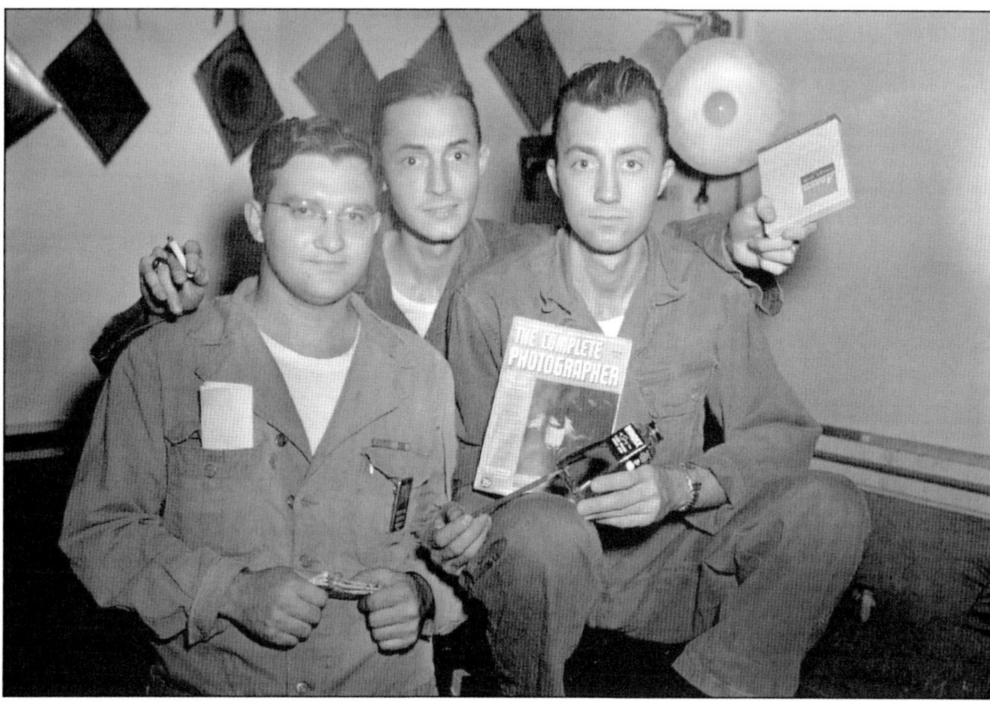

Lab photographers Stan Zembaty (left) and Joe Gluth (right), with lab assistant Conway P. Coe are framed by the cigarette and color film. The guys were part of the Provisional Engineering Detachment (PED) and usually worked in areas such as maintenance and utilities but each found his way to the photo lab.

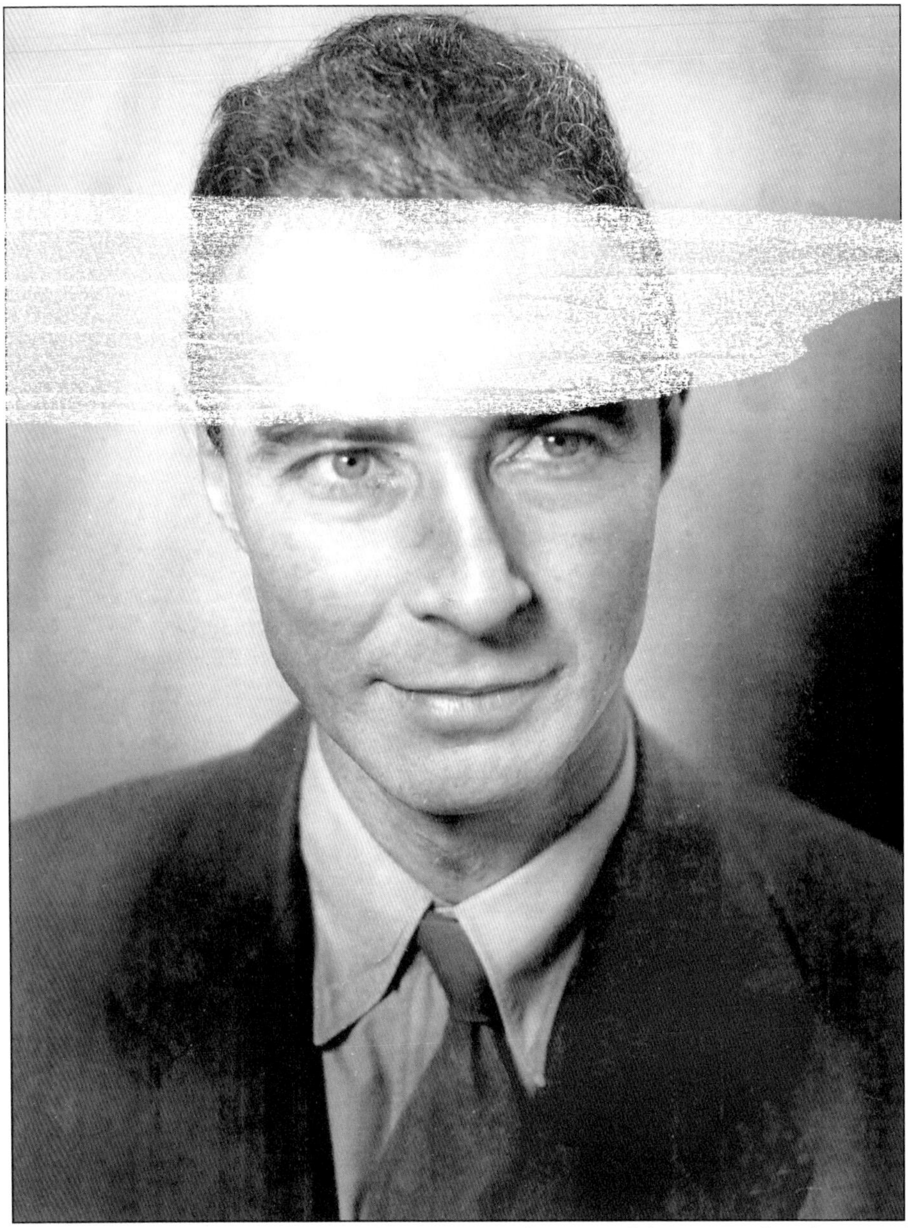

This photo of Robert Oppenheimer, taken between the time of the Trinity bomb test and the drop of the first atomic bomb on the city of Hiroshima, was in preparation for the anticipated press release. Oppenheimer was a professor at Berkeley and a theoretical physicist when Gen. Leslie Groves chose him as the director of the Los Alamos Laboratory. His brilliant mind and keen sense of people combined to gather a unique group of scientists and lead the Project to completion. After the bomb was dropped on Japan, his concern about its use was framed in letters to several friends, and he began to lobby for international control. In 1947, Oppenheimer accepted the position of director of the Institute for Advance Study at Princeton. In 1963, he received the Atomic Energy Commission's highest honor, the Enrico Fermi Award, for his contributions to atomic science. Oppenheimer autographed this photo for John Michnovicz, the photographer.

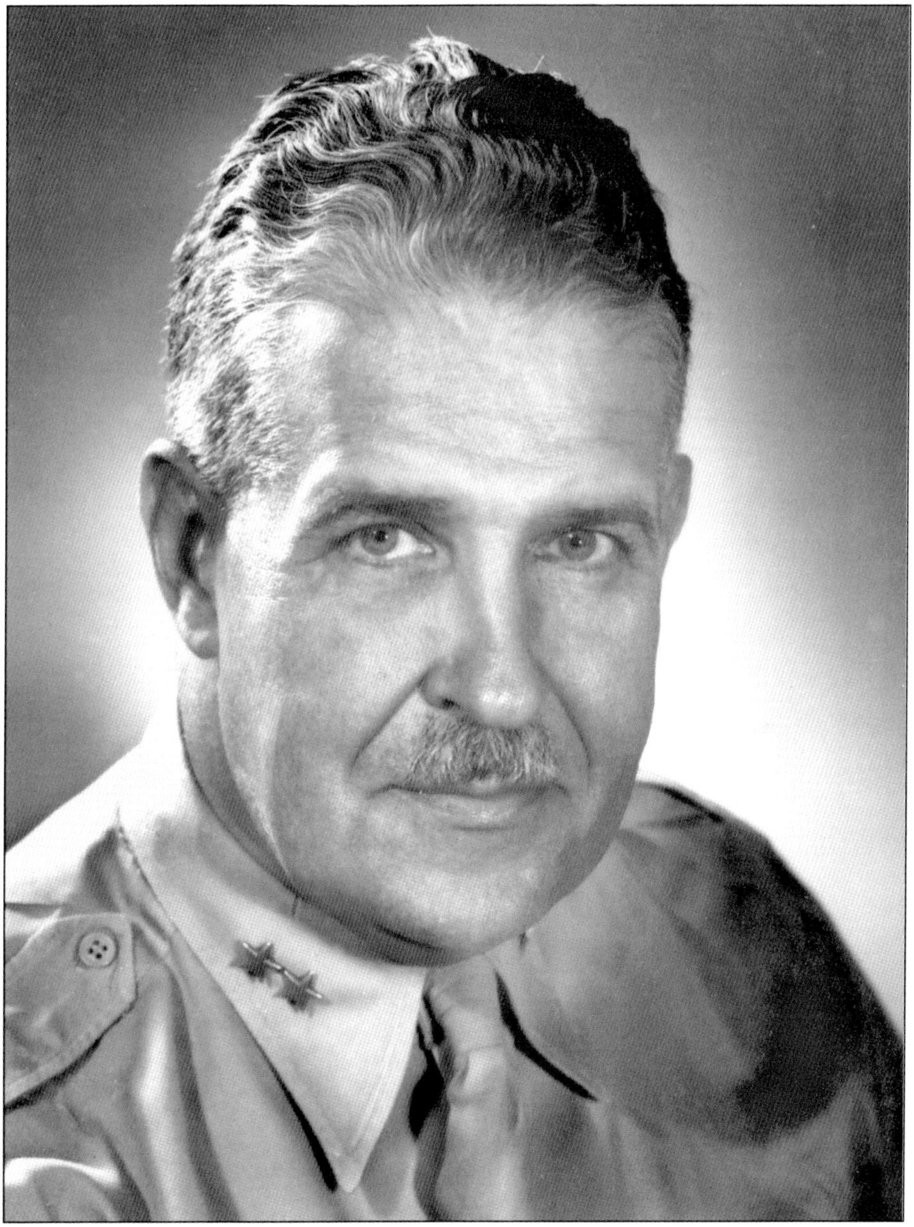

Maj. Gen. Leslie R. Groves was the military force behind the Manhattan Project. After he finished supervising the building of the Pentagon, he was asked to take command of the Manhattan Engineer District, which included Site W in Hanford, Washington, Site X in Oak Ridge, Tennessee, and Site Y in Los Alamos, New Mexico. The Manhattan Engineer District offices were in New York City, thus the code name Manhattan Project. When Groves chose Oppenheimer as lab director, he "thought he was the best theoretician around and knew just about everything except about sports." The general wanted to run the lab with all military procedure in place but bumped against the scientists' openness and academic airs. It was not always an easy arrangement, but his hard driving determination and abilities were essential for the Project's success. Groves did not reside in Los Alamos, but on one of his visits, his portrait was made.

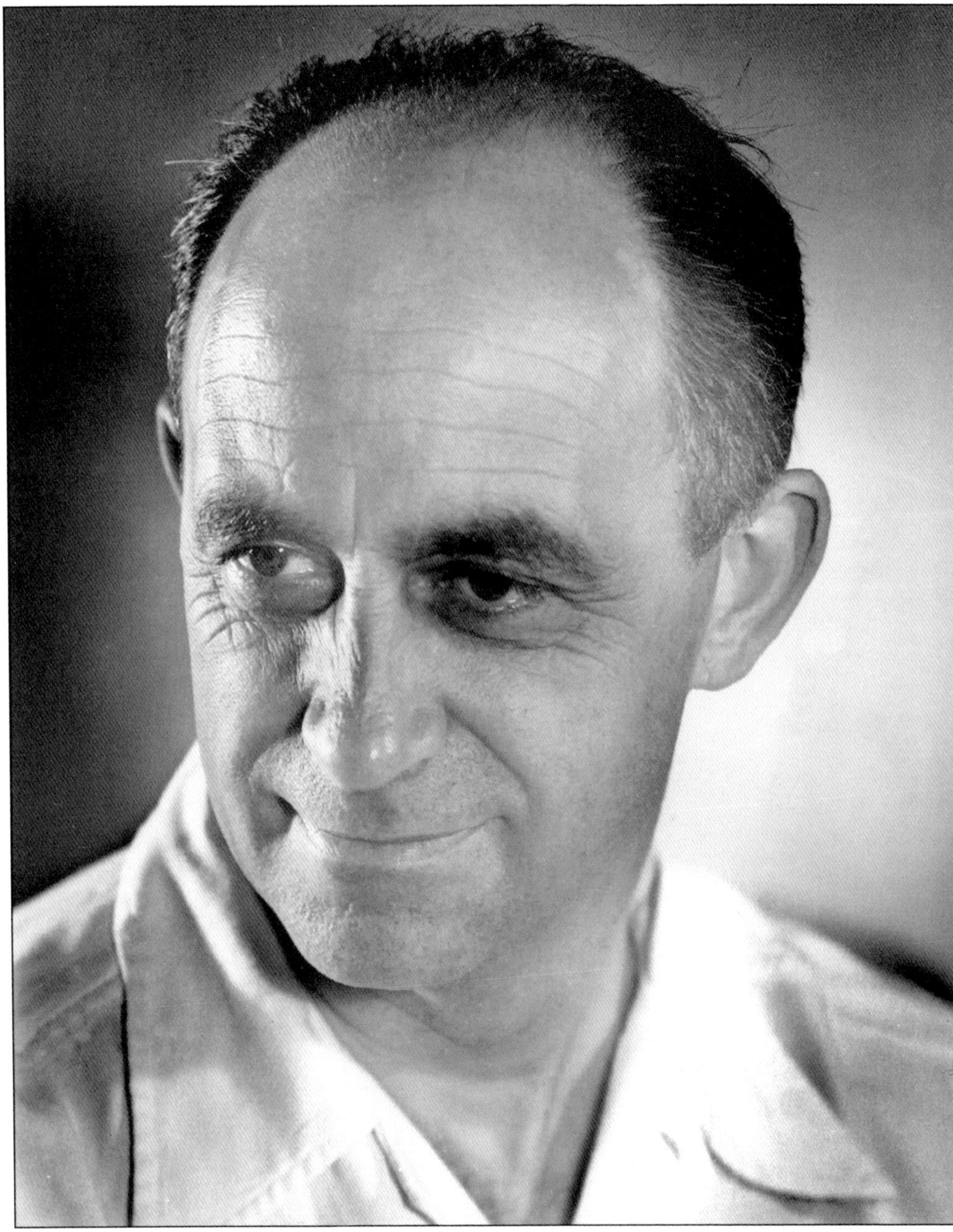

Enrico Fermi was one of the leading physicists on the Manhattan Project, having arrived in Los Alamos via Columbia University and the University of Chicago. Like many other European-born scientists, he fled fascism in the 1930s, following his acceptance of the Nobel Prize. Fermi was the first to demonstrate a self-sustaining nuclear chain reaction and for this achievement, he received the Congressional Medal of Merit in March 1946. Rachel Fermi, granddaughter of Enrico Fermi, wrote to the photographer that this portrait was prominently displayed in her grandmother's home. The Enrico Fermi Award was established in 1954 by the Atomic Energy Commission to honor Fermi and was modeled from this portrait.

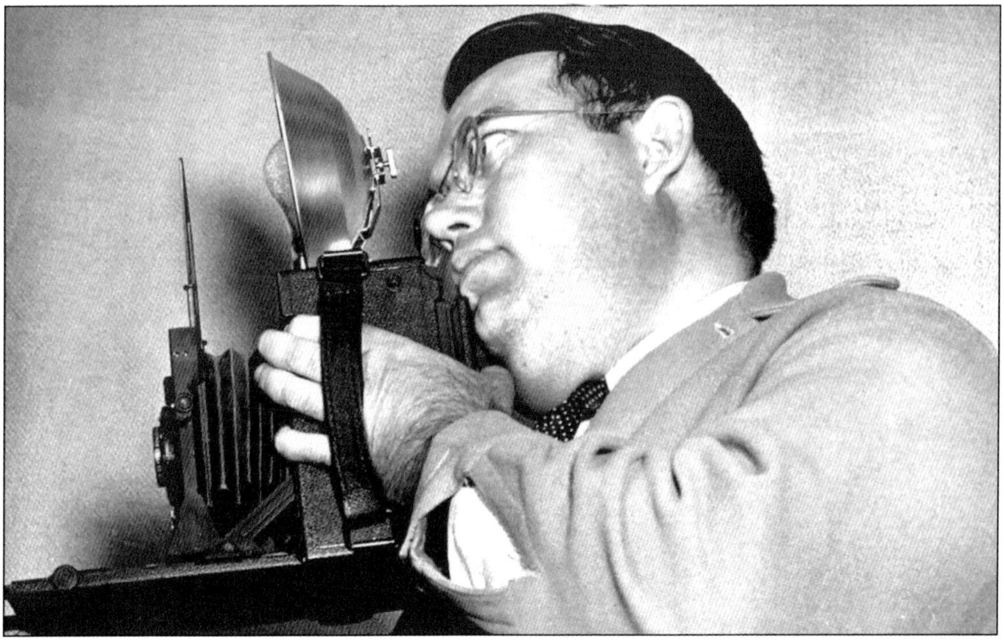

John Keller, with his Speedgraphic camera in hand, was the leader of the documentary photography section at the Project from 1943 to 1945. Keller was examining the service records of incoming GIs in order to snag photographers when John Michnovicz arrived in October 1944. Michnovicz expected to be doing technical work, but Keller noticed the GI's photographic experience at Southern Illinois University and had Michnovicz assigned to his section.

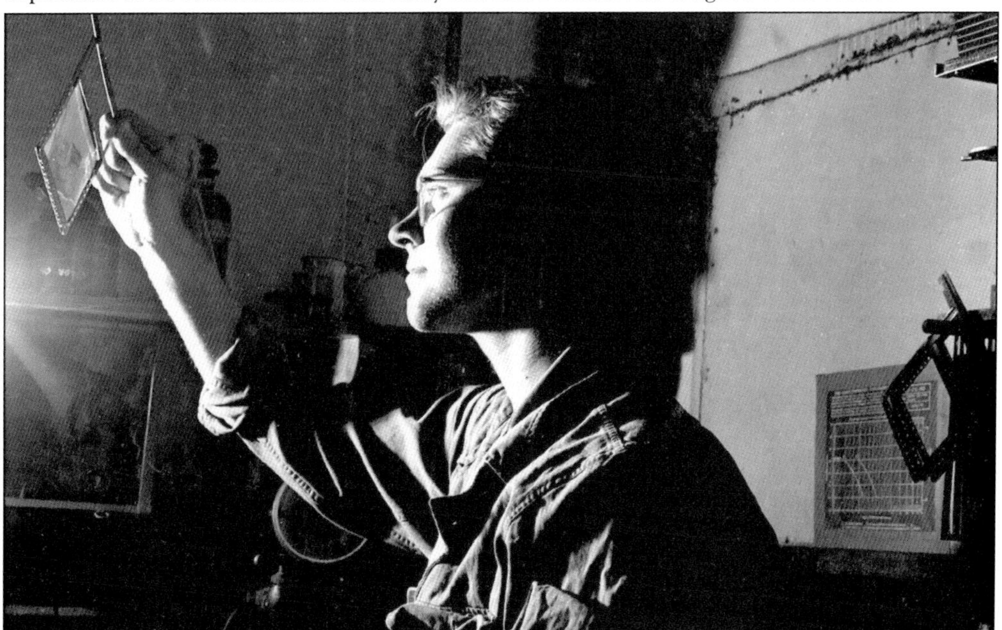

The members of the photography unit set up a number of shots to document their work and equipment and then took turns posing in the pictures. In this simulation, John Michnovicz stands in the darkroom inspecting a negative positioned in a metal holder that was used to immerse the negative in the different tanks of developing chemicals.

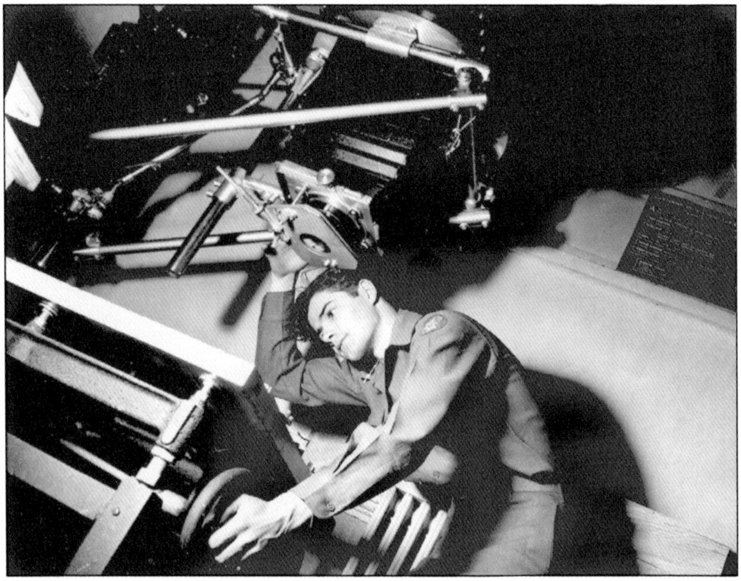

George Kochaniec began in the lab in January 1946 after doing aerial photography for the Army for five months at Sheppard Field, Texas. This angular shot of him in the Building A photo lab documented the equipment used to enlarge photos.

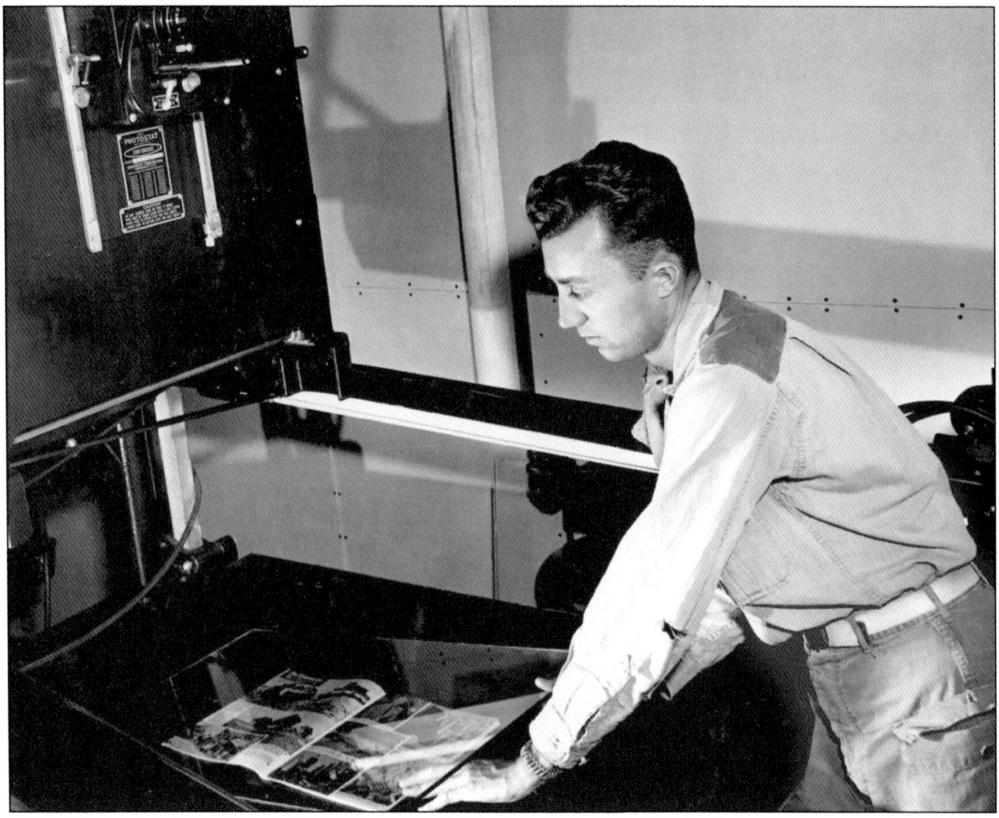

The Photostat machine produced readable copies either in negative (white on black) or in positive (black on white) and could reduce or enlarge prints. Joe Gluth positioned material ready to be copied at the Photostat and posed for the lab camera crew. Other photo lab equipment included a Speedgraphic camera, view cameras, a 16-mm motion picture camera, several enlargers, mimeograph and ditto copiers, and the Ozalid, a dry developing, white print machine.

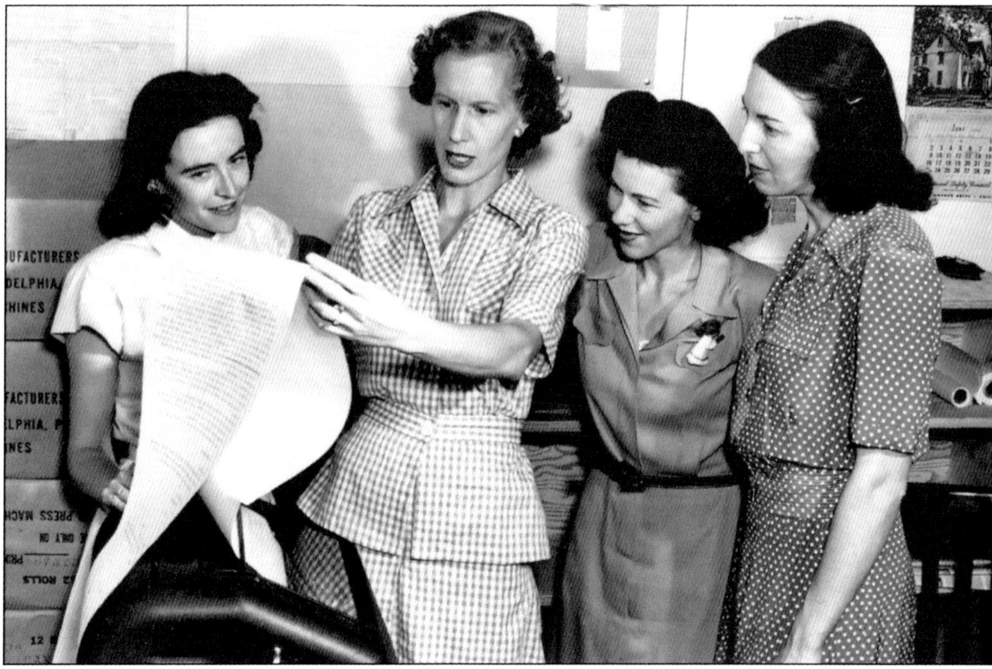

Peggy Thompson, on the left, joined her friends to read the teletype that detailed the results of a 1946 South Pacific bomb test. After months of preparation in Los Alamos, the fourth atomic bomb was exploded over the Bikini Atoll near the Marshall Islands. Reports indicated no injuries or damage to equipment, and relief was evident in the readers' faces. The use of atomic bombs was still new and as yet untested over a body of water, so the *Los Alamos Times* questioned, "Will a Navy be necessary with atomic bombs?"

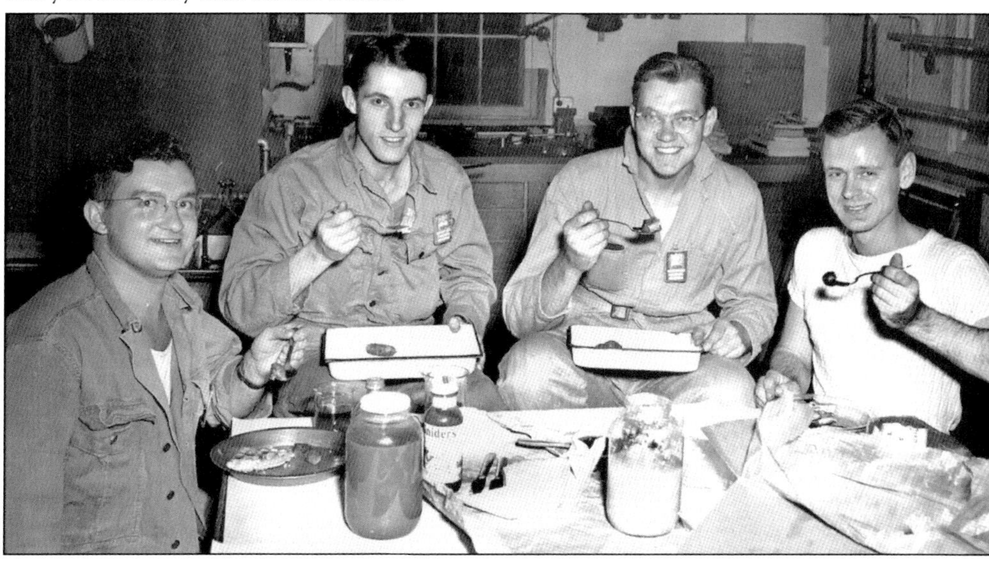

Gathering for a snack at midnight in the photo lab, from left to right, are Stan Zembaty, Paul Farrar, John Michnovicz, and an unidentified friend. Access to the Tech Area was not limited to daylight hours, and if there was a deadline to meet or a large workload, the men stayed until the job was done. So, makeshift dishes that were handy—developing pans and jars—were filled with waffles, sausages, and drinks from the Tech Area PX or the mess hall, and dinner was ready.

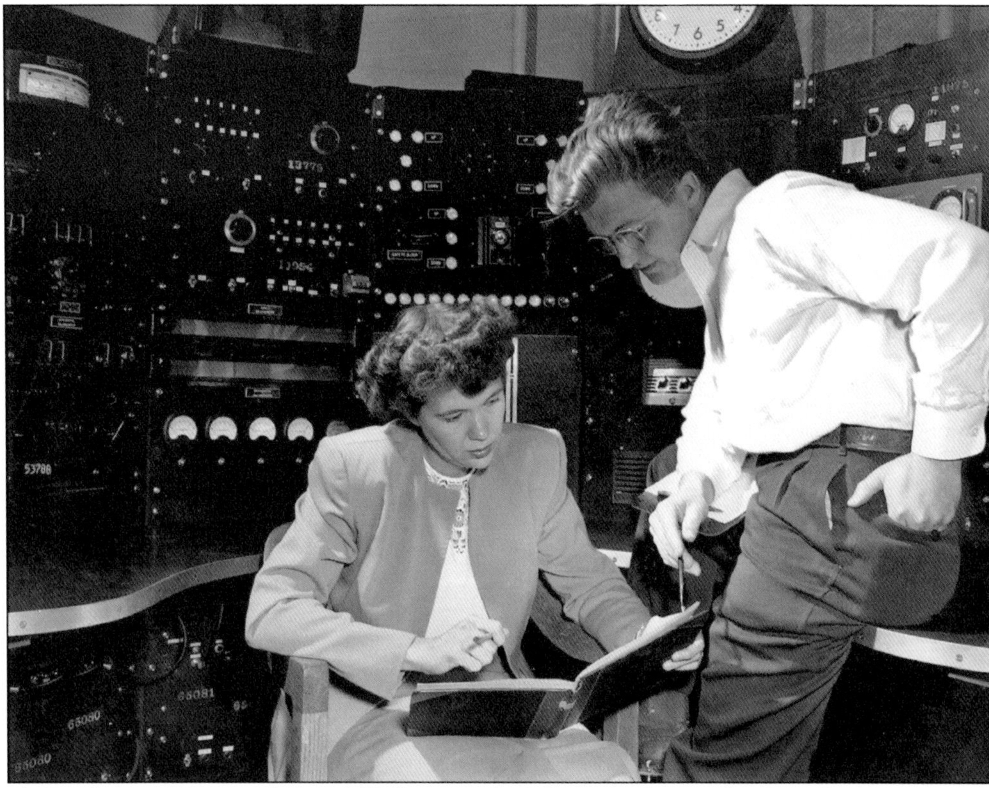

Ph.D. physicists Jane and David Hall married while in graduate school at the University of Chicago and acted as consultants in initiating the first uranium production piles in 1944–1945 at Site X in Hanford, Washington. In November 1945 they moved to Los Alamos. Jane worked with explosives and tested the shock velocities of metal plates. In 1947, when their son Malcolm was two years old, the Halls served as group leader and alternate group leader in one physics division of the lab, and they continued at the lab until retirement.

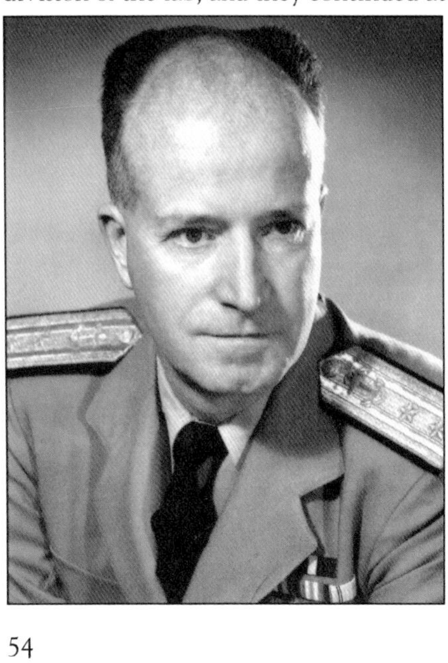

William "Deke" Parsons joined the Project in June 1943 as a Navy captain and was later advanced to admiral. The Annapolis graduate and physicist headed the Ordnance Division. He was responsible for designing the bomb shapes that would fit the B-29 and training the crews that manned the flight. Parsons flew in the *Enola Gay*, the plane that carried the "Fat Man" atomic bomb, and armed the weapon just before its drop on the city of Hiroshima.

In January 1946, Loris Gardner was hired to be in charge of the Los Alamos photo lab. His news career at the *San Jose Mercury Herald* had begun unsuccessfully as a reporter, but determined to stay on, he filled in for a vacationing staff photographer. In spite of inexperience he moved to the position permanently when the staff member did not return. As a novice he was known to try anything, so he got several scoops for the paper and made some notable photographs. Gardner enjoyed life and was well liked by his staff.

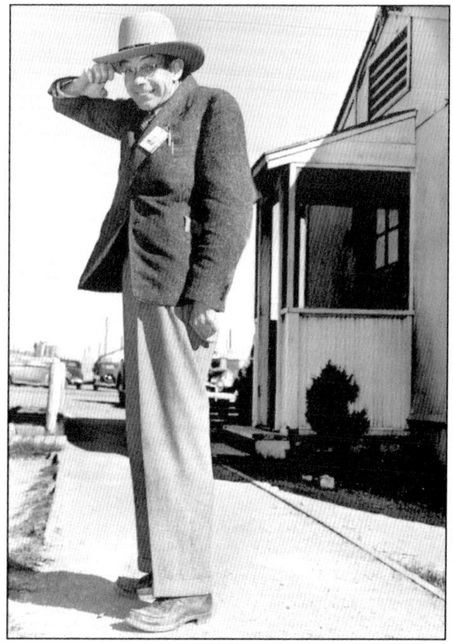

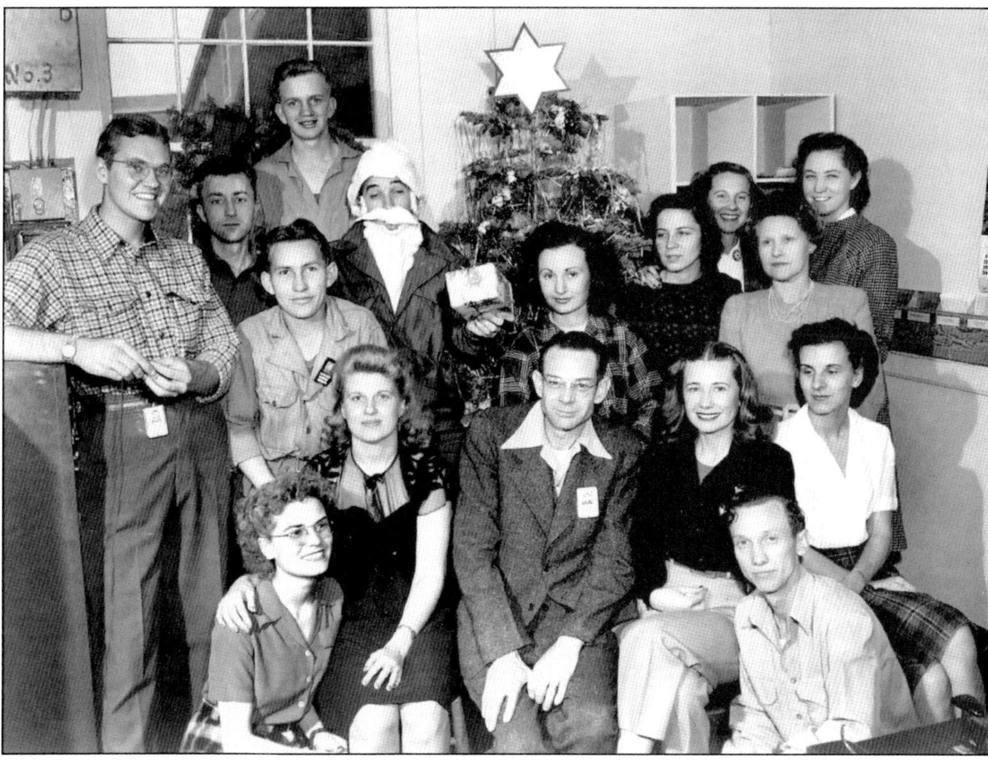

The photo group gathers around Loris Gardner at the Christmas celebration in 1946. Look closely to see the wire attached to the camera shutter held by John Michnovicz at the far left. He set it up so that he could take a photo of the bunch and include himself. Joe Gluth stands behind Michnovicz, and at the very back is Elmer Donor. Ruby Langham sits to the right of Gardner, and at the front right is Carl Somers.

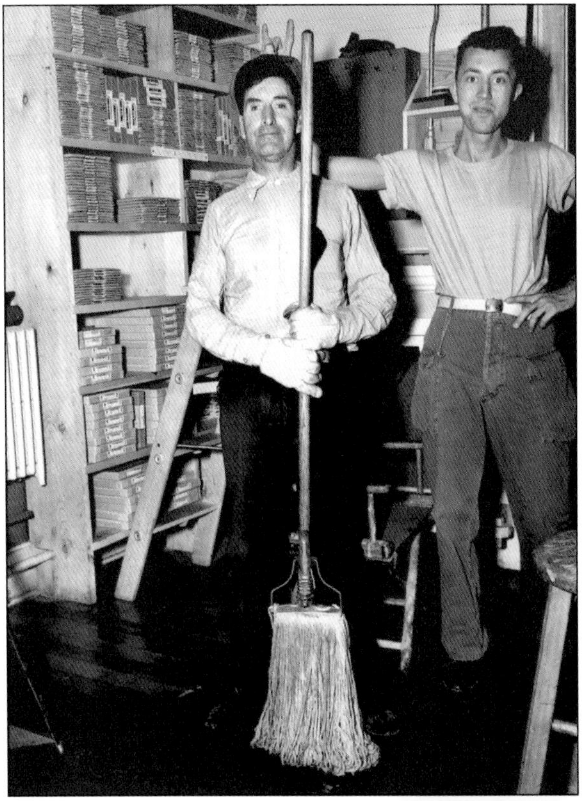

In the photo lab, everyone had an opportunity to be in a picture. The janitor on the left was nicknamed "Sergeant Billie" by his photo lab buddies. He hailed from the Espanola Valley and headed on the bus daily to Los Alamos for work. Here he is with Joe Gluth, whose nickname was "Jose," as they pose in the supply room. The Project work was a priority, so there was ample supply of black-and-white, Ansco color, and Ektachrome film available.

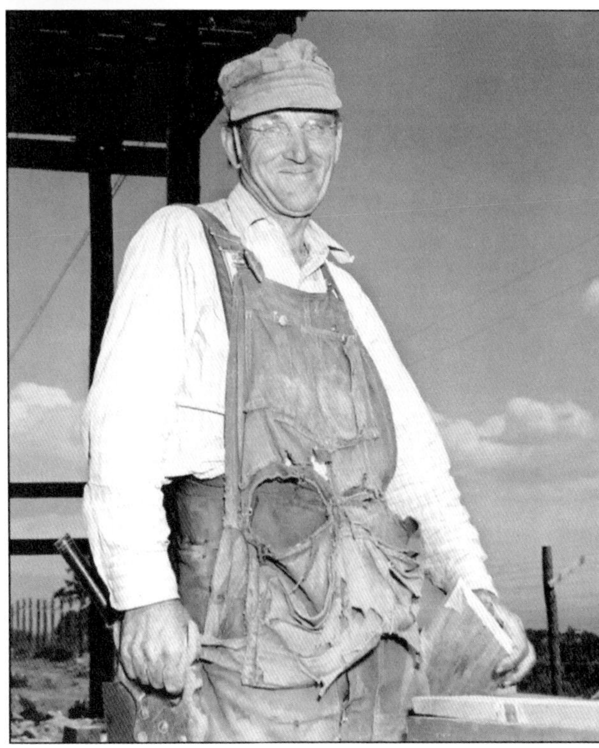

Although this gentleman doesn't look too old and grizzly, this photo was titled "Old Grandpa Carpenter at DP Site." In an isolated world of young GIs, he must have seemed ancient, and the tattered clothes probably added to the impression of age. Working with plutonium involved potential health risks, so a separate area for plutonium processing—the DP site—was constructed some distance from the main Technical Area. Early plutonium work was done in D Building, which may have contributed to the name.

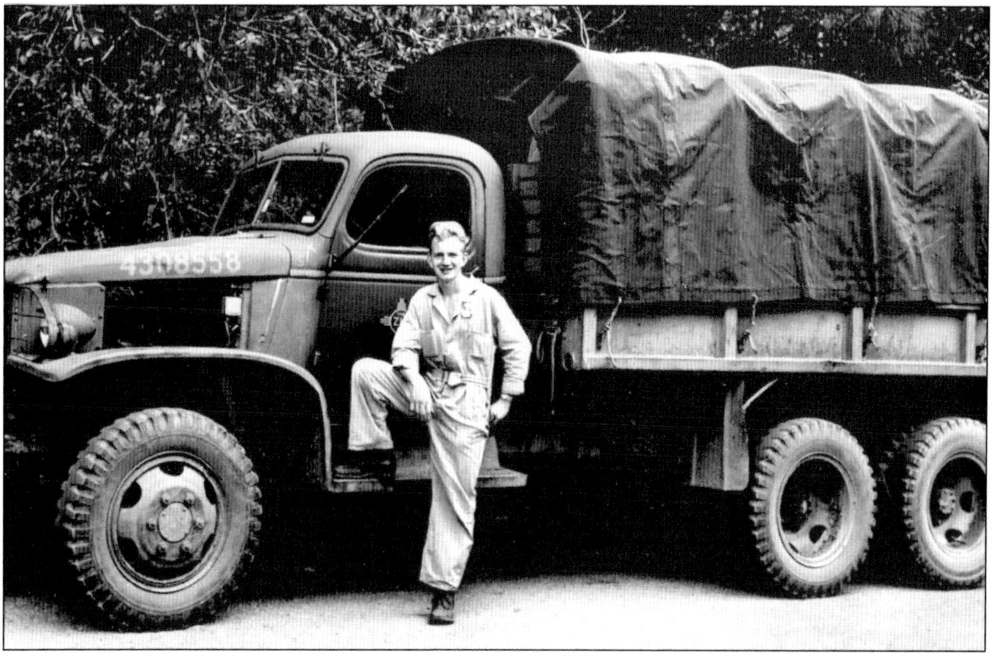

Elmer Donor enlisted in the Army in November 1945 and was sent to Los Alamos the following January. While he waited for his security clearance, he "made a weekly run to Salt Lake City . . . with several trucks with plutonium" (Donor, October 2004). After seven months he was assigned to the photo lab and worked there until his discharge from the Army in February 1947. Donor immediately returned to Los Alamos as a civilian photographer and stayed for several years.

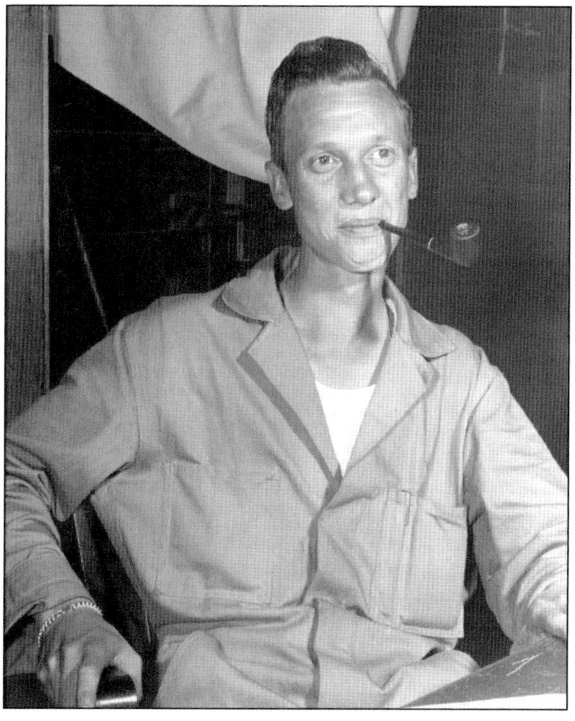

A new choice of prop—the pipe—was used by Carl Somers for his portrait, and the photographers all agreed that the pipe gave a look of distinction whether the subject smoked or not. Somers was the Photostat and Lithoprint Section leader. Lab equipment like the Photostat and the Ozalid were useful in making reproductions of positives and negatives; reducing, enlarging, and making negatives from paper copy; and making prints from the microfilm.

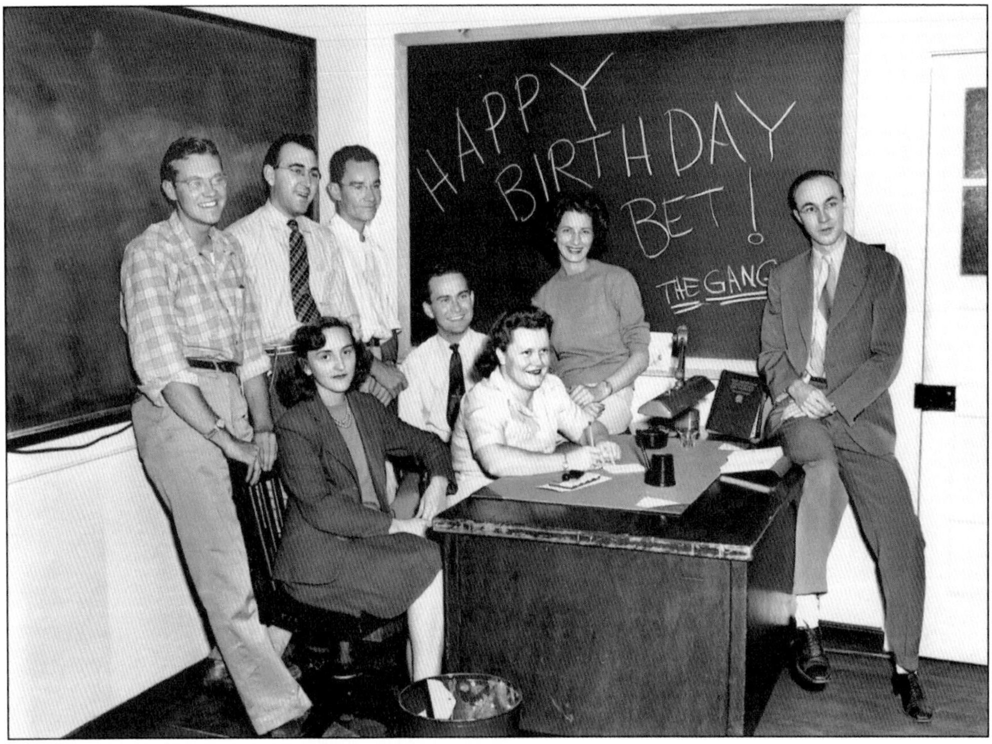

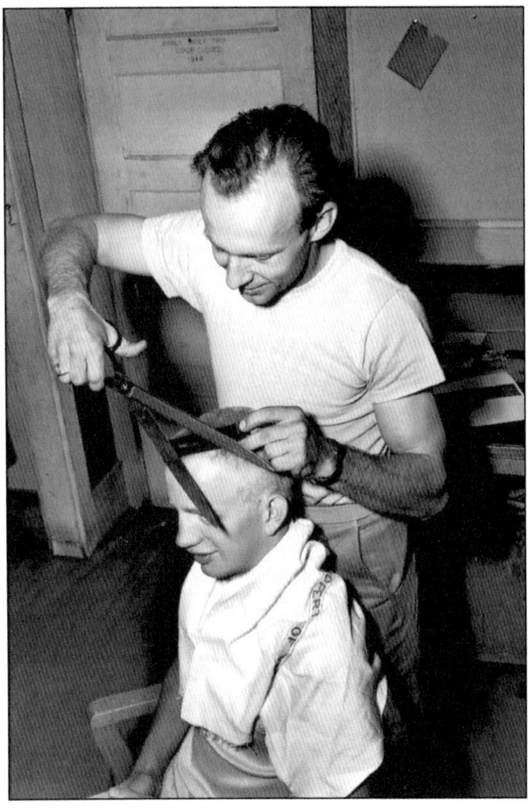

Betty Canfield sits at the back surrounded by birthday well-wishers. The "gang" includes, standing, John Michnovicz and Chuck Canfield. Nondice Jackson, seated at the desk, was known for "having made travel reservations for more world famous scientists than the reservations desk at Grand Central Station," claimed the *Los Alamos Times*. On her desk sits Ray Powell. These civilian employees, who chummed around socially, made invaluable contributions during wartime work hours.

"For the sheer fun of it, Roy Stone was shearing the locks of fellow photographer Elmer Donor," the *Los Alamos Times* of 1947 reported. Stone joined the photo lab late in 1946 and took up scissors in exchange for a camera for this practical joke. Surely Donor hoped it might be the first and the last cut at the hands and scissors of this eager barber. Both men were photographers in the Los Alamos photo lab. (Photo by Lab Photo Group.)

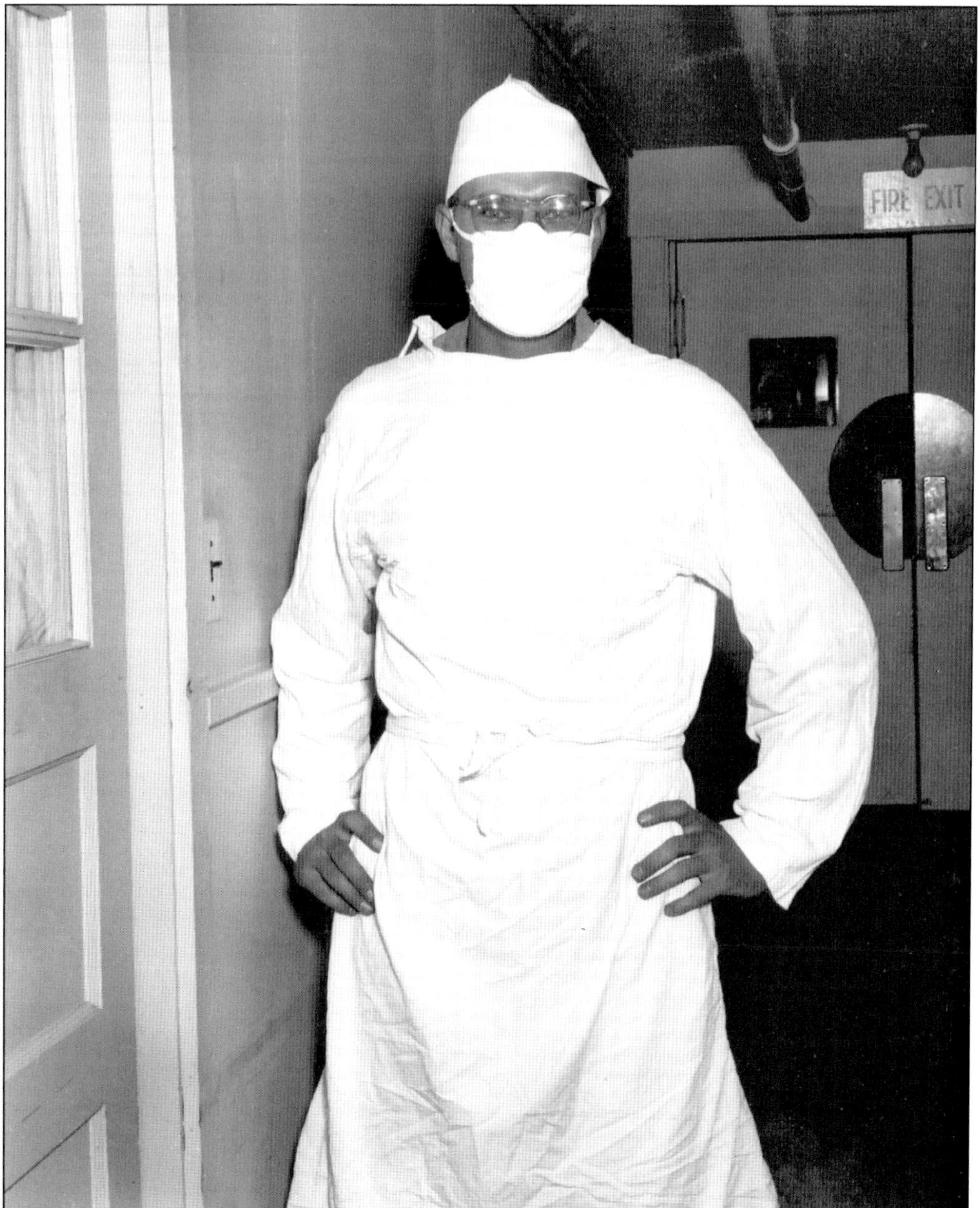

The premature deaths of Harry Daghlian and Louis Slotin from an overexposure to radiation happened in Los Alamos after the war. In separate incidents, critical assembly experiments were being conducted when a momentary slip caused a super dose of radiation to occur. John Michnovicz photographed both men during their hospitalization and, upon their deaths, was asked to document the autopsies. He is shown at the hospital just before the autopsies were to take place. Dr. Louis Hempelmann wrote a commendation to the photo lab supervisor about the work. He stated, "T/5 Michnovicz' manner in dealing with the patient and doctors was both discrete and pleasant . . . His photographs have good composition, clarity, and lighting, giving them excellent illustrative value . . . He is one of a few photographers on the site who could have done the excellent job that was done for us concerning the recent Omega accident."

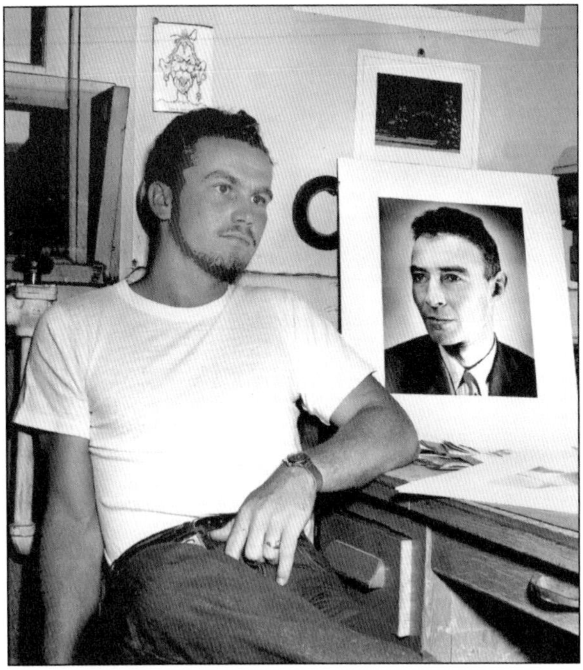

It seems that the lab was proud of its photo of the Project's most famous resident, Robert Oppenheimer. Other favorite prints were hung on the walls, and they all surrounded Harry Snowden, lab technician, who posed in the office area of the lab.

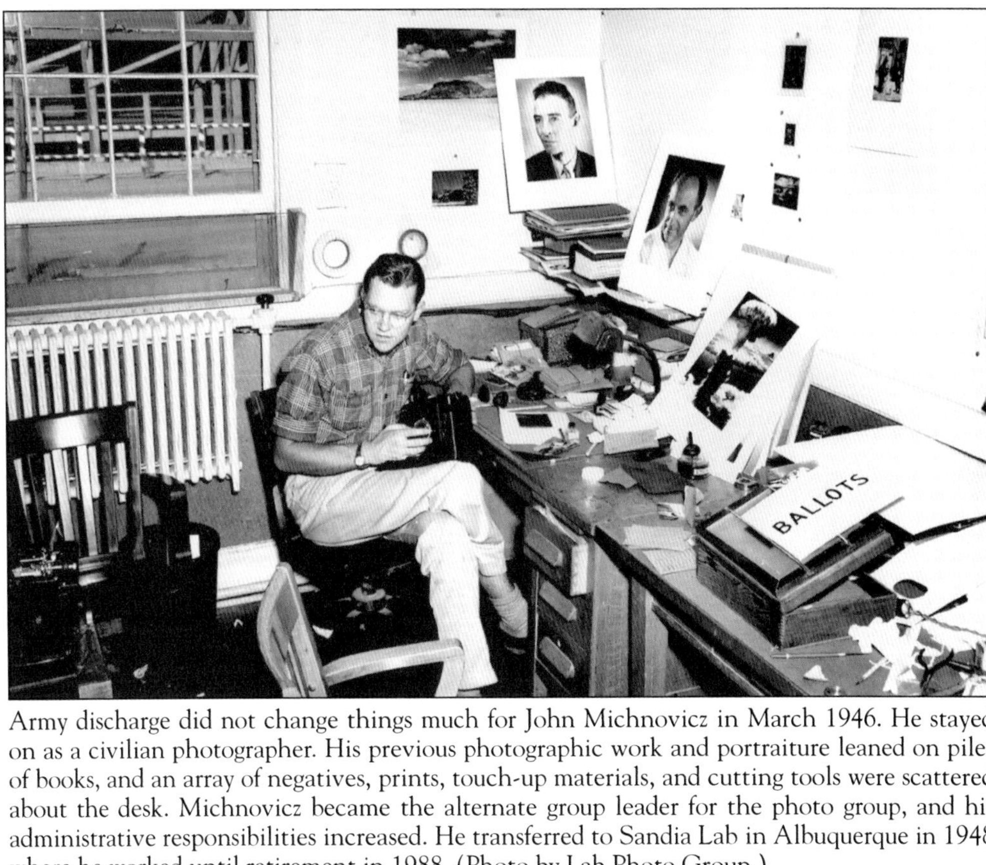

Army discharge did not change things much for John Michnovicz in March 1946. He stayed on as a civilian photographer. His previous photographic work and portraiture leaned on piles of books, and an array of negatives, prints, touch-up materials, and cutting tools were scattered about the desk. Michnovicz became the alternate group leader for the photo group, and his administrative responsibilities increased. He transferred to Sandia Lab in Albuquerque in 1948 where he worked until retirement in 1988. (Photo by Lab Photo Group.)

Five

DANCING, ROMANCING, AND MORE

Scientists at Los Alamos worked feverishly, under great strain and pressure, to complete their goal to end the war. Everyone felt the heat. At times, therefore, it was necessary to step out and burn off some steam, go dancing and partying for the evening, perhaps play some football in the afternoon, or, go ice skating or skiing before returning to one's all-important tasks.

As innovative as they all were on the Manhattan Project, they were equally determined to find new ways to have a good time when not busy with work. So, what was there to do on and off the Hill?

Music and dancing were probably the most important sources of enjoyment at Los Alamos. Many members of the community were musicians, and they used every opportunity to express themselves. Some played live music over the local radio station, and some organized themselves into bands big and small—trios, quartets, sextets, and ultimately, the "Big Band." And if you had a good voice, nobody would stop you from getting up on the stage. All of this music was regularly available for everyone to enjoy.

Also, revelry was essential to the young men and women in this small community. This meant organizing parties with lots of beer and homemade Tech Area punch. The latter was made from fruit juice and some "extra" ethanol that the boys in the warehouse somehow managed to procure.

Pranks and gags were also a regular occurrence on the Hill. Men and women lived in very close proximity to each other, and they were always seeking novel ways to break up the boredom or loneliness. It might mean creating a whole new award, such as the "Fairly Good Conduct Award," or, it might involve some goofy skits.

There were holiday parties, birthday parties, office parties, going-away parties, outdoor parties, picnics—just name it, and somebody would start organizing the event. There were mountain trails to explore, both on foot and on horseback. The ancient Indian ruins only a few miles from the gates made for an interesting excursion. Important scientific discussions took place along these isolated secure trails.

And the romance? Plenty of that took place, too, judging by the number of children born during the Project years. Perhaps that story is best left to the imagination.

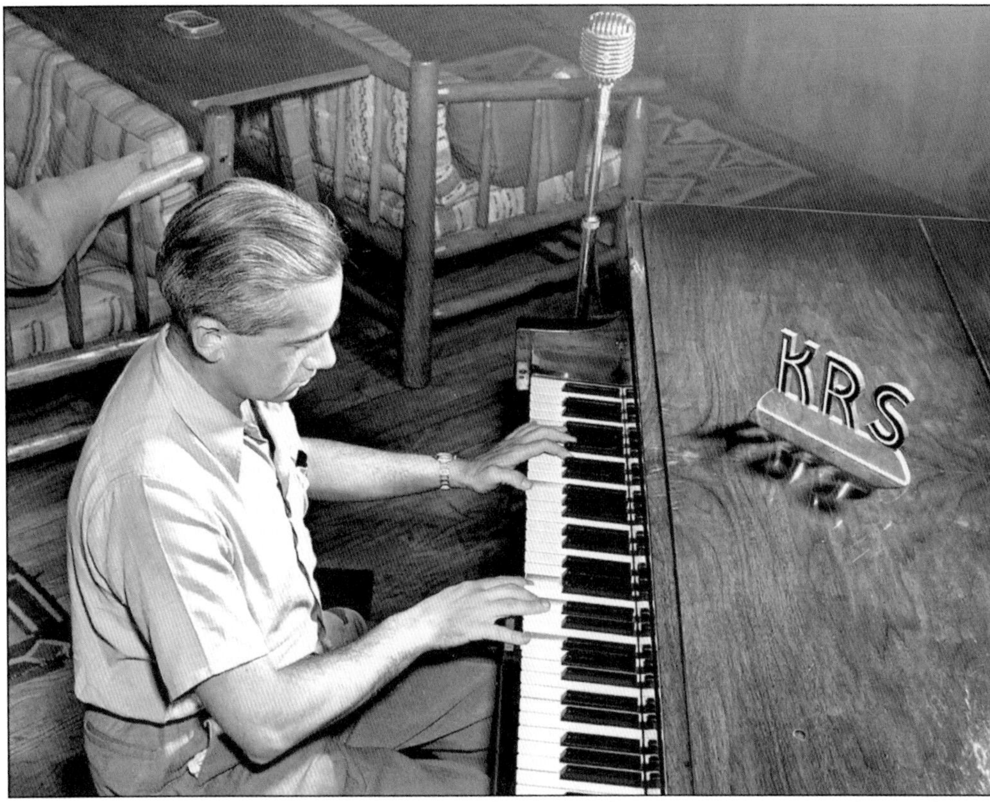

Austrian-born Otto Frisch was forced to abandon his work in Germany in 1933 during the rise of Hitler's Nazism. He immigrated to America via England and found his way to the Los Alamos Manhattan Project. His aunt, Lise Meitner, one of only a handful of female physicists in the 1930s, encouraged him to concentrate his studies on physics and not music. Nonetheless, his skills were such that he was able to serenade listeners regularly on the piano during local Radio KRS broadcasts of his live performances.

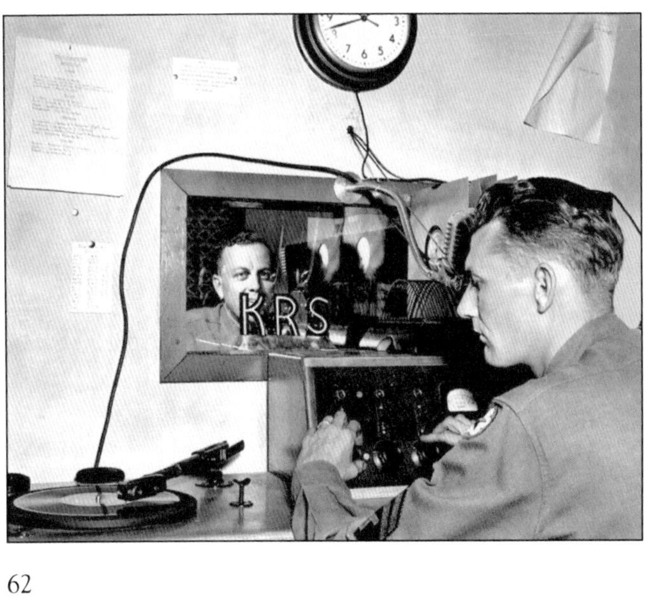

Bob Porton, the Radio KRS station manager behind the window, was the first announcer on the new "closed circuit" radio station, and Tom (Al) Fike engineered the program. Live and recorded entertainment carried by the telephone lines filled the airwaves. The Army Recreation Department and residents supplied the records for a daily show called *Music of the Masters*, its play list tacked to the wall. Contact with the outside world was tightly controlled, so the homegrown entertainment was welcome.

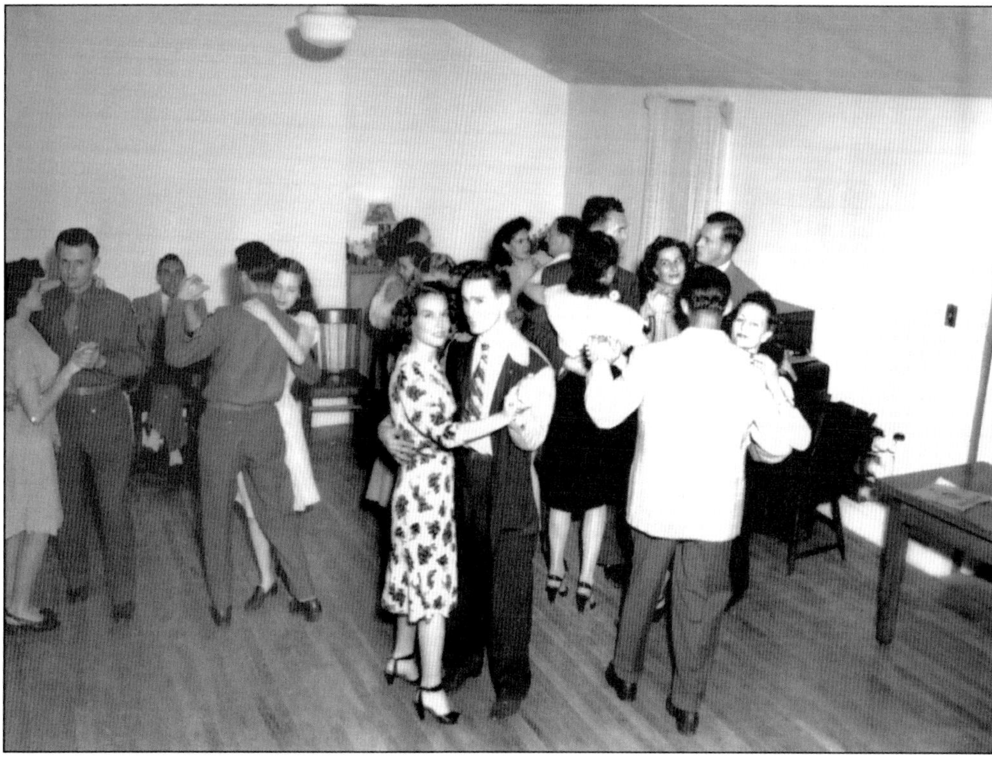

Dormitories housed some married couples as well as singles. This party took place in the common room of the married couples' dorm. "Dorm parties," wrote Bernice Brode, "were the biggest and brassiest. The boys took out all furniture from the common rooms to make room for dancing. Then there was the hardy punch often with all kinds of mixed liquor in one bowl . . . and some fruit juice for style. Despite such wicked punch, there was little unseemly behavior."

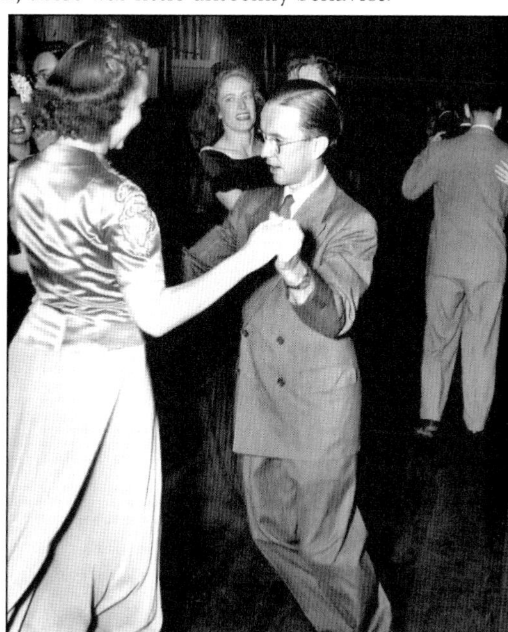

Marion Konopinski, sister of physicist Emil Konopinski, danced at a formal occasion with boyish-looking Willie Higinbotham in Fuller Lodge. The work, the weather, and the isolation convinced the population that casual attire was not only acceptable but preferable, but for the formal dances, women dressed in a grand fashion. Higinbotham was a scientist and bachelor, and he fulfilled multiple ancillary roles on the Hill, including square dance caller, accordionist, and barbershop quartet member.

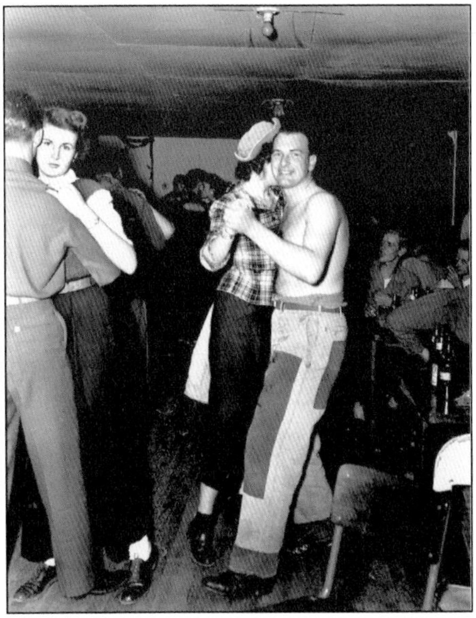

Military uniforms were cast aside for the Non-Commissioned Officers' (NCO) Costume Party. Sergeant Drake decided to do without shirt and costume and enjoy the evenings' festivities bare-chested. GIs and WACs who ranked technician fifth grade (E-5) or higher could join the NCO Club for the $1 per month dues. Military hierarchy prevailed for guests, and only the GIs' girlfriends or the WACs' boyfriends could be invited to the club.

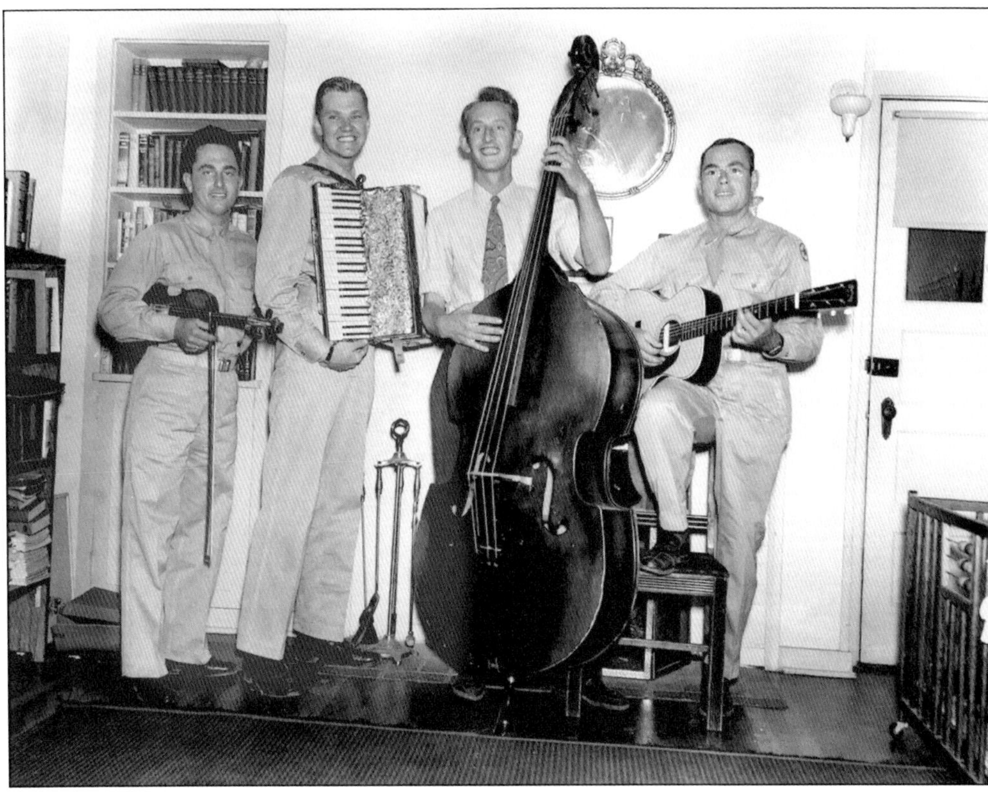

On June 25, 1945, the mimeographed *Daily Bulletin*, a local circular, alerted its readers to "keep your eyes and ears open" for the debut appearance of Los Cuatros (The Four), a group of musicians consisting of three servicemen and a civilian machinist. The members included, from left to right, Ray Gallo on violin, John Michnovicz on accordion, Locky Lockhart on bass, and Keith Gard on guitar. A portrait of the group was taken in the home of leader and bass player Locky Lockhart. Note the playpen on the right. (Photo by Joe Gluth.)

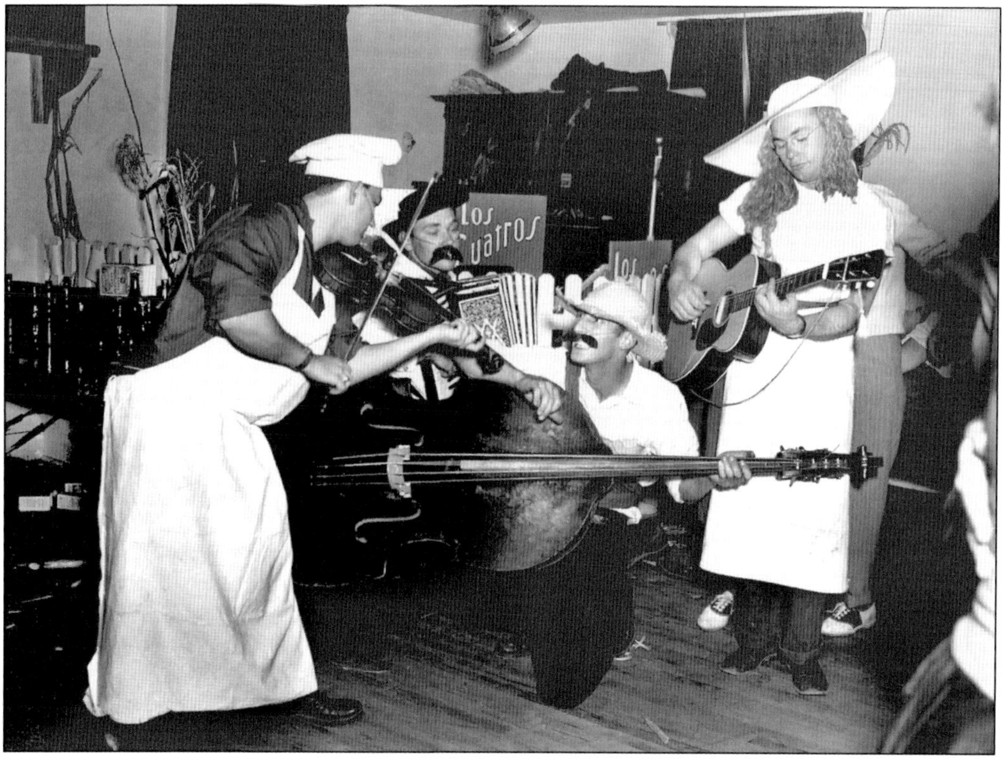

Los Cuatros entertained at dances and included novelty acts such as silly costumes and Locky Lockhart playing the bass like it was a guitar! He booked engagements for Los Cuatros, but phone service was limited, so interested parties contacted him by writing to P.O. Box 1663, Santa Fe. Lockhart's car was handy for "touring" different venues on the Hill. They often played at the Officer's Club, WAC Barracks, Service Club, and NCO Club. (Photo by Lab Photo Group.)

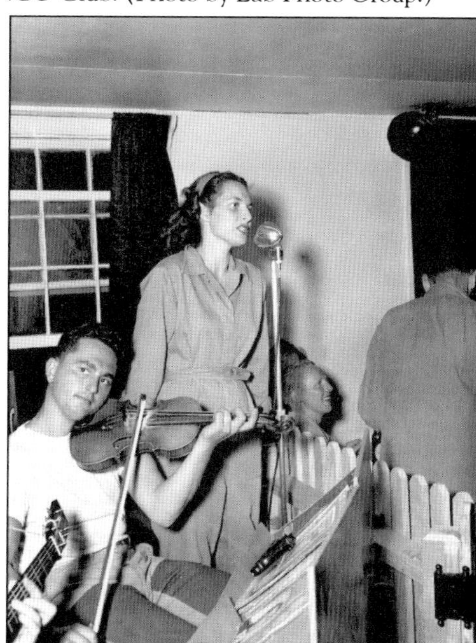

It was a family affair when vocalist Lois Lockhart performed here with Los Cuatros. Themed dances were created, and this one was the "fatigue" dance, so the vocalist dressed the part. She also appeared regularly with the Keynotes and the Sad Sack Six. Dances were scheduled on several weeknights and every weekend, which supplied ample work and kept the Lockharts, who were the parents of three children, six years old and under, quite busy.

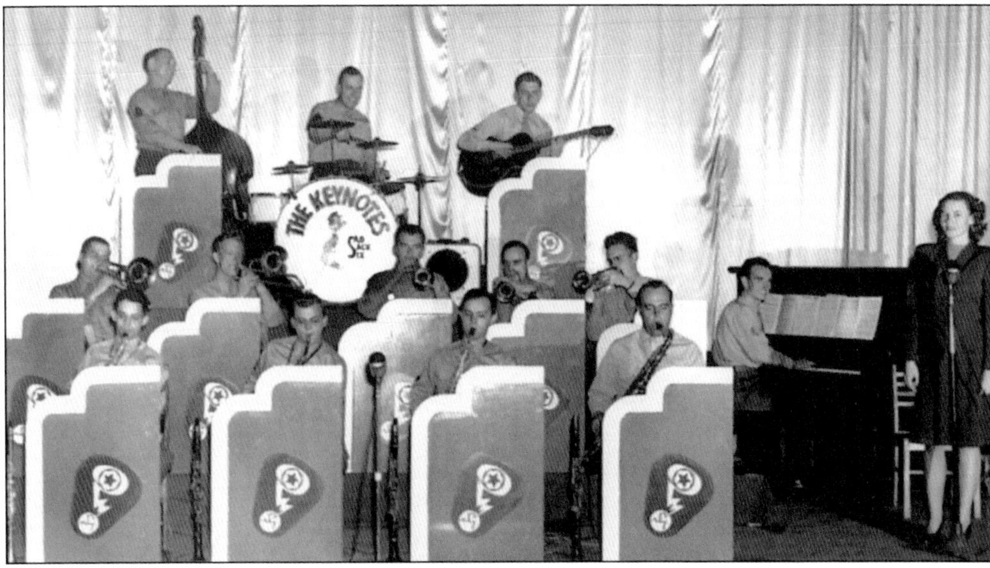

"It was Saturday night . . . dance night again at Theater #2 with music by the band you made popular, The Keynotes," announced the *Daily Bulletin*. The Keynotes included, from left to right and from the top down, Hal Fishbine (leader and bass player), Bob Porton (drums), Sam Macaione (guitar), Ray Thill and Jerry Scheiderick (trombone), Arnie Roensch, Tom Carmen, and Don Lovelace (trumpet), Jack Hanett (tenor sax), Fred Kusta and Lou Calderelli (alto sax), Harold Wheeler (tenor sax), Clay Stebbins (piano), and Mary Lane "Weezie" Antos (vocals).

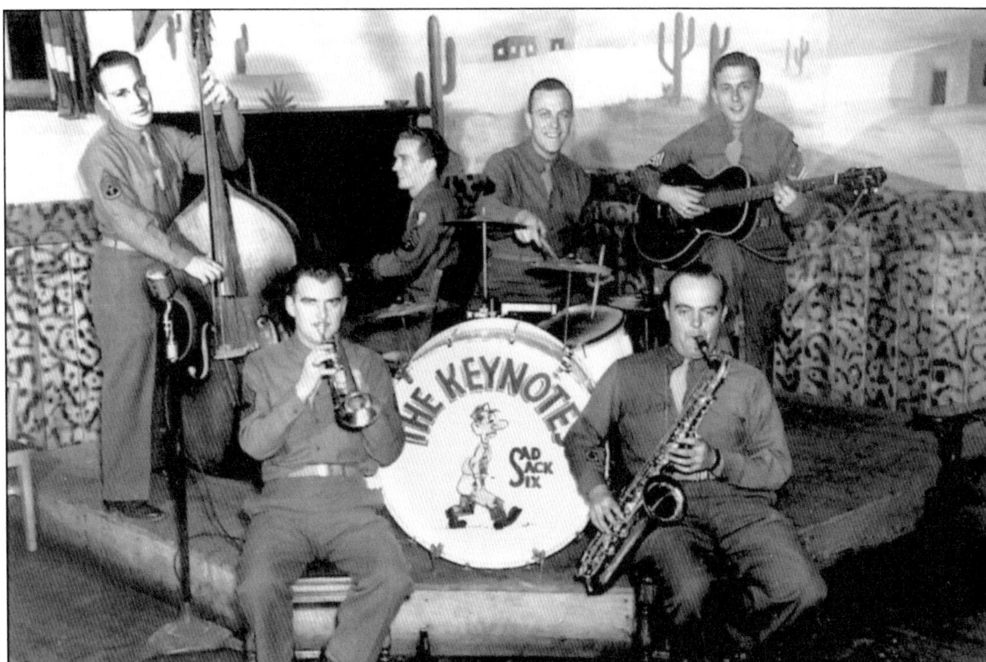

Another ensemble of musicians on the Hill called the Sad Sack Six was composed of members of the Keynotes. Musicians included Hal Fishbine (leader and bass player), Clay Stebbins (piano), Bob Porton (drums), Sam Macaione(guitar), Arnie Roensch (trumpet), and Harold Wheeler (tenor sax).

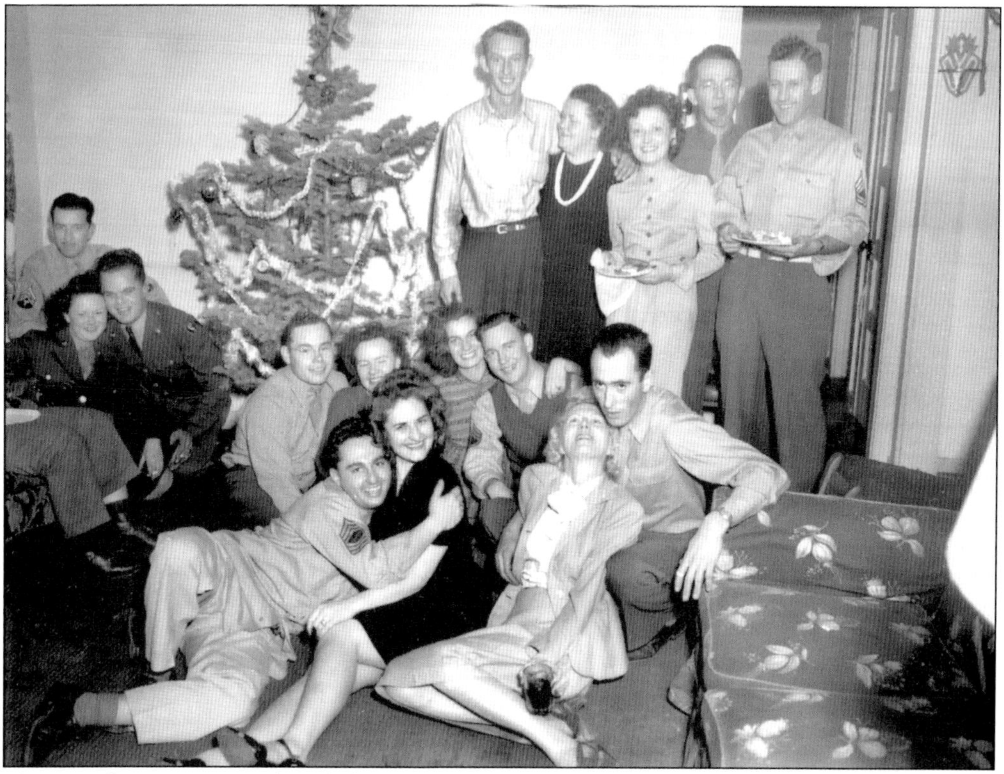

The spindly tree came right off the mesa for the Christmas party hosted by the Lockhart's for Los Cuatros and friends in December 1945. Lockhart stands tall at the back, Ray Gallo is sweet on his girl as he leans in closely on the floor, and just to his left are Keith Gard and his date. The war was over and Gallo and Gard would join the exodus of many military and civilians from the Project and bring Los Cuatros to its end.

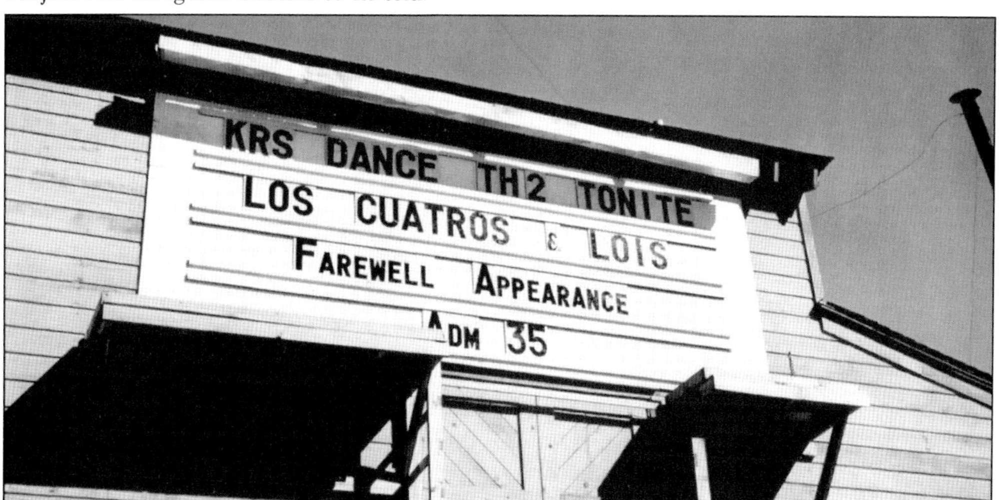

Radio KRS sponsored the last appearance of Los Cuatros with a special appearance by Lois Lockhart. Los Cuatros lasted from June 1945 to March 1946, and though many left Los Alamos at war's end, the lure of this enchanted land was too strong for Locky Lockhart and John Michnovicz. They stayed on the Hill for a few more years.

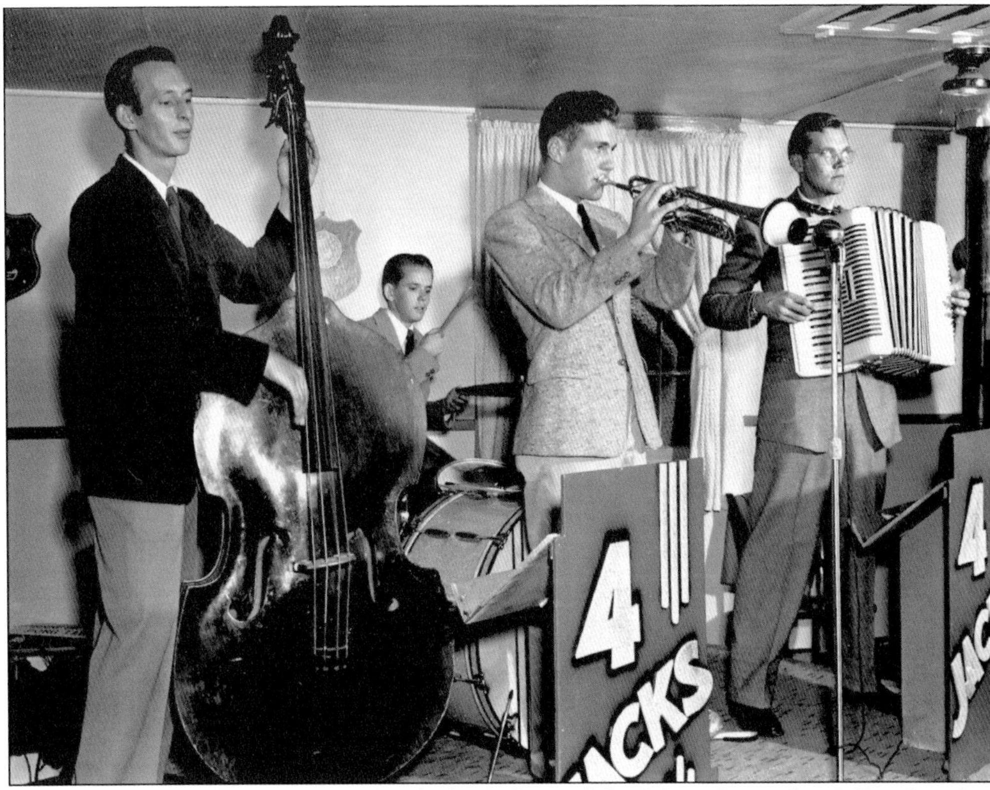

A story in the *Los Alamos Times* on April 26, 1946, noted the debut of a new band. Don Lovelace on trumpet and Tommy Hines on drums joined Locky Lockhart and John Michnovicz, and The Four Jacks appeared on the dance scene in Los Alamos. As soon as a vocalist could be found, the band intended to call itself "The Four Jacks and a Queen."

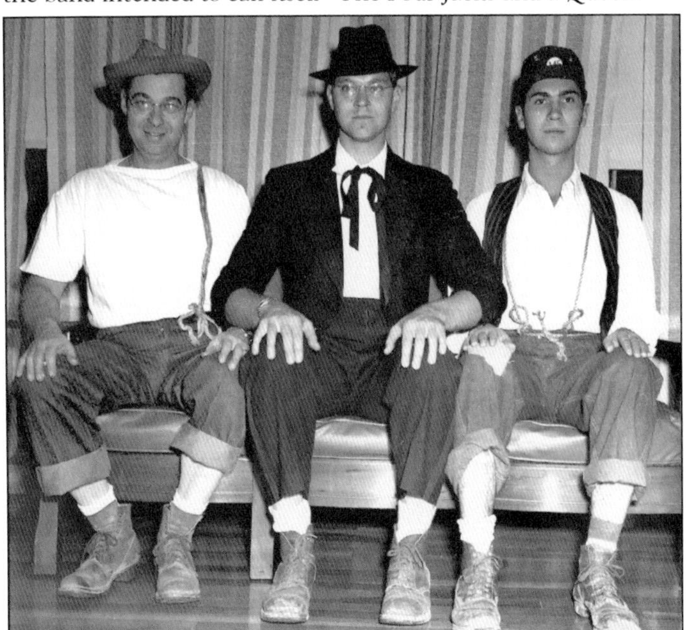

When Locky Lockhart and his family returned home to California, John Michnovicz got together with Herman Lacey (left) and Leo Gonzales (right), and the JAMIC Trio was born. They were in costume for this portrait as they prepared to entertain at the Civic Club. The group stayed together for a couple of years, their popularity increased, and soon they were performing in Santa Fe and Taos. (Photo by Elmer Donor.)

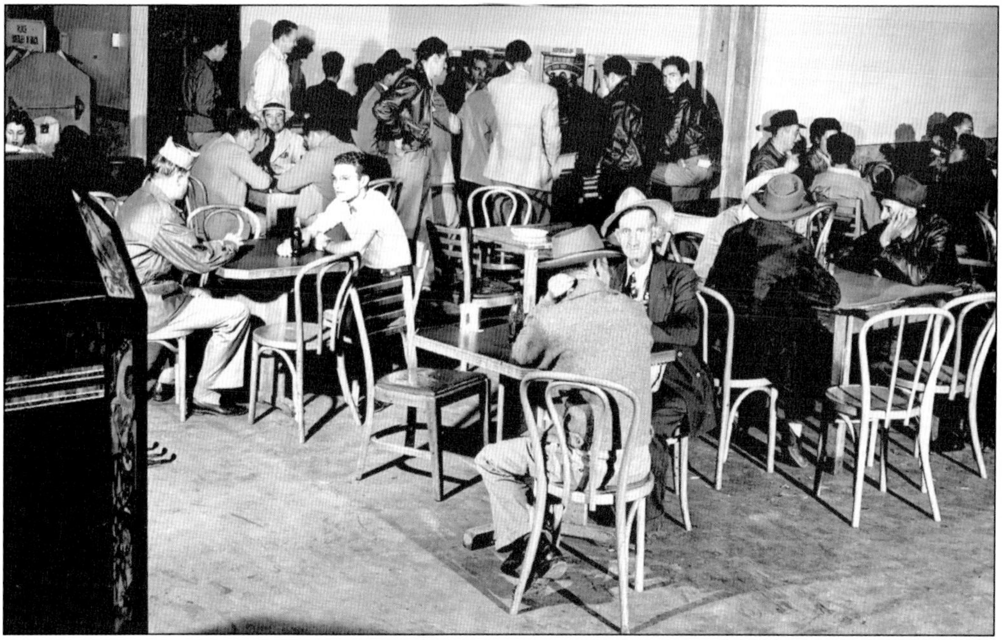

In 1946, of all the gathering places in Los Alamos, the real melting pot was the Service Club. Pictured here are the layers of social strata that existed in Los Alamos as the town began to define itself in the postwar period. Military folks, scientists, laborers, technicians, and clerks sipped cokes or beer and downed fried egg sandwiches. The jukebox and pinball machines were ready and all were welcome—Indian and Hispanic, immigrant scientist and Midwestern Ph.D., military and civilian, young and old.

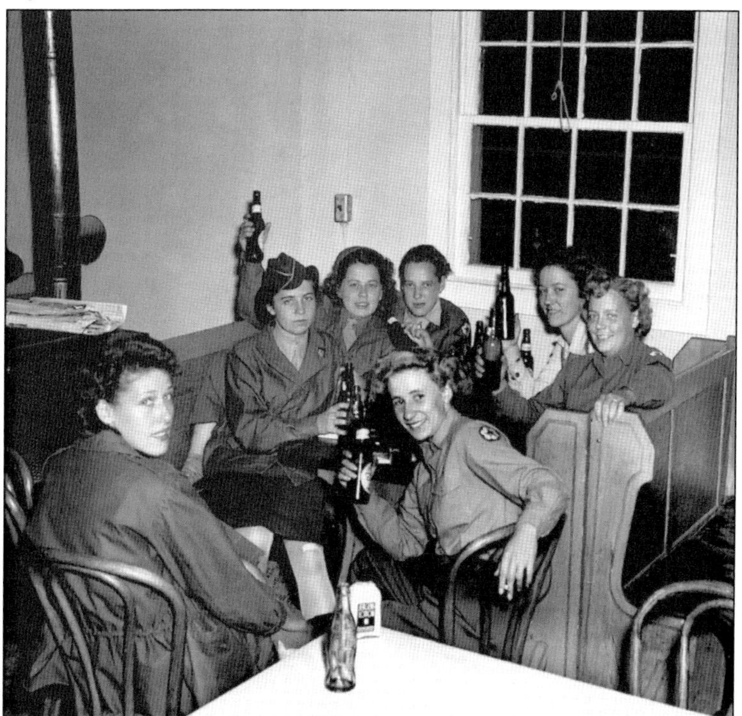

Los Alamos was considered an Army post, and so the system of post exchanges (PX) was maintained. These included the SED (Special Engineering Detachment) PX, the MP (Military Police) PX, and a PX across from the fenced Technical Area simply called the Tech PX. The WACs in this picture did not have their own PX, so they were welcome at the SED PX, which offered refreshments, sundries, and a place to meet friends, relax, and have a beer.

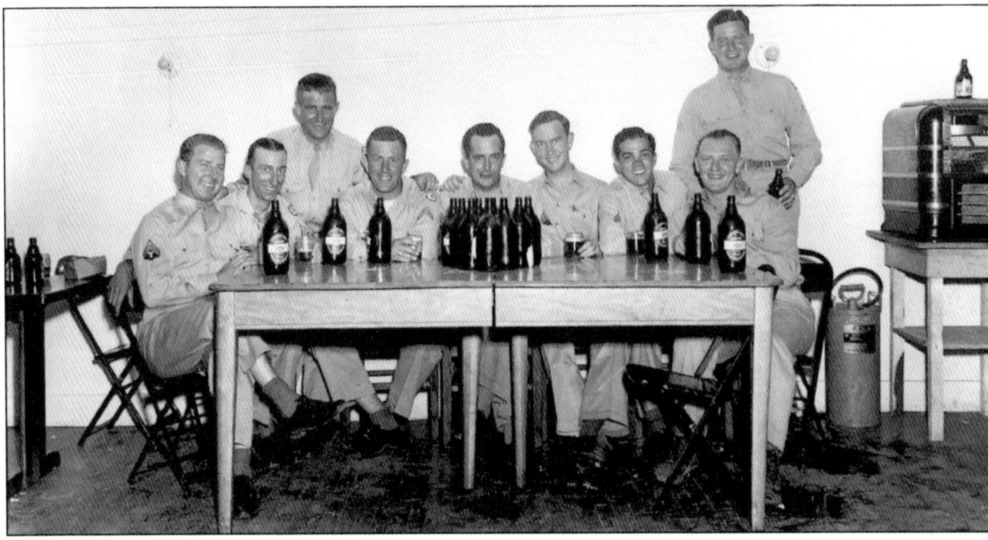

A couple of beers each for a bunch of Army guys and that adds up to a lot of beer. In mid-1946 the local paper announced that "although beer is rapidly becoming scarce in the outside world, 10,000 cases of beer were to arrive in the next sixty days." Two hundred cases per month were destined for the NCO Club, pictured here. The PX procurement officer reported that 300 cases of beer per day were consumed at the Service Club. "You can see what we're up against," he remarked.

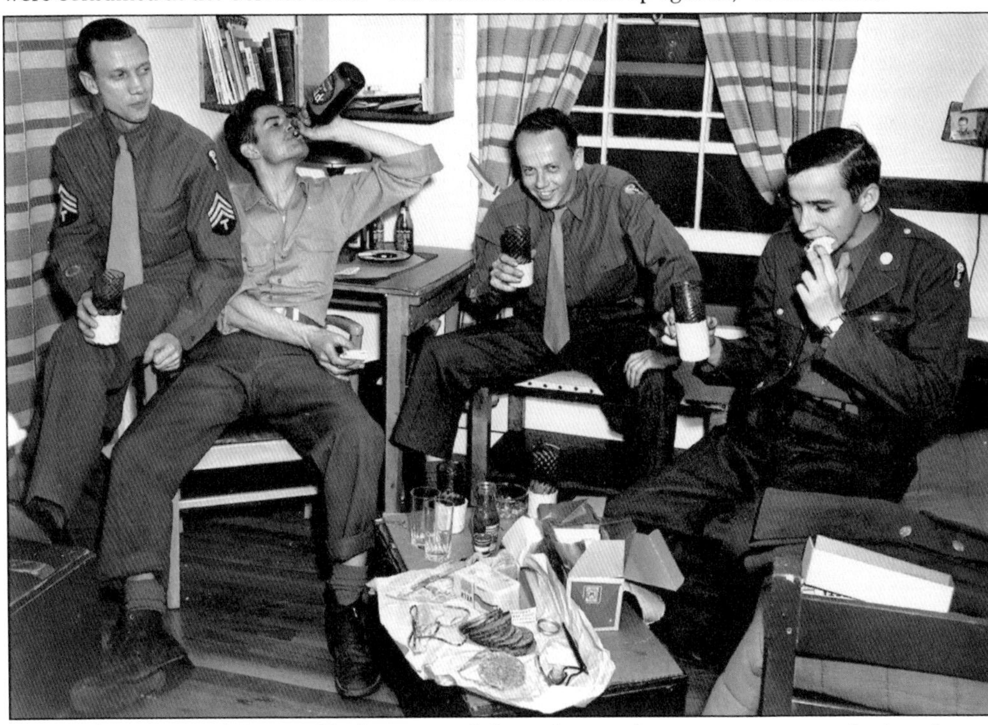

GIs Carl Somers and George Kochaniec, at left, and two other guests enjoy a relaxing change from the barracks as they party in a friend's room in 1946. Civilian dorm rooms were better furnished and more spacious, and obviously lines of hierarchy did not exist between these Army and civilian friends. They partied with some cheese, sausages, crackers, and beer that cost only 10¢ a bottle.

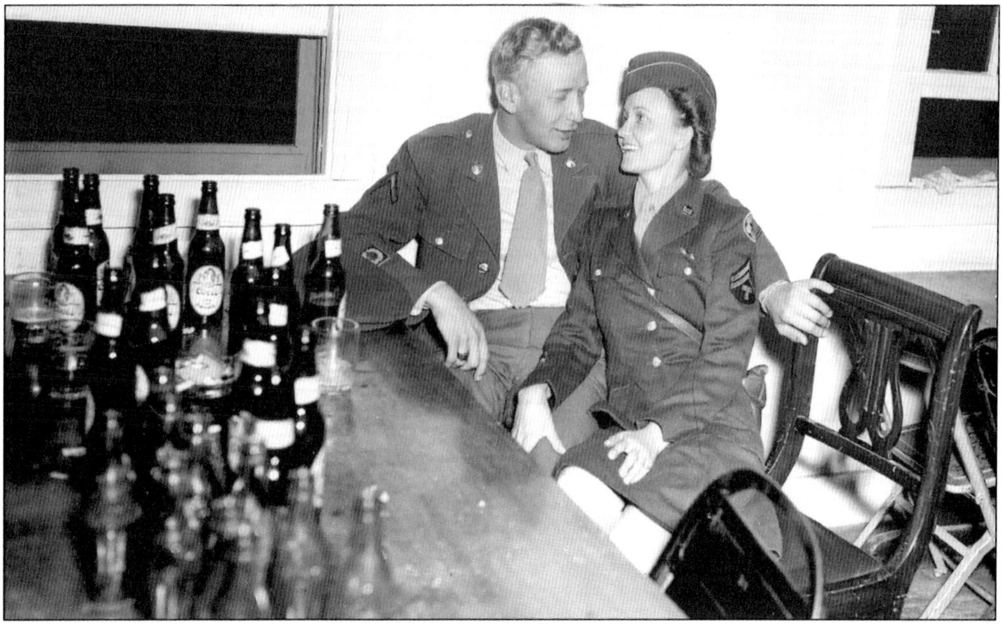

The others had departed, the beer bottles remained, and at the end of the evening these two sat tenderly with each other. Had they met their one and only? Lucky him, if so, because there were ten men to every woman at the Project. Cpl. W. Wellhausen in his notes on SED life in the *Los Alamos Times* complained about a couple of fellow soldiers who behaved so well during the work day but came to blows after 5 p.m.—over women!

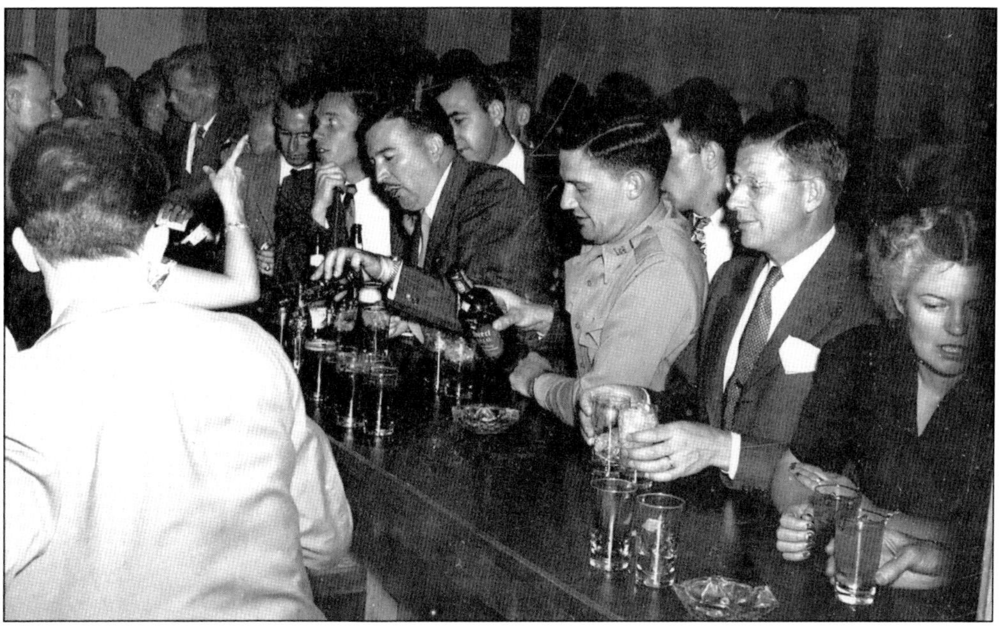

In the postwar period, many of the original newcomers to the Hill chose to make Los Alamos their permanent home. Several residents felt the need for a private club. They organized and in time, a constitution was written, dues were collected, and the Civic Club was formed. Members renovated the closed North Mess Hall to house the popular club. By 1947, the Civic Club—a place for dining, dancing, and drinking—was thriving.

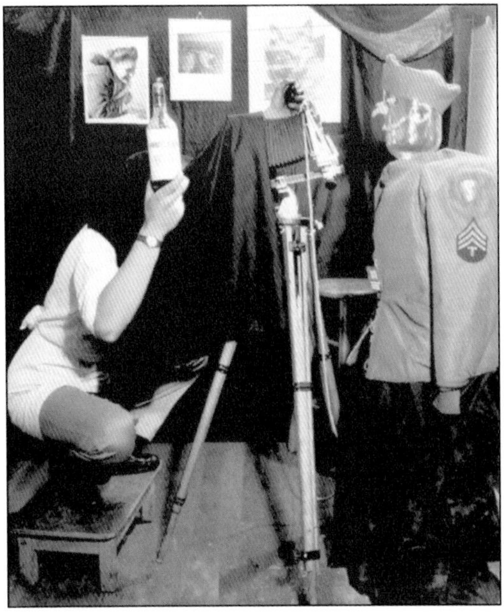

Would the whiskey bottle make the empty-headed GI smile as he posed for the cameraman? The shrouded photographer crouched quietly, paying careful attention to light and focus under his dark cloth. From this View camera came many historical photos, but John Michnovicz had a penchant for silliness, so while he waited in the dark, his subject posed patiently and so did he. (Photo by Joe Gluth.)

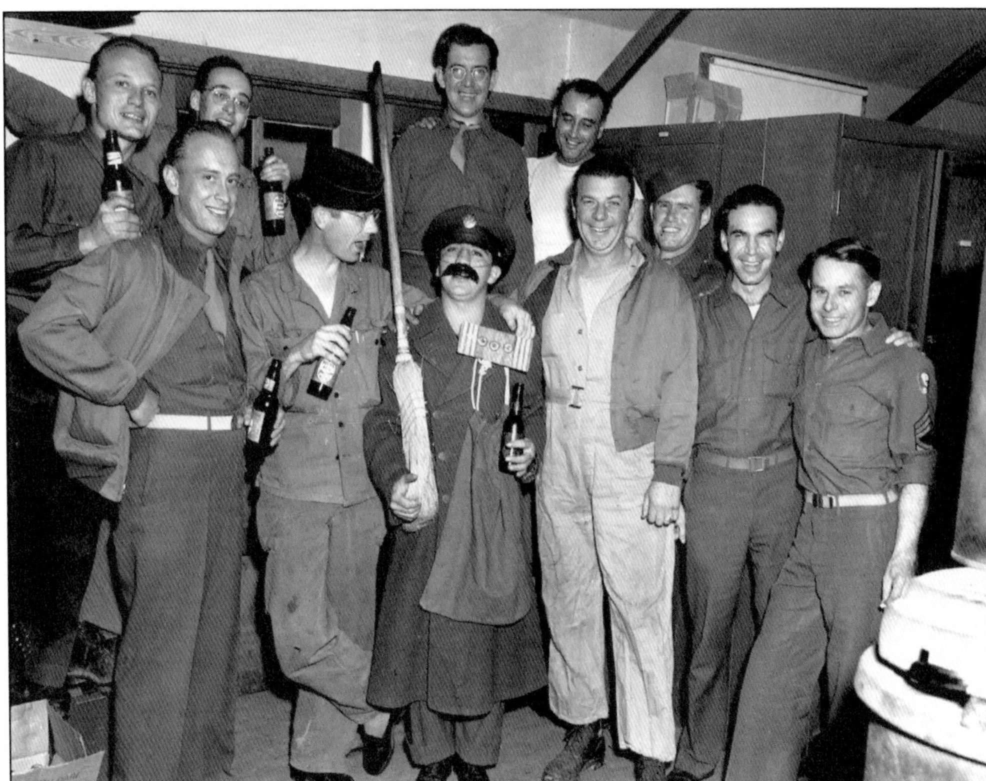

In this photo, GIs have fun at each other's and the Army's expense. Jim Cavelli, surrounded by his barracks mates, is the decorated soldier in the center receiving the "Fairly Good Conduct Medal" on his "Barracks Bag Cluster Award." Spoofing the Army's "Good Conduct Medal," Cavelli stood proudly with beer and broom in hand!

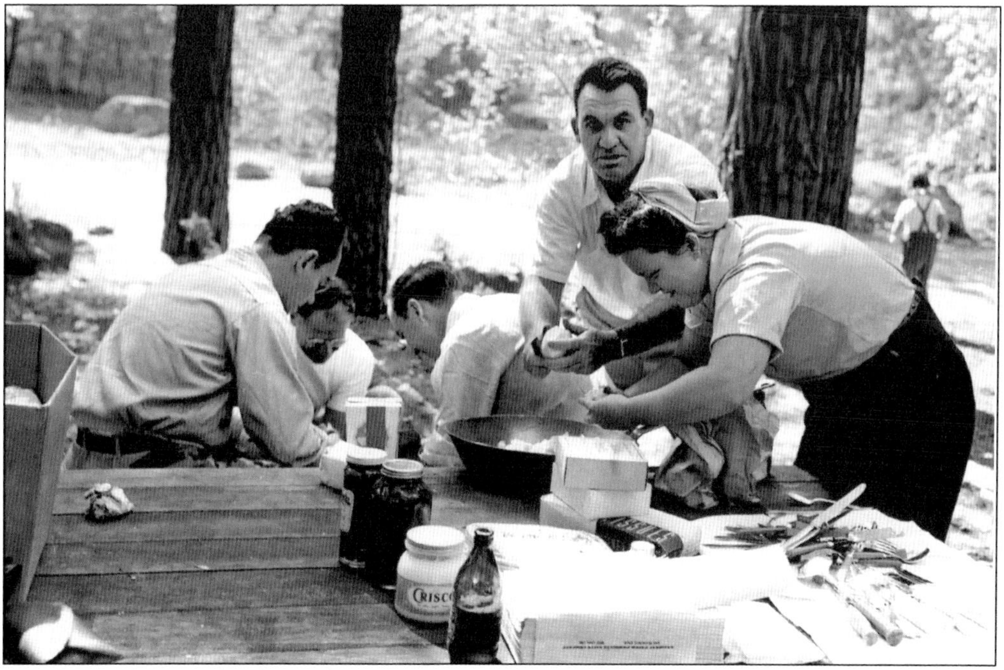

Nondice Jackson and Bob Hill busied themselves with potato peeling while others built the fire, set the table, and readied the food. Fried potatoes and steak never tasted so good, and the setting was perfect for a day of relaxation. It was easy to see why many of those at Los Alamos decided to stay in New Mexico, having caught the bug that convinced them that life back home could not compare to the bright sunshine, mountains, and warmth that this place had to offer.

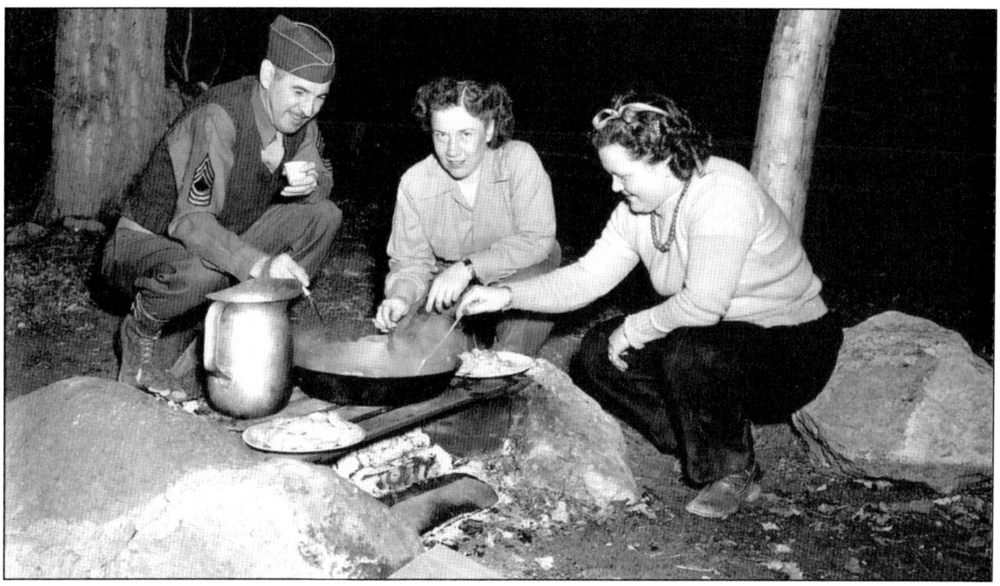

The weather must have been promising for this steak party in Frijoles Canyon on March 24, 1945. Evening picnics gave many a chance to imbibe some Tech Area punch. GIs assigned to the warehouse would "moonlight" requisition the alcohol, and at parties and picnics, it was combined with grapefruit juice to make a powerful but delicious punch. Thick steaks and punch made the mass-produced meals in the Army mess halls become a distant memory.

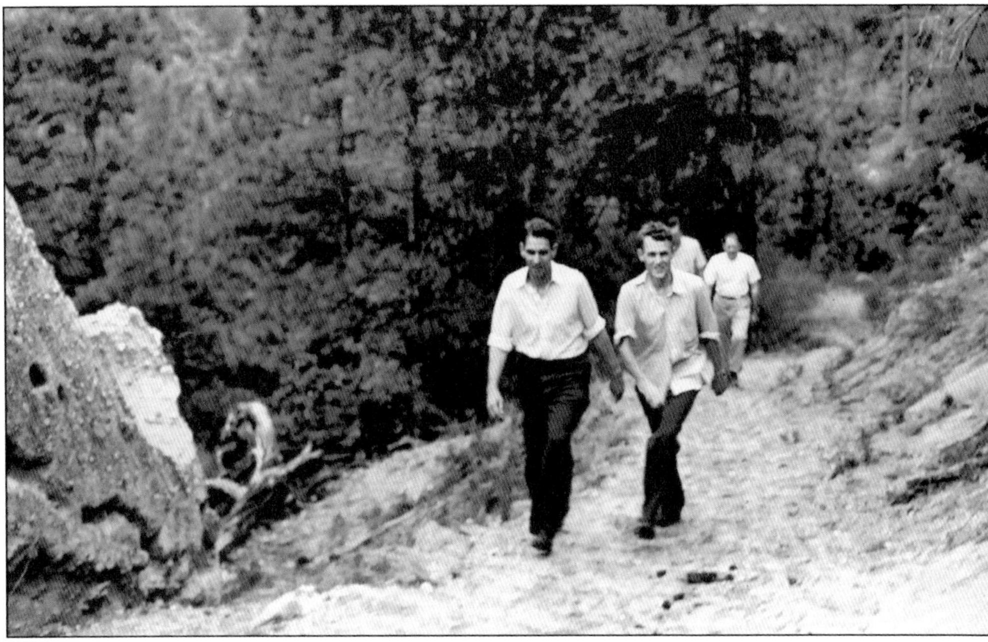

The cliffs of Frijoles Canyon are visible in the upper left corner and the hiking path that trailed through the canyon was worn down by many a Manhattan Project resident. This foursome—Les Seeley, John McGee, Gil Campbell, and J. Clark—walked the path on a summer outing. The Army administration saw the need for organized recreation in this isolated setting, but until that was functioning, the vast Pajarito Plateau provided its own playground for hiking and picnicking.

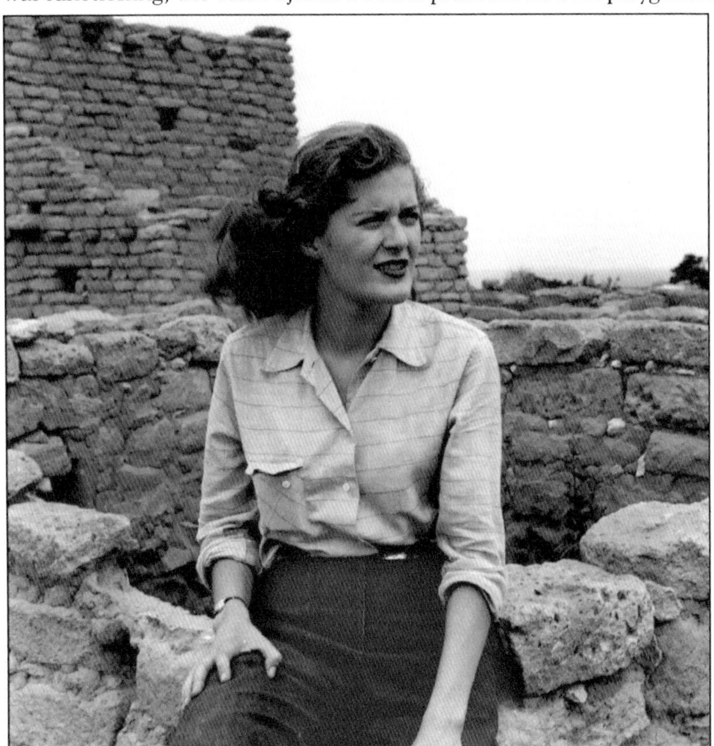

On the same Pajarito Plateau but to the north was another ancient Indian ruin known as the Puye Cliff Dwellings. Mary Louise Maloney, shown here, enjoyed visiting the site. She was one of the many young women recruited from Las Vegas, New Mexico, to fill personnel needs in Los Alamos during the war. Maloney worked in the commissary and the motor pool. She met John Michnovicz at a Valentine's Day dance in 1947, and they married the following year.

This wind-up pitch by Bill Bannon opened a new season of softball in Los Alamos after the war. The men played on teams called the Exploders, the Plutons, and the Bombers, and the women's teams included the Sad Sockers and Atomic Dodgers. Games commenced after work hours and rounds were played, with the batting averages and standings published weekly in the *Los Alamos Times*.

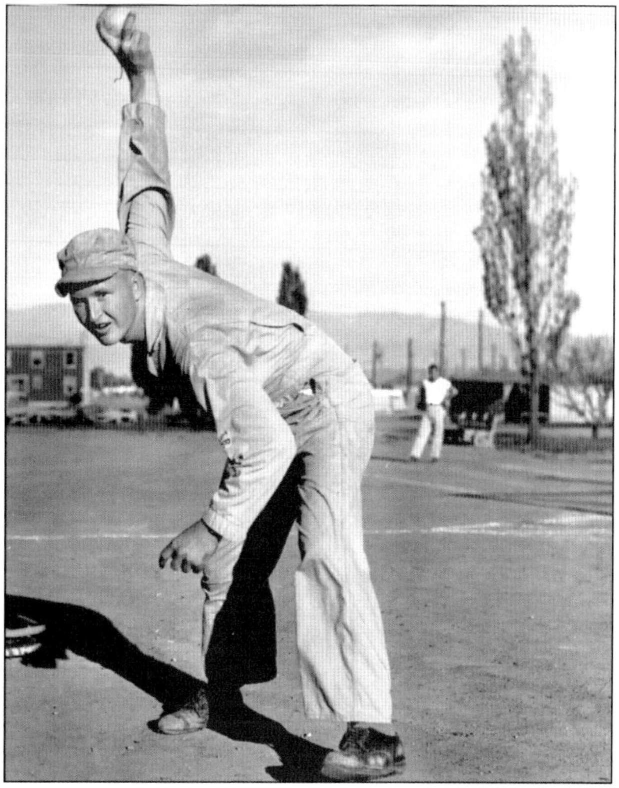

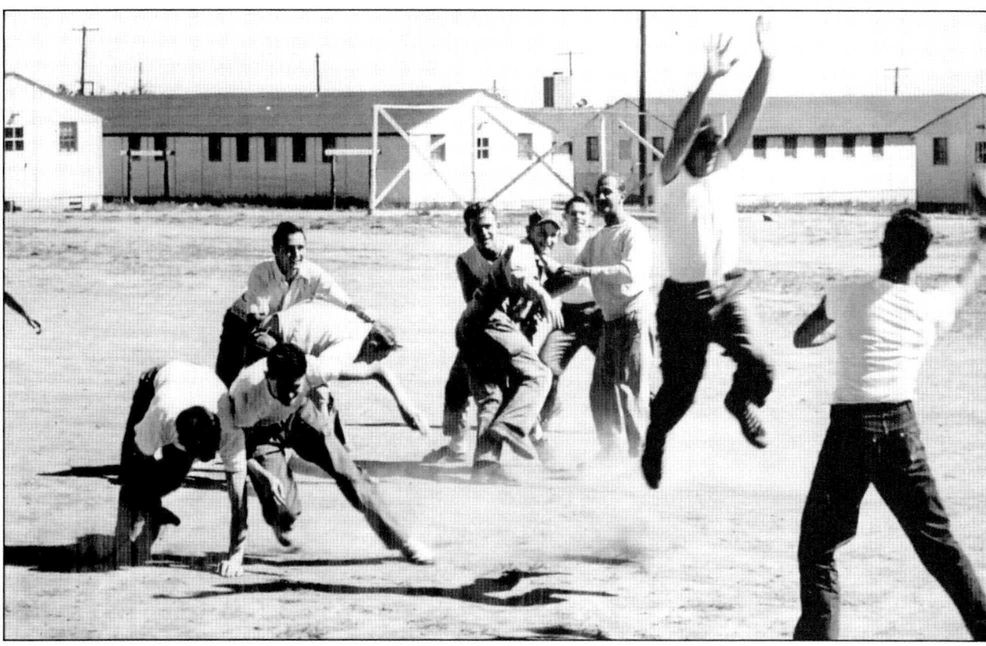

Joe Gluth, on the right, goes back for a pass in a pickup game of football played on the best surface available, a dirt lot. In the closed world of top-secret work conducted six days a week, a touch football game, no matter the conditions, was a welcome change from the routine. Barracks and dorms line the background of the photo.

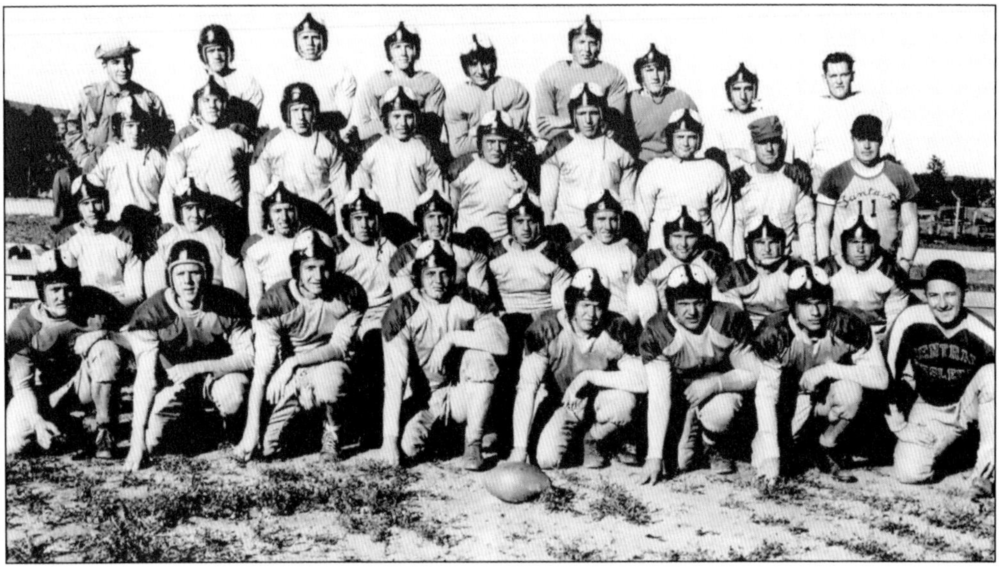

The Manhattan Project's entry in the Fourth Army Football League in 1946 was this team with a familiar name—the Atomic Bombers! They competed with teams from White Sands Proving Grounds and Brooke Army Medical Center in San Antonio as well as the University of New Mexico "B" team. Midway through the season, a practically new team took the field because of so many GI discharges. A "one win" record did not deter Coach Haynes Richardson from predicting that next year's squad would be a threat in the league.

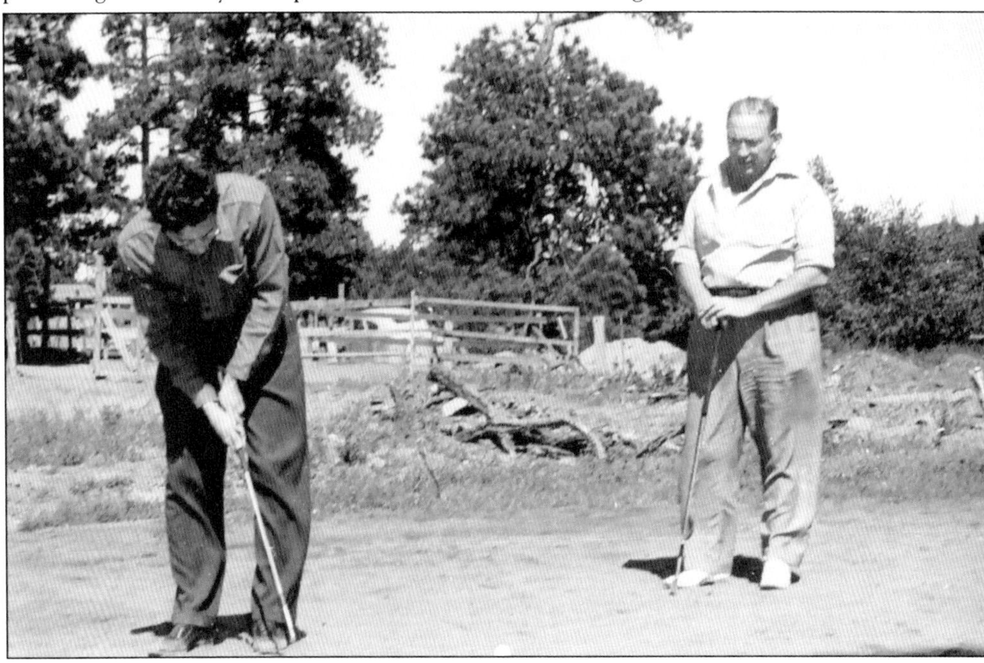

Two fellows tee off from the dirt and scrub on the Los Alamos premier golf course of 1946. An odd combination of determination and imagination was required to play on the golf course that doubled as a horse pasture. Sand traps abounded—well, it was mostly sand anyway—and the "greens" were made of loosely packed, oil-treated earth enclosed by a fence to keep the horses out. The fenced green had no gate so players had to climb over to sink the ball.

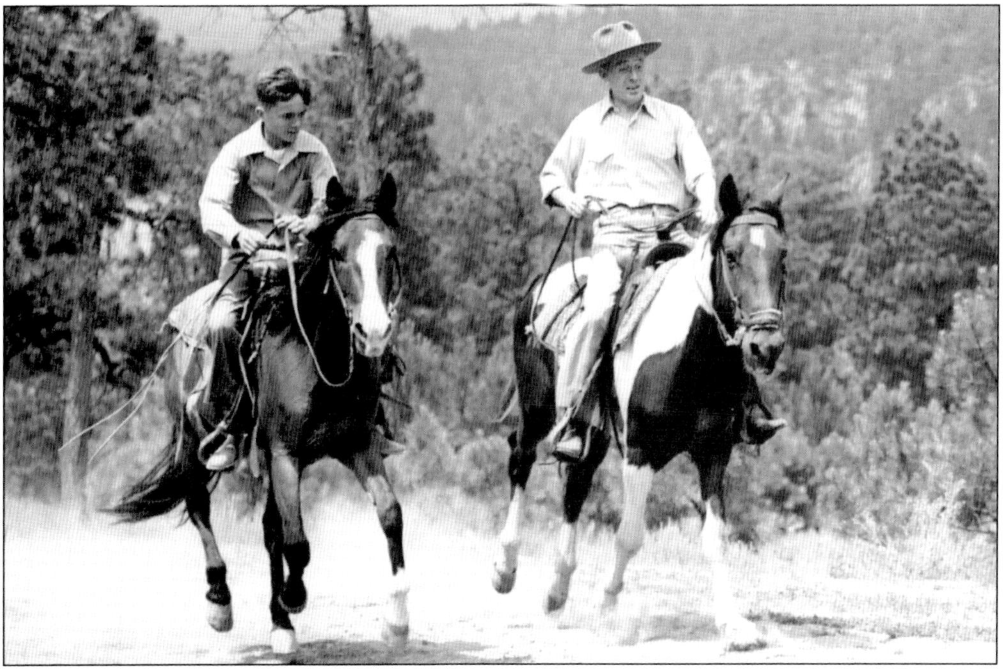

Charlie Robinson and his son, Robbie, took advantage of the riding opportunities that existed on the Hill. Horses had been corralled during the Ranch School days, and they became government property at the time of the takeover. Some residents were able to purchase additional horses, and exploration of the mountains and surrounding area was a popular pastime.

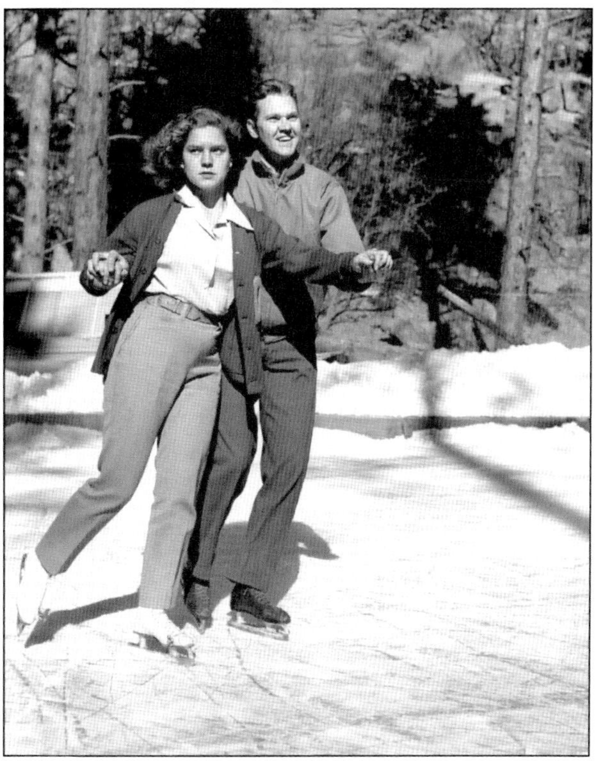

Betty Williamson and John Michnovicz cut the ice at the pond in Omega Canyon. The sunshine in this photo lasted briefly, and then the pond deep in the canyon would stay frozen most of the winter. The Army obliged its customers and tried to scrape the snow from the ice, but an uneven surface remained. Little matter as the soldiers and scientists, mommies and children, teens and friends would still try their skills at a spin and a figure. (Photo by Elmer Donor.)

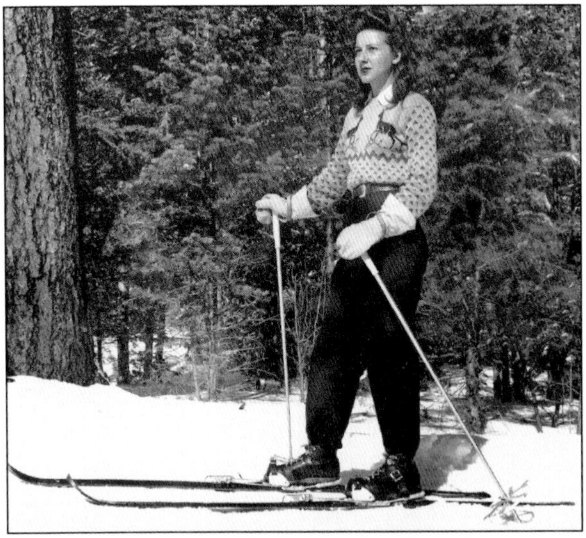

Interest in skiing began the second winter of the Project with homemade runs. This skier made the situation appear far more efficient than it really was because most of the skier's time was spent climbing the hill in order to ski back down. The first ski run was a narrow path on Sawyer's Hill west of town that was cleared during Ranch School days by the students and teachers. As skiing increased in popularity, more acreage was required, so volunteers spent weekends clearing brush and trees. George Kistiakowski, a Manhattan Project chemist and explosives expert, helped to blast some areas clear.

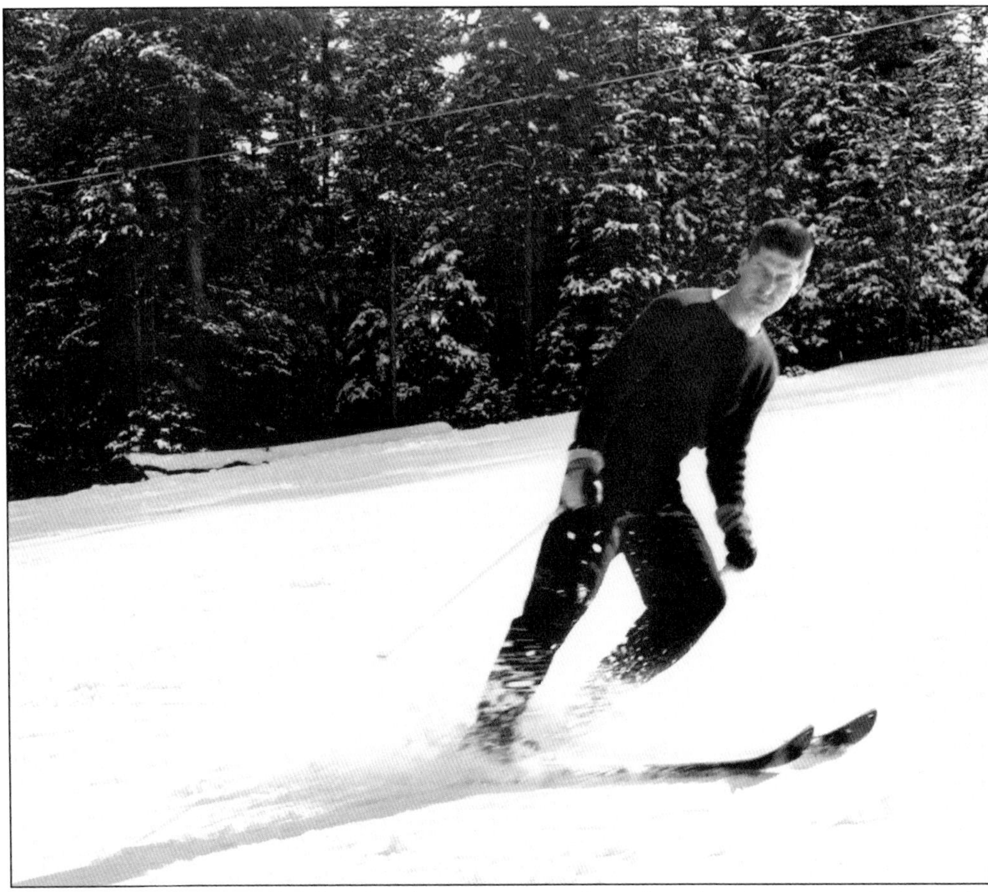

Eventually the Sawyer's Hill Ski Tow Association was formed, and volunteers worked together to build a rope tow that could haul the happy skiers uphill. Many of the European-born scientists who helped build the bomb had grown up on Nordic slopes and thoroughly enjoyed the skiing and the vistas and adventures that went along with it.

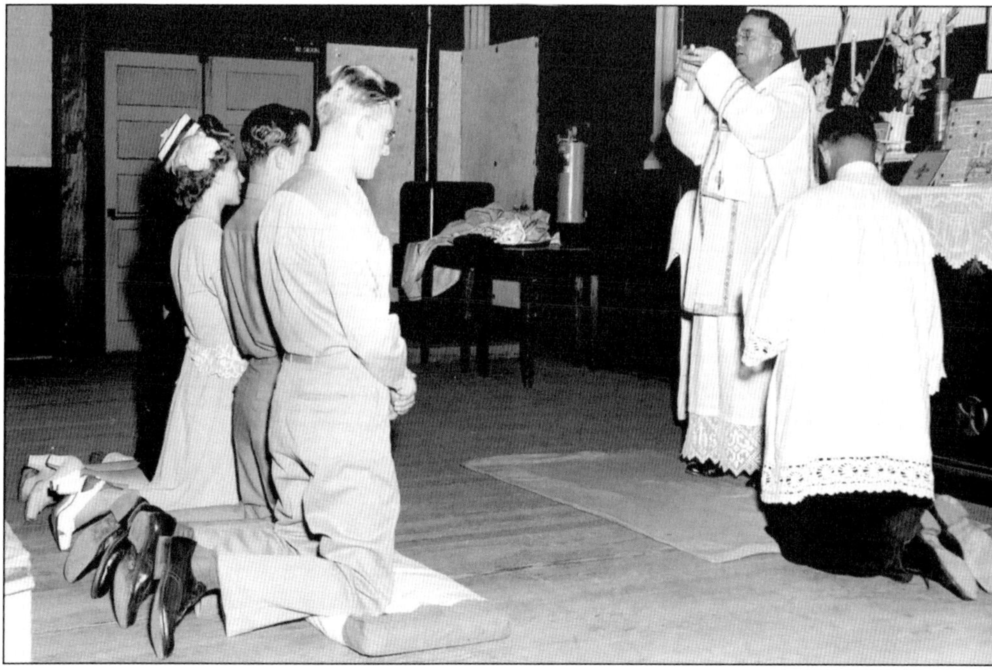

The wedding scene was a regular thing on the Hill as couples met and married. This couple, attended by friends, prepared to receive communion at their ceremony in Theater No. 1 during a Catholic mass. Weddings were held in Theaters No. 1 and No. 2, the chapel, the chaplain's office, churches in the surrounding communities, and in private homes.

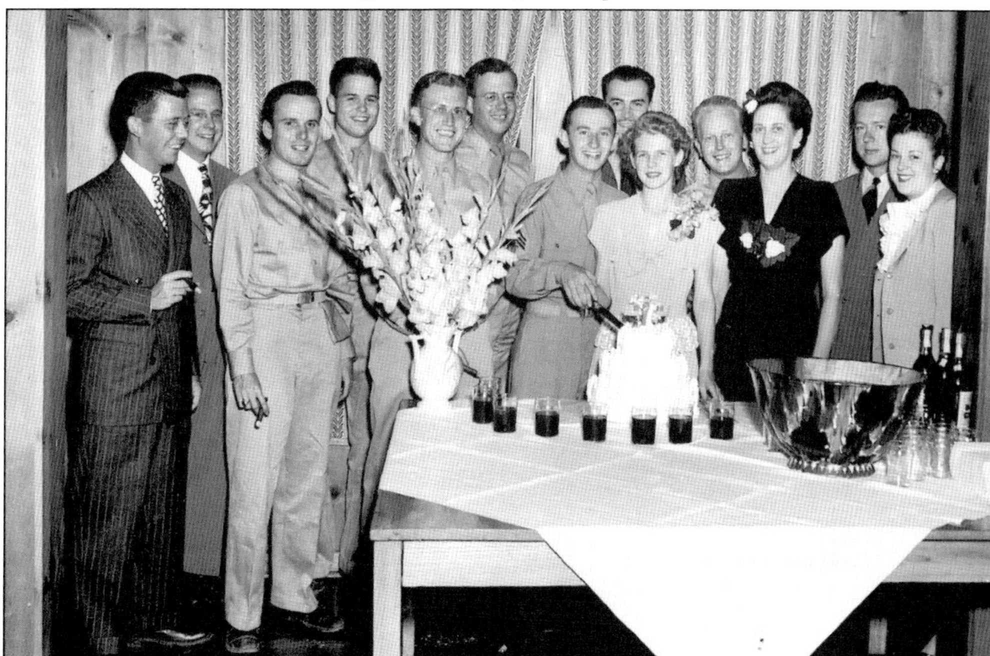

This couple followed their ceremony with a cake and punch reception in the NCO Club. The scrubbed look of the GI and his new bride and the elegant little cake surrounded by smiling friends were good omens of a happy future.

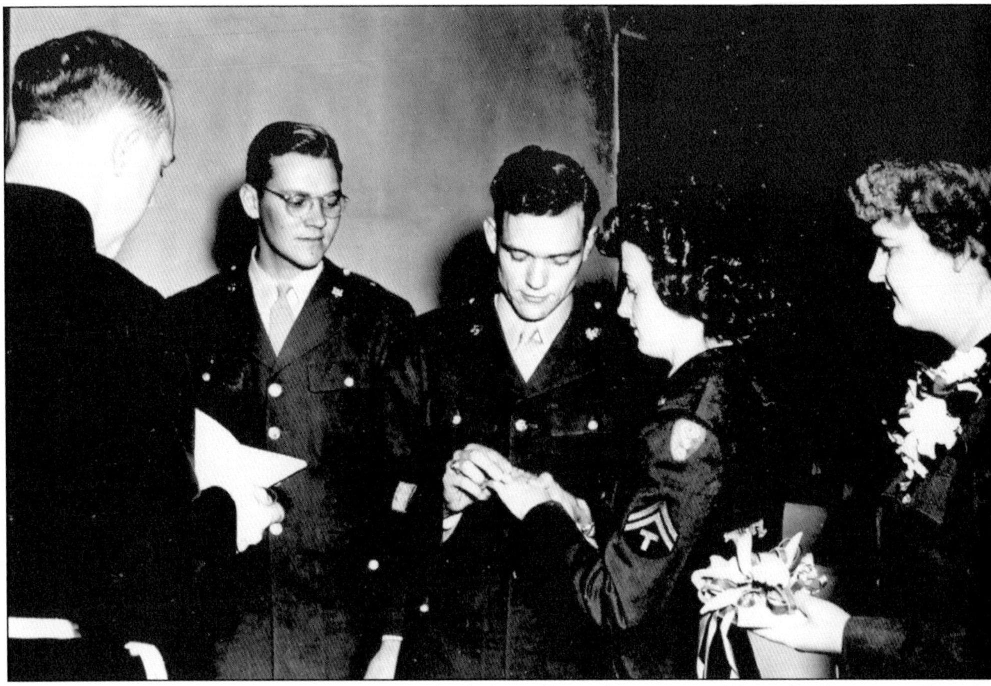

Roger and Jane Rasmussen were married while still in the Army, although this was after the war because the shoulder patch on the bride's uniform shows the postwar design of the question mark splitting the atom. They exchanged rings at a Catholic church in Santa Fe.

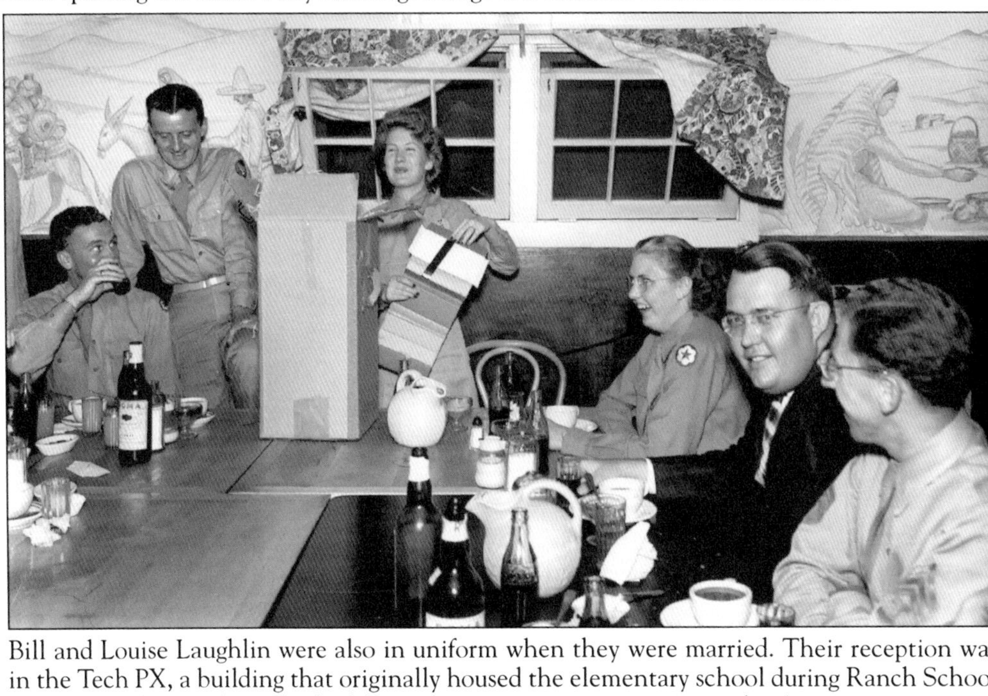

Bill and Louise Laughlin were also in uniform when they were married. Their reception was in the Tech PX, a building that originally housed the elementary school during Ranch School years. Complaints about the building's dreariness were common, so the Army commissioned a Swedish artist who lived in Santa Fe to liven up the place with the Mexican landscapes on the walls.

Six

CULTURAL LIFE OUTSIDE THE GATES

Place a finger randomly on a map of the United States. Pick any small town, any *really* small remote town. How many have ever heard of Hurricane, Utah, or Sugar City, Idaho, for example? Choose one, and then pump in $200 million (in current dollars) and 6,000 people in two years. This is what happened to the tiny community of Los Alamos, New Mexico, in 1943.

Every town in America can claim to be unique and fascinating in its own way. Yet, northern New Mexico—the original community outside the gates of Project Y—has a blend of culture and geography unlike anyplace else.

The desert Southwest is home to dozens of surviving Indian communities, including the Pueblos and the Navajos. These people are the descendants of a more ancient culture that is abundantly evident in petroglyphs, excavated ruins, and abandoned cliff dwellings.

Living alongside these Indian communities is a second indigenous culture—Spanish-speaking people descended from the conquistadors of New Spain. Francisco Coronado originally visited this region in 1540, and the town of Santa Fe was founded in 1598 and relocated to its present location in 1610. These are old towns, indeed.

Workers at the Project encountered this unique cultural blend from the day they arrived. Many of their co-workers were bused in each day from nearby pueblos, and even more arrived each day from New Mexican towns with distinctly Spanish names, like Española, Bernalillo, and Las Vegas.

Everyone enjoyed an occasional trip to civilization in the form of a visit to Santa Fe. Cultural exchanges were also set up periodically between local pueblos and other groups on the Hill, most notably the Old Timers Square Dance Club. These events were very important in helping the two groups understand and work alongside each other.

Lastly, a third, very different culture was integrating itself into New Mexican history. This new community brought technology, military bases, and government research facilities that were here to stay. This was the "new" New Mexico, and it began inside the gates of the Project.

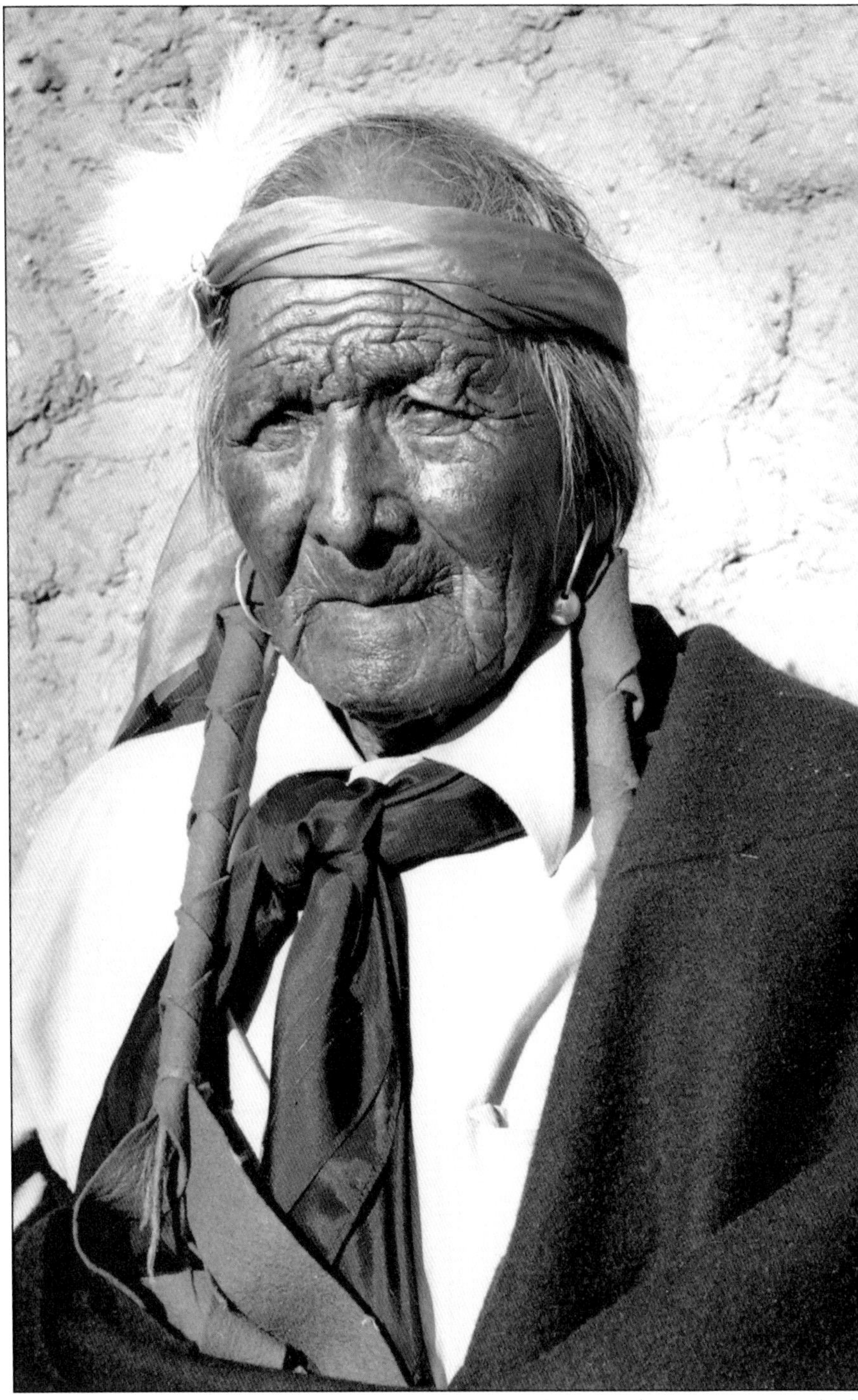

Ever on the lookout for interesting subject material, the photographer's eye was surely drawn to the mysteries carved into the face of this Indian from the Santa Clara Pueblo. It was the custom for tribal elders to pose for the camera for a nominal fee. Santa Clara Pueblo is situated to the northeast of Los Alamos. Like the potters from San Ildefonso, Santa Clara potters were famous for their high-quality work.

San Ildefonso Pueblo and its central plaza, pictured here, was located to the east of Los Alamos. A wide-open square, with an ancient cottonwood tree and acres of space, greeted visitors. Bernice Brode writes that the benched area around the tree became an easy rendezvous point for residents of the Hill to meet friends and relatives lacking security clearance to enter the Project. The pueblo itself extended into the distant hills and was home to several hundred residents.

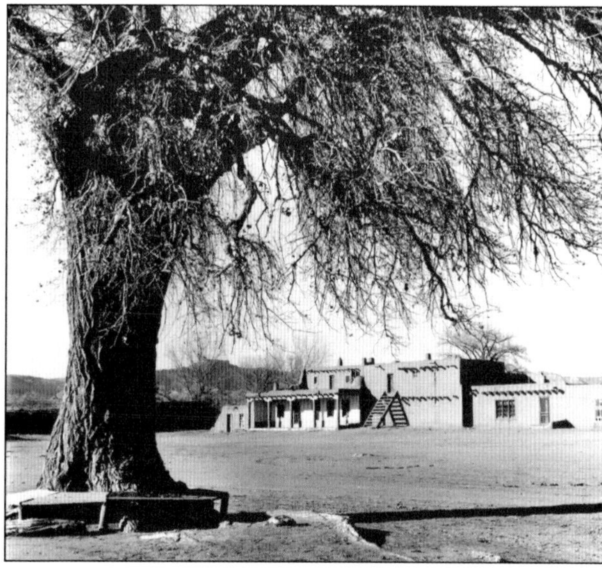

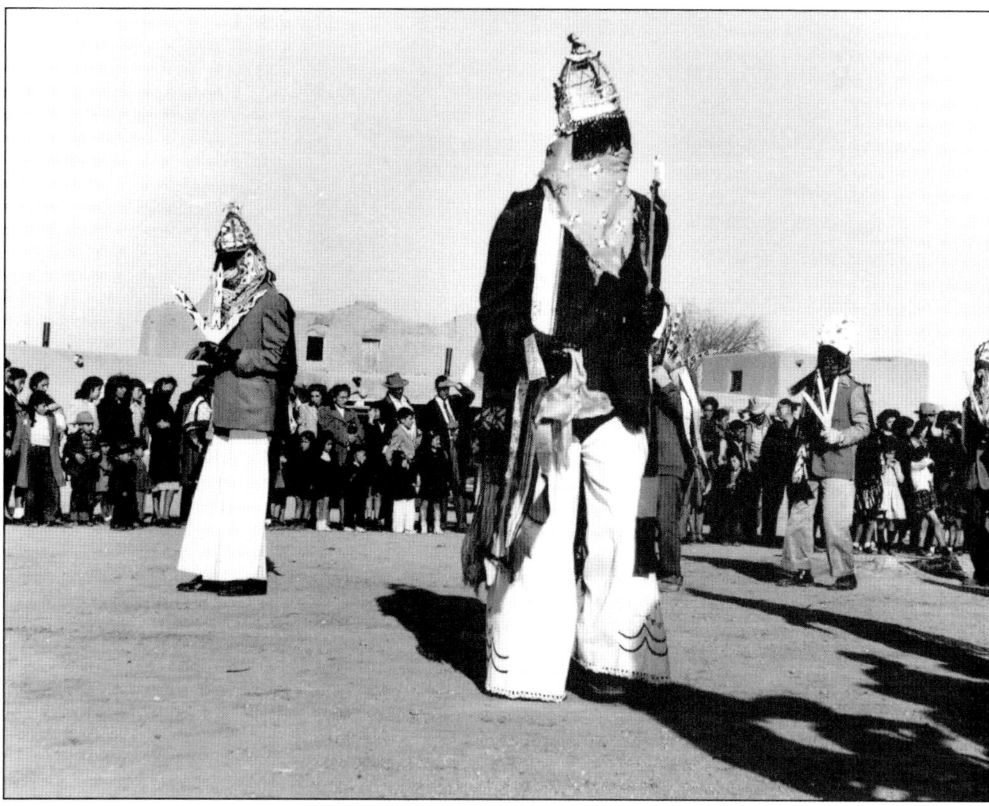

Visits to nearby pueblos allowed residents of Los Alamos to witness traditional Indian dancing. One popular dance was Los Matachines, which took place around Christmas at several of the pueblos and Hispanic villages in northern New Mexico. This dance represented a struggle between good and evil, and its historical tradition could be traced from Mexico's conquistadores back to Spain. Permission was always necessary before taking photographs at these events.

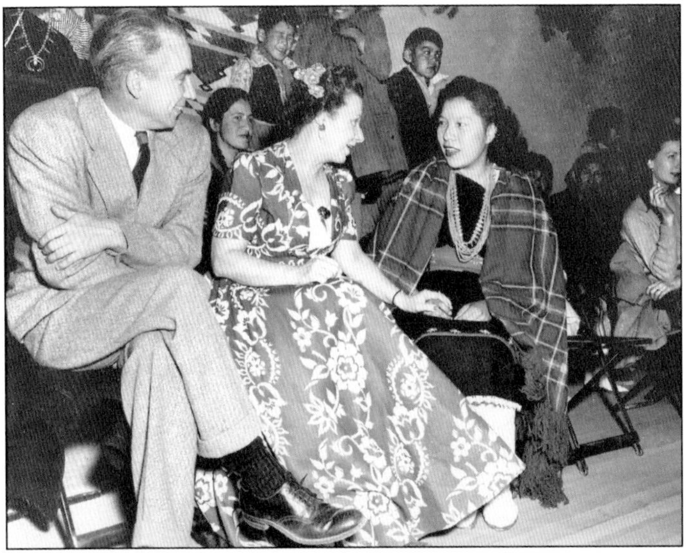

Norris Bradbury assumed the scientific leadership of the Los Alamos lab in late 1945. Here he is pictured with his wife and an Indian hostess at a cultural exchange between residents of the Hill and the local Pueblo Indians. The Old Timers Club, a group of Hill square dancers, were joined by their guests and traveled in December 1945 and again in December 1946 to participate in a joint dance celebration at the San Ildefonso Pueblo.

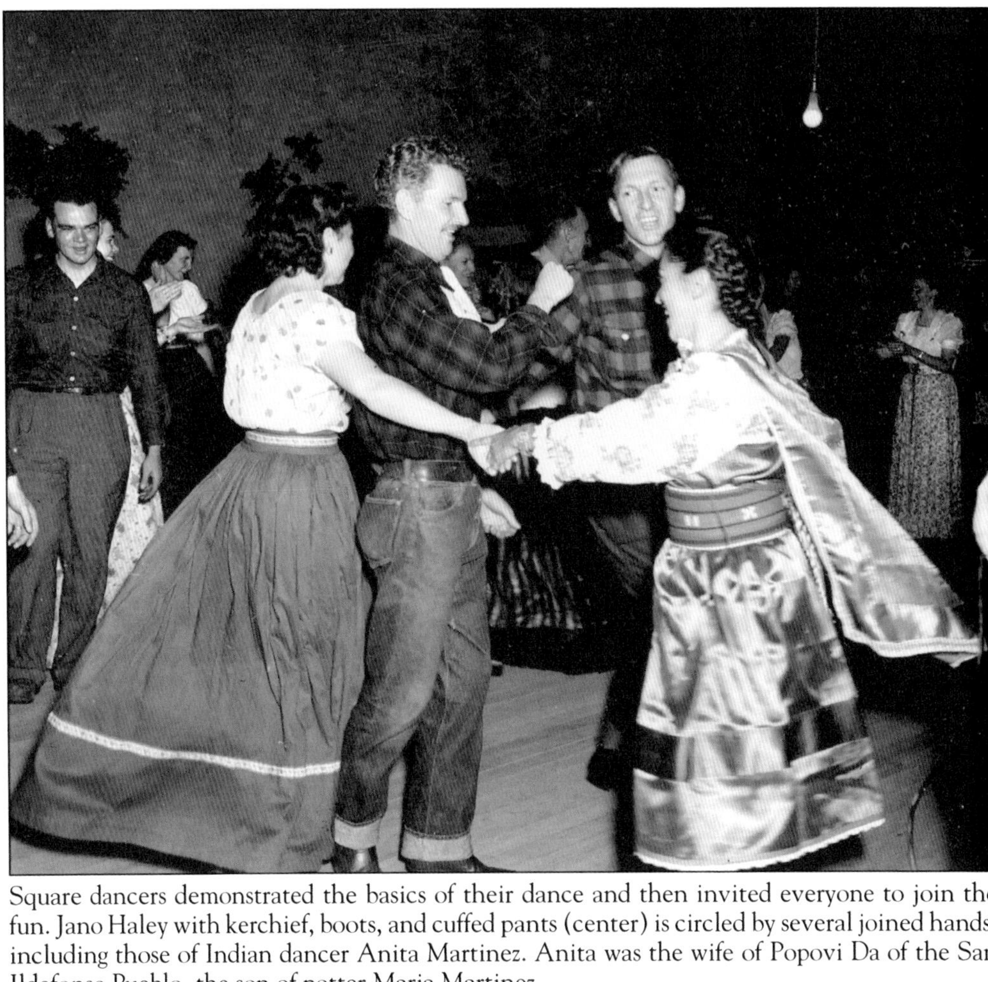

Square dancers demonstrated the basics of their dance and then invited everyone to join the fun. Jano Haley with kerchief, boots, and cuffed pants (center) is circled by several joined hands, including those of Indian dancer Anita Martinez. Anita was the wife of Popovi Da of the San Ildefonso Pueblo, the son of potter Maria Martinez.

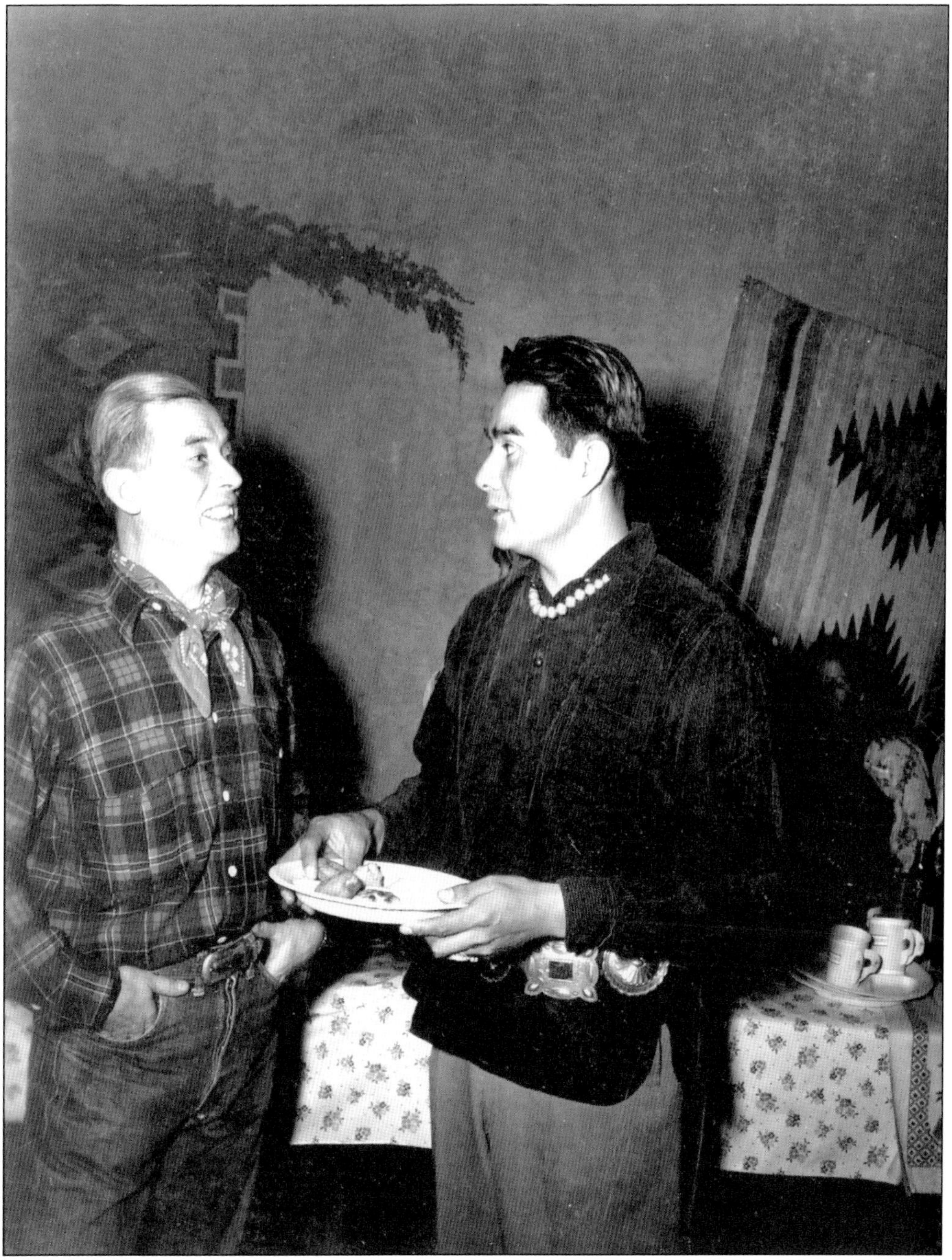

Good will was clearly evident between Charlie Robinson, at left, president of the square dance club, and Pueblo Indian Popovi Da, at right. Popovi Da was a remarkable individual. A native of San Ildefonso and son of the famous potter Maria Martinez, he joined the Army and was luckily stationed on the Hill. He successfully bridged the two worlds and helped bring about these opportunities to mingle. After the war, Popovi Da became an influential potter in his own right.

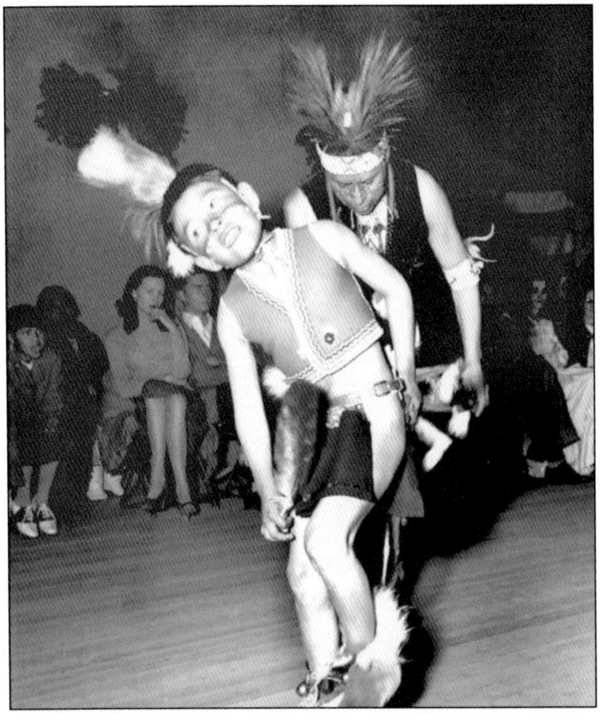

When the dancers from the Hill mingled with dancers from the pueblo, everyone, young or old, had a chance to show off their best moves. This young native of San Ildefonso demonstrates to the curious onlookers just how much he knows of his tribe's traditions. From the look on his face, it was an exhilarating evening.

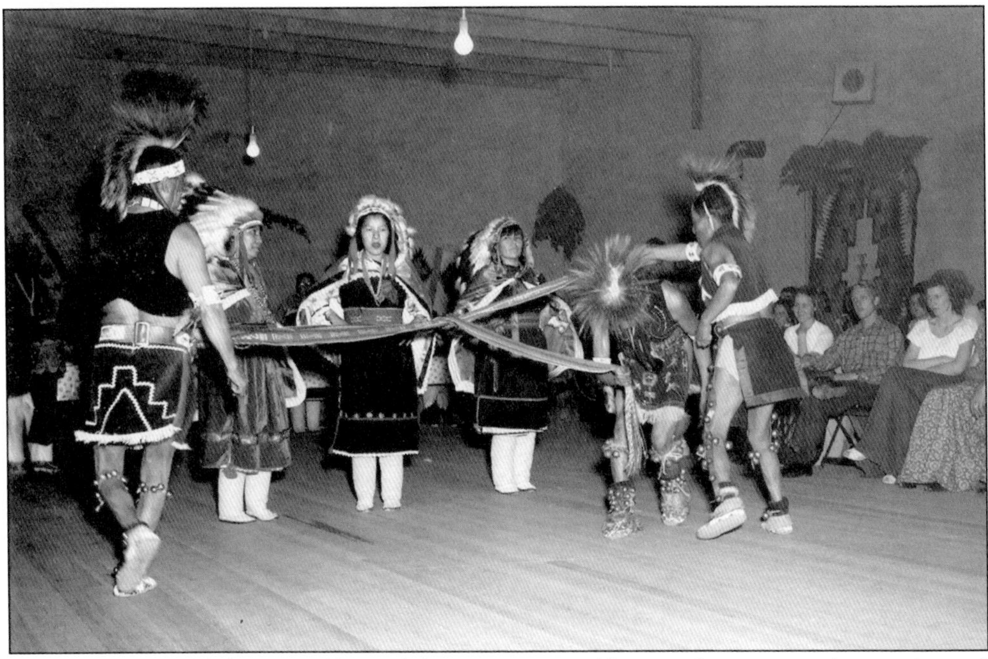

Members of San Ildefonso Pueblo used the event pictured here to demonstrate their traditional dances, such as the Dance of the Braided Belts. The beginning of the dance was marked by the jingle of bells, and then male and female dancers would weave a collection of belts together, carefully and rhythmically. Onlookers lining the walls of the vast hall watched in fascination. This building had been unused for some time, but for this festive occasion, walls were decorated with pine boughs and Navajo rugs.

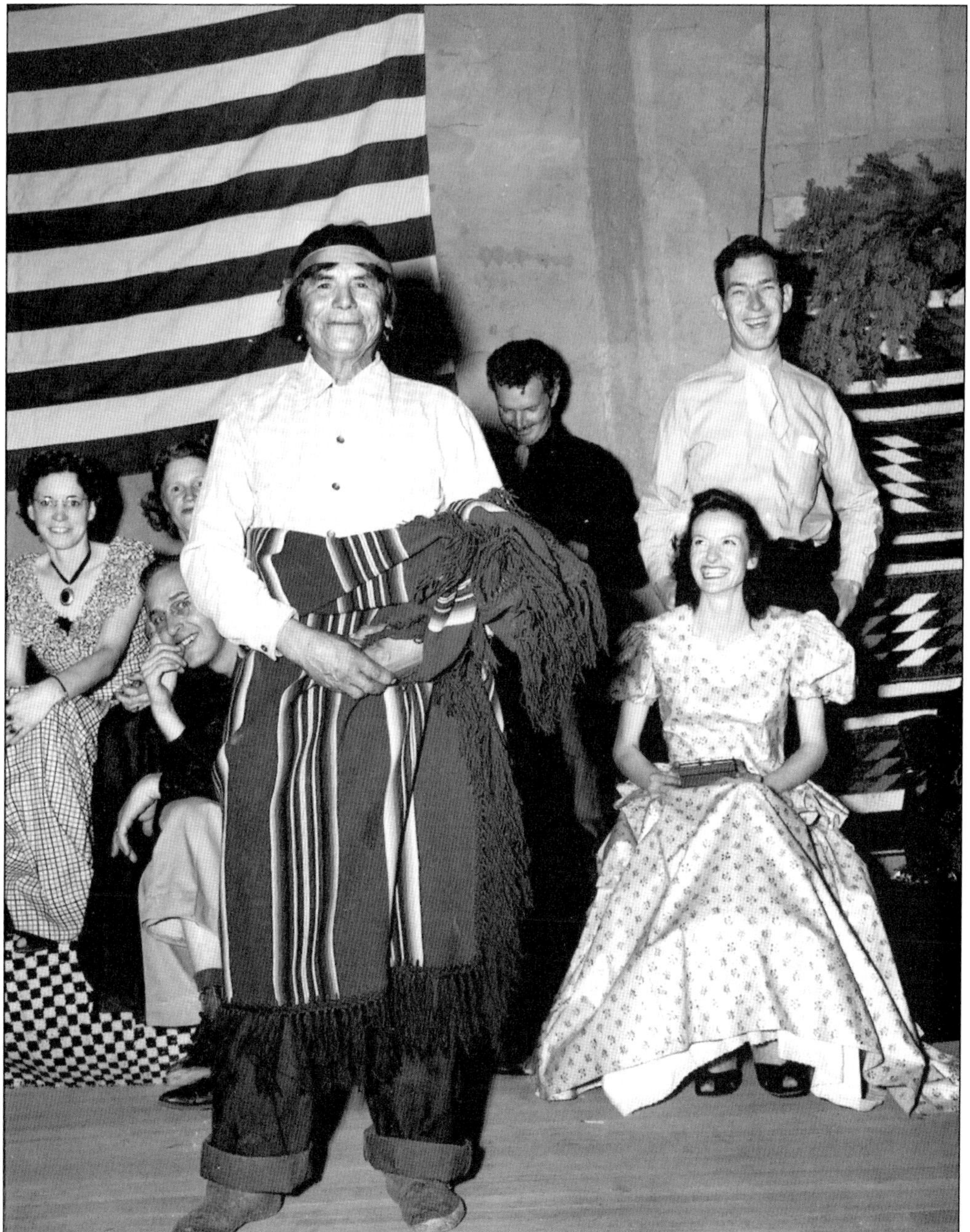

At the beginning of the festivities, prominent members of the local tribe, as well as visitors, would step forth to be introduced by Popovi Da. He would address the crowd, first in his native Tewa and then in English. Jane Wortmann, at right, and other members of the Project are clearly enjoying the introductions. The unidentified Indian at center smiles proudly.

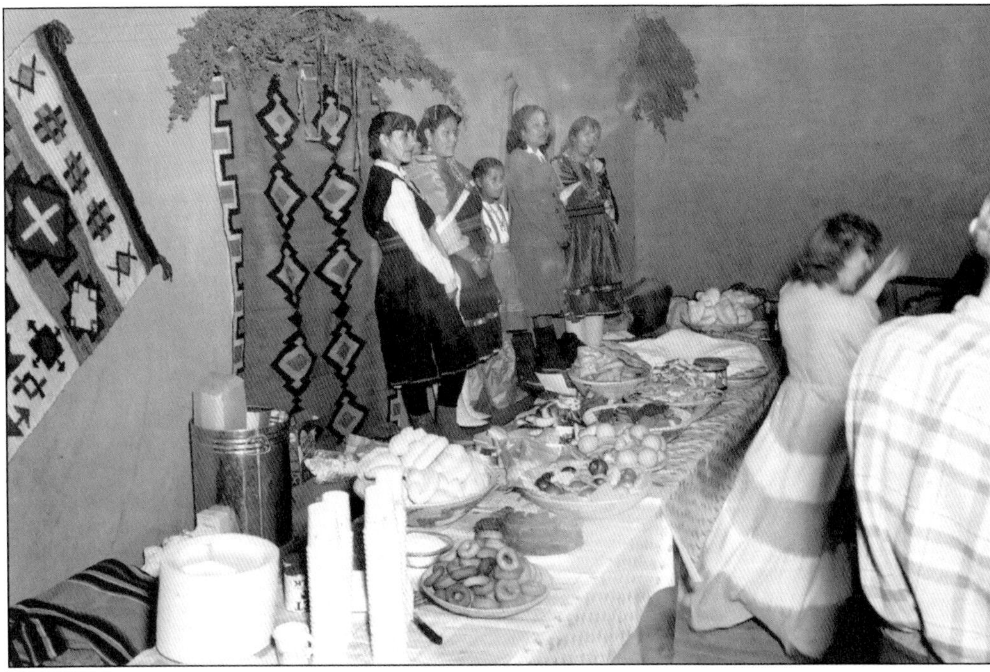

After a full evening of dance and ceremony, participants would be famished. The oilcloth-covered table was piled high with the pueblo's favorite selections: fruit pies, tamales, chile dishes, tortillas, and bread baked in the outdoor ovens or hornos. Hill participants added hotdogs and Coca-Cola. Lots of coffee and juice were available for the thirsty dancers.

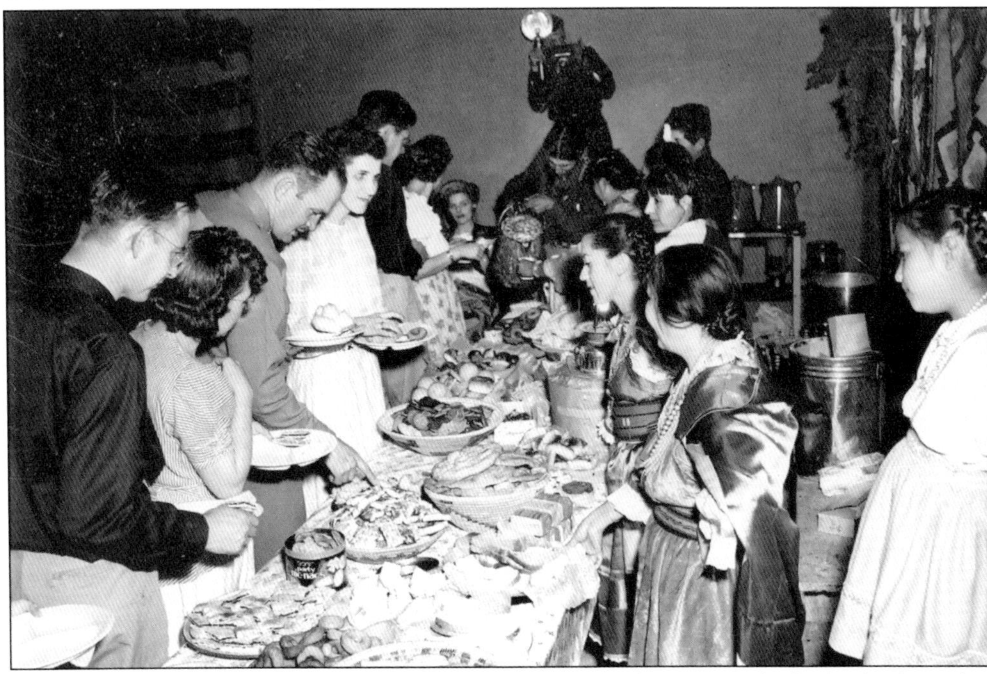

Once the intermission was announced, everybody joined the line to sample the food. The Indian women had prepared several traditional recipes. In their colorful native dress, they answered questions and guided their guests in their selections.

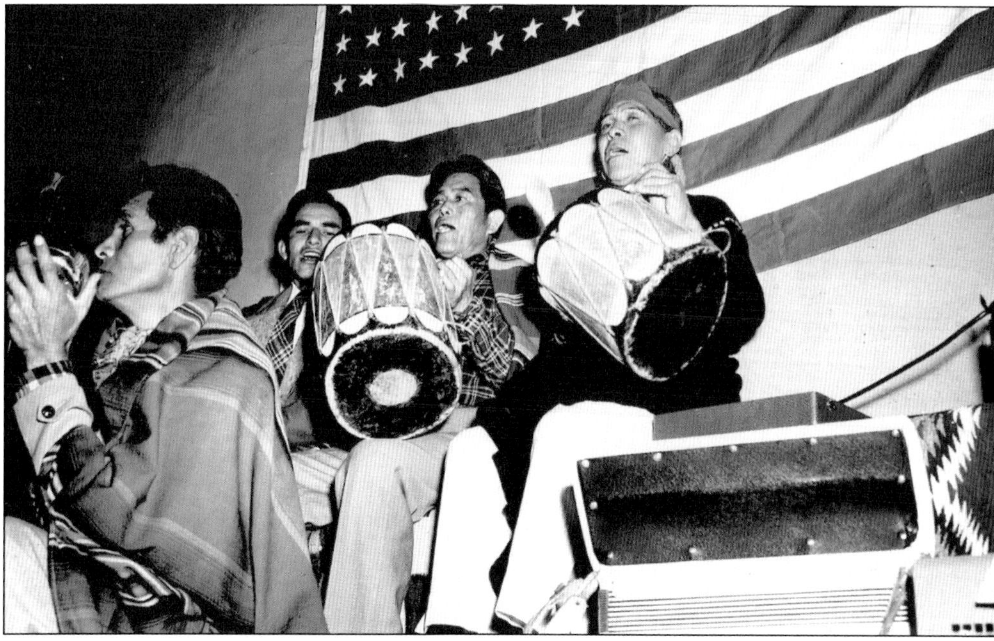

Indian drummers played a crucial role in traditional dances, keeping a strong steady rhythm for the dancers. Holding their drums are singers Charlie Montoya and Miguel Martinez. John Michnovicz had his accordion on the occasion (visible in right foreground), so he accompanied George Hillhouse, the square dance caller for a number of dances.

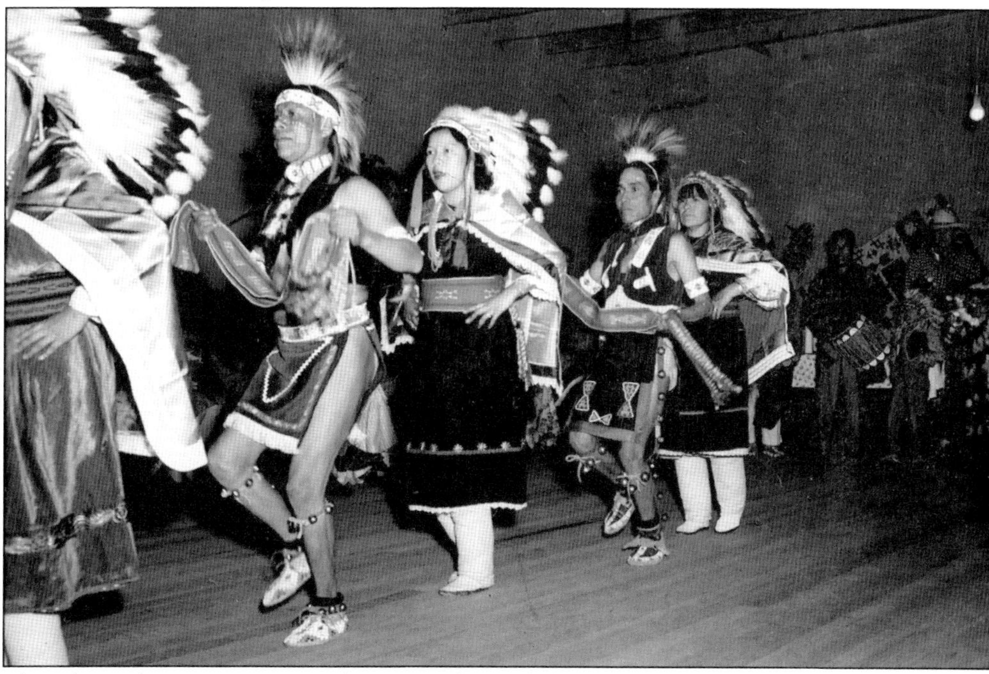

This photo demonstrates one of many traditional dances performed for the visitors from the Hill. Dances included were the Hoop Dance, Horse Tail Dance, War Dance, and Toe Dance. Scientist Bob Brode had originally initiated this evening of cultural exchange during the war and hoped that it would become an annual event.

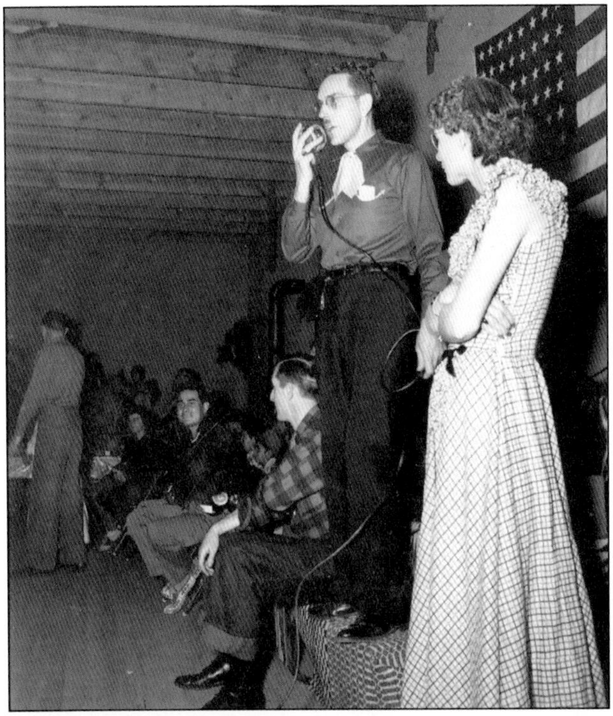

George Hillhouse stands next to his wife as he calls out the rounds for a lively dance. He was the manager of the commissary warehouse, and his wife taught second grade in the elementary school. This couple came from Santa Fe to the Manhattan Project in May 1943. Through their efforts, both natives of the pueblos as well as natives of the East Coast, were introduced to the fascinating world of American square dancing.

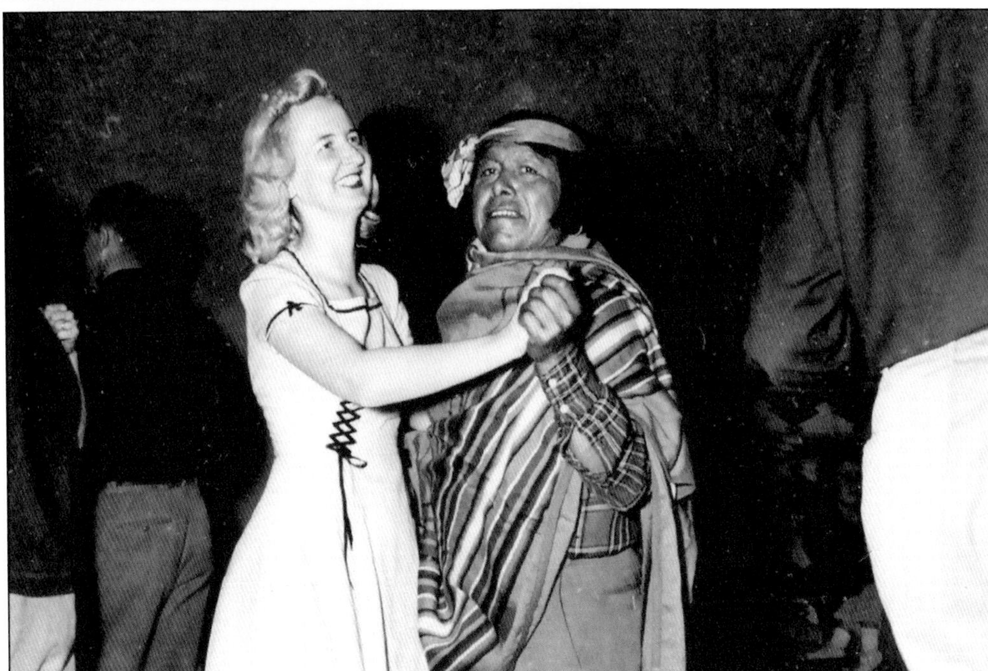

Mrs. John Reide was a member of the Old Timers Club, the premier square dancing club at Los Alamos. In this photo, Mrs. Reide and her Pueblo Indian host twirl the dance floor in one of several dances of the evening. Square dancing was interspersed with traditional Indian dances. A wide variety of dances introduced by the visitors from the Hill would include the Virginia Reel, the Schottische, the Varsuviana Promenade, and the Mexican Raspa. (Photo by Joe Gluth)

Maria Martinez was San Ildefonso's most famous resident. She and her husband, Julian, revived the art of pottery in the pueblo and perfected their signature black-on-black ware viewed by millions since 1918. Her pieces were first shown at the St. Louis World's Fair in 1904 and decades later at the Smithsonian Museum. Maria continued to fire her pots in the traditional method. This process involved burying the unfinished pot in a fire in the ground, covered tightly with sheep or cow dung for fuel. The amount of air reaching the pottery determined whether the clay remained red or instead turned completely black. Members of Maria's family continued to make further innovations in the technique. Many of her pieces are housed today at the Millicent Rogers Museum in Taos.

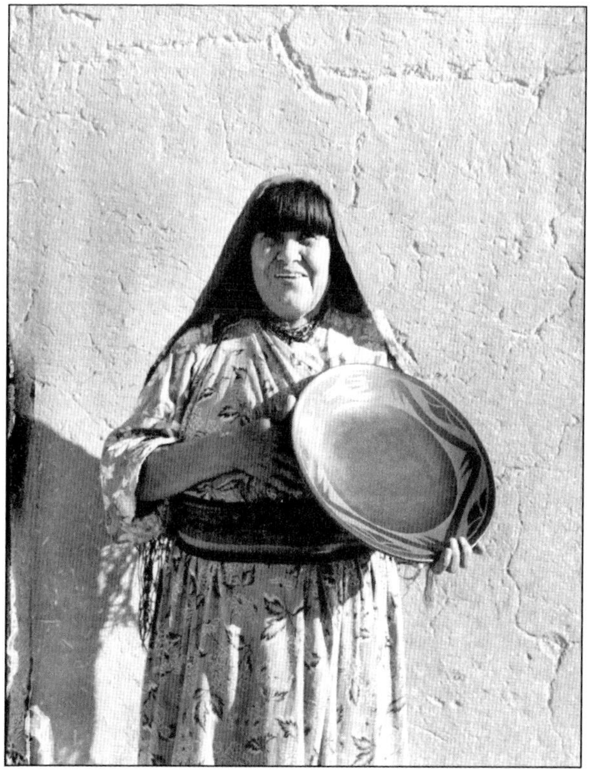

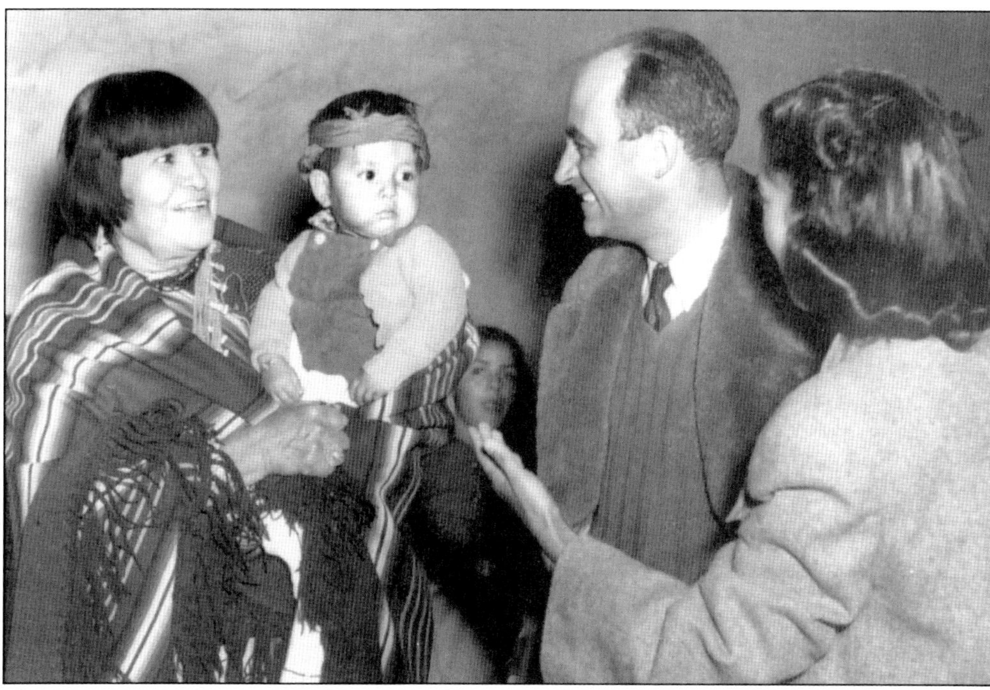

There were several meetings of great minds at Los Alamos between 1944 and 1947. One such occasion is shown here, as Enrico Fermi, the Italian-born scientist and Nobel Prize winner, is introduced to world-famous potter Maria Martinez. Maria is holding one of her grandchildren.

The Spanish settled the northern village of Ranchos de Taos in 1716. This photograph shows the mission church of St. Francis of Assisi, completed in 1815. The church is a prominent example of early adobe architecture, with fortress-like walls four feet thick and massive buttresses supporting each of the two towers. Generations of Taoseños have plastered and replastered the mud walls over the centuries. The Ranchos church continues to have a magnetic attraction for artist and photographer alike.

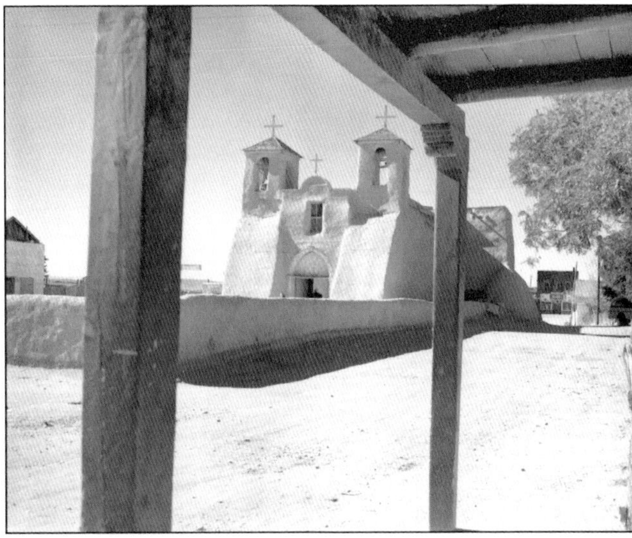

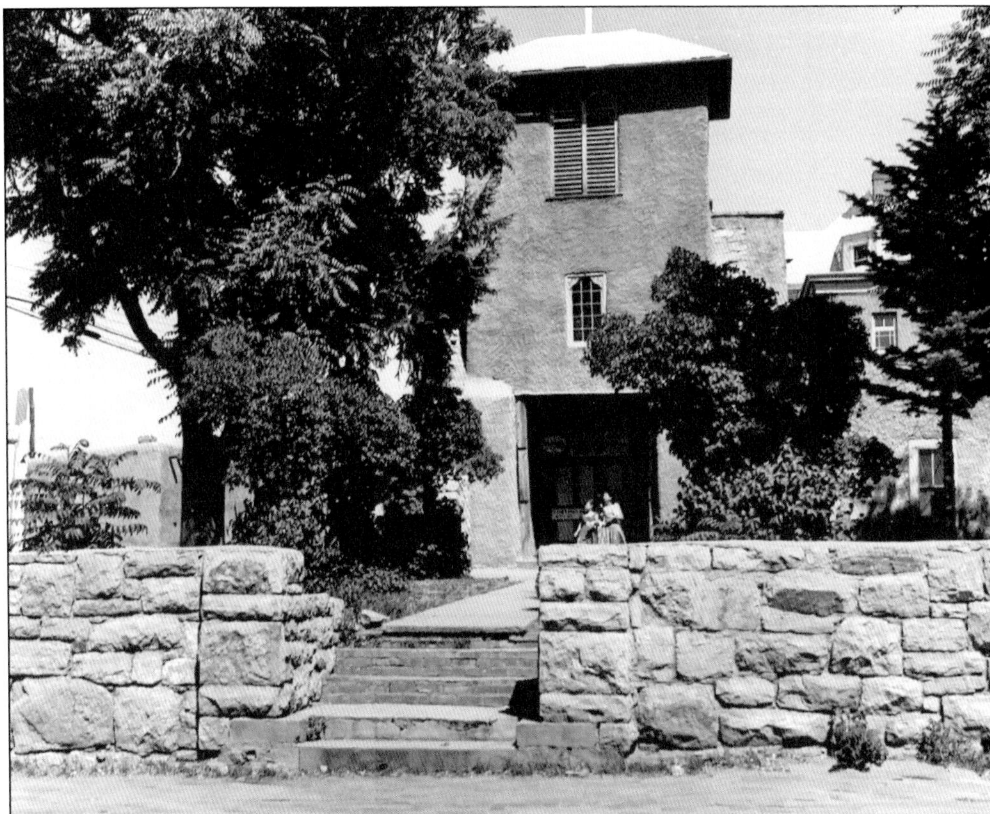

The Chapel of San Miguel, shown here, was first built in 1626. During the Pueblo Revolt of 1680, much of the church was destroyed. After the Spanish reconquered in 1710, it was rebuilt, but the chapel has undergone several restorations since then. Today its appearance differs from this 1947 picture. A bell tower sits where the louvered windows are seen, and the pitched roof has been replaced with a flat one in the adobe style. The chapel is situated in the Barrio de Analco, one of the oldest European settlements in Santa Fe.

The San Juan Pueblo lies along the Rio Grande, 30 miles to the north of Santa Fe. Continuously inhabited for over 700 years, San Juan is today the seat of the Northern Indian Pueblos Council. At the pueblo, one sees Our Lady of Lourdes Chapel that is built quite differently from other mission-style churches. A distinctive feature is the use of volcanic tuff in the facade. Deep layers of this volcanic rock extend for many miles around the Valles Caldera.

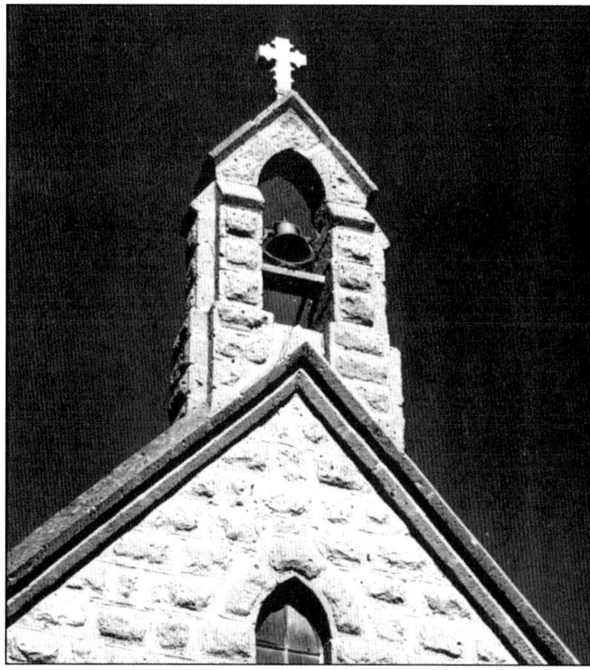

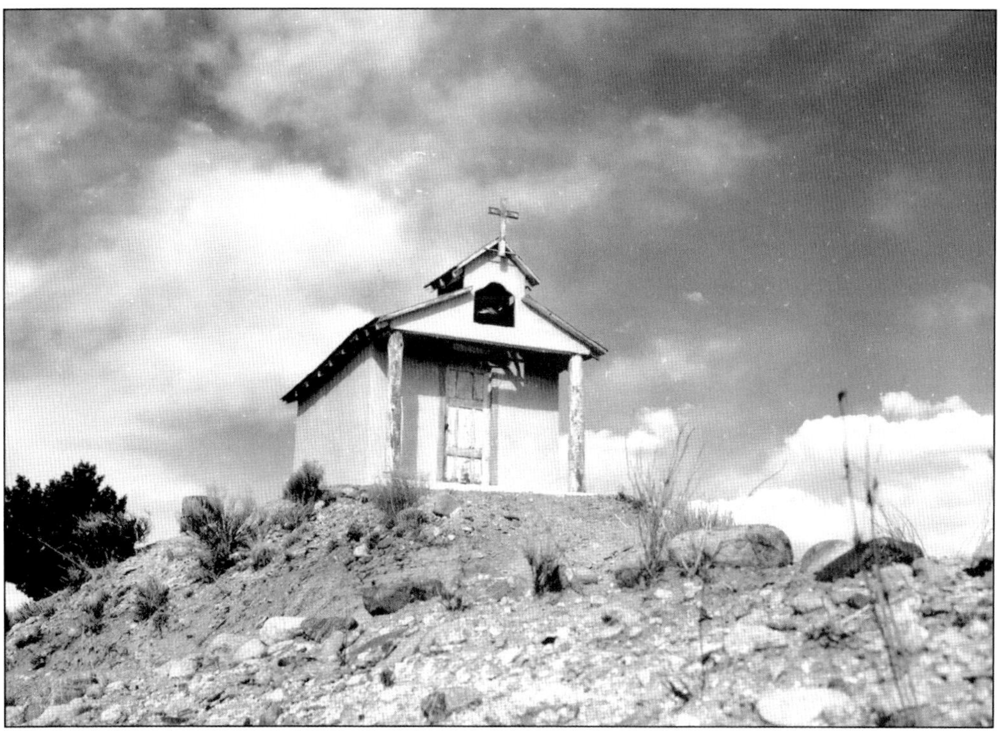

This is a photo of a private chapel, or *capilla,* built near Chimayo. During colonial times, New Mexican villages were spread out over long distances hugging the Rio Grande or other rivers. To avoid a long trip to Santa Fe, villagers needed a nearby chapel or sanctuary to conduct important religious rites, such as baptism. If a prominent family could afford it, they might consider erecting their own chapel and have it blessed by the priest on his next visit.

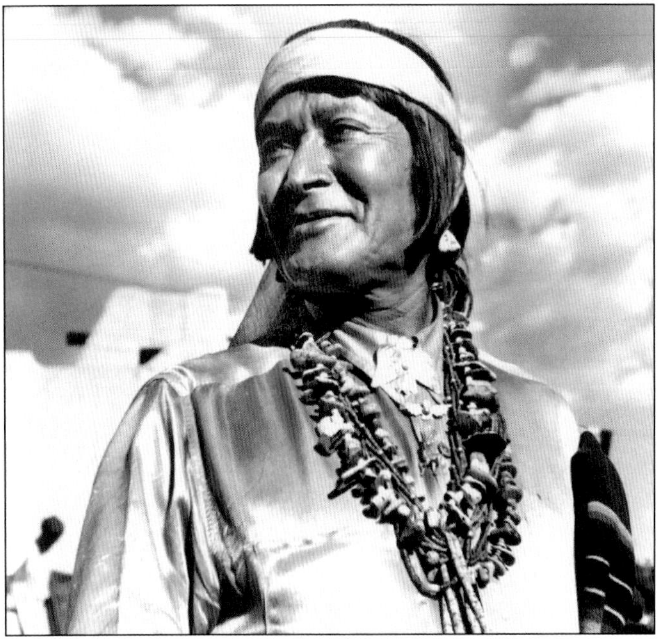

This gentleman might have earned a tidy sum on the weekend just by standing still long enough to have his photo taken. He certainly cast a fine pose, complete with traditional headband, woolen shawl, and Indian-style necklaces made of turquoise and carved fetishes. Even here, the photographers would experiment with different poses, shooting this one from below the subject. Cultural life outside the Los Alamos gates held many wonders for the band of young soldiers from the photo lab.

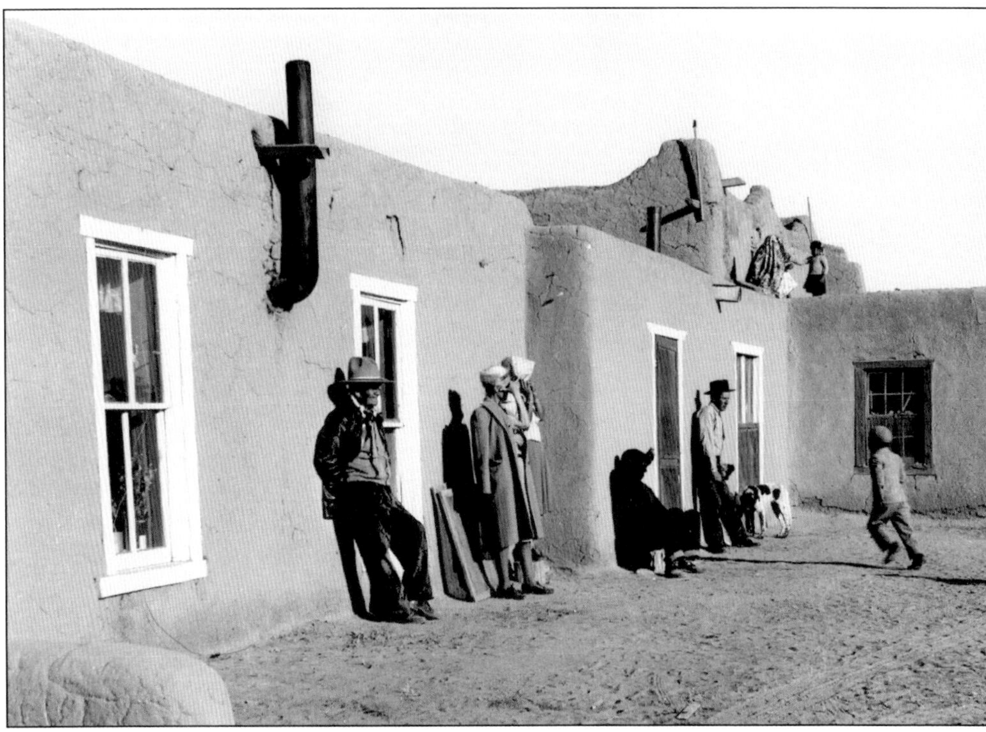

When the day came to visit the pueblo to witness a traditional dance, not everyone preferred to crowd the plaza up close near the dancers. Here, the photographer captures a couple of ladies mingling with the townspeople at a building just off the main plaza. This vantage point allowed them to take in a whole different scene, with children running about and others up on the roof attending to some important family business. Notice the brilliant sunlight slowly baking the dry adobe walls.

Seven

AFTER THE BOMB

It is so easy in the present day and age to view the development of the atom bomb as inevitable. However, Project scientists argued about whether or not their device would work until the very morning of the famous test explosion at Trinity site in the early hours of July 16, 1945. Until that moment, nobody dared to contemplate how much life would change "after the bomb."

It is also nearly impossible, given our contemporary biases about nuclear power and nuclear proliferation, to imagine the pride and relief that was experienced that day in July. These physicists had accomplished, at breakneck speed, a hopelessly complex task, and they had done so before an enemy power could get there first.

Almost immediately after the bombs exploded over Japan, the curtain of secrecy began to lift at the various sites of the Manhattan Project. The entire world learned the outlines of what had been done for the past few years. But perilous times lay ahead, and many secrets still needed to be kept close to the vest. Dr. Oppenheimer knew this, stating in a memo shortly after the Hiroshima bombing, "I know that it will be some comfort to all of you to have the general purpose of our work known, and to be able to admit your association with it; beyond that, no information about our work may be made public."

Yet, despite this somber tone, the celebrations were about to begin. In short order, displays of the Trinity test site were set up at the New Mexico State Fair (alongside prizewinning cattle and blue-ribbon pies!). There were parades through the ancient streets of Santa Fe, with soldiers and civilians making light of these long and difficult years. There was a week-long physics conference, in which the scientists could finally share their groundbreaking discoveries into the makeup of the atomic nucleus.

Other important tasks lay ahead: the forging of a civilian Atomic Energy Commission, the relocation of thousands of personnel to their previous homes and lives, the dismantling of military control over the Pajarito Plateau, and finally, the true development of Los Alamos as a modern city, complete with bathtubs!

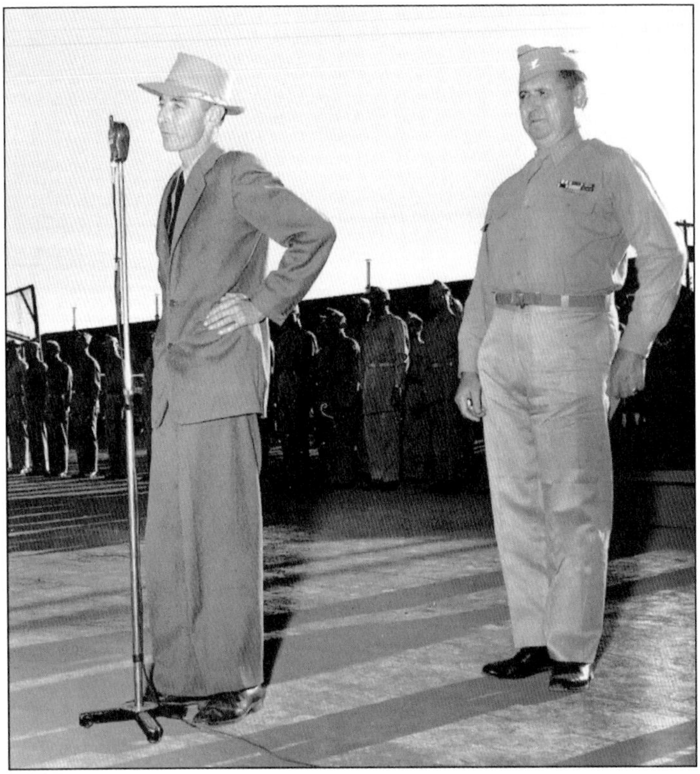

The Trinity bomb test had been successful, and in early August of 1945, the decision had been made to drop the atomic bombs. The cruel result of the war had been indescribable death and suffering, but the war was soon to end. Back on the Hill there was an Army parade and ceremony to award the Meritorious Service Award to the military personnel who had been part of the Manhattan Project. At the ceremony, Robert Oppenheimer thanked the soldiers for their effort, and Colonel Tyler stood behind him.

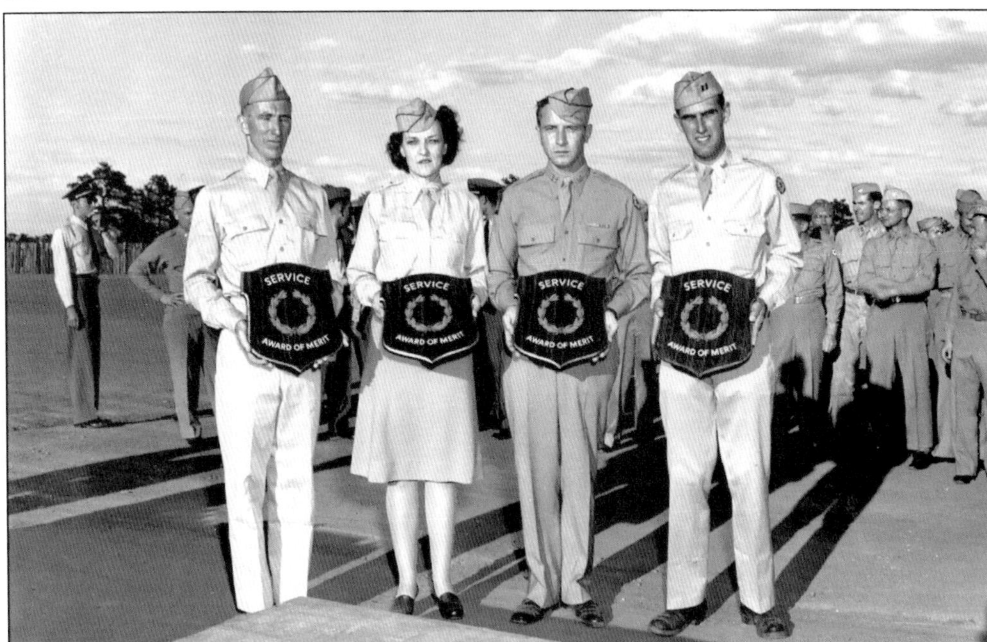

Each military detachment had a representative receive the wreathed plaque, and individuals were awarded the patch and the pin of similar design. The award was symbolic of good conduct and was given to symbolize a job well done. The fact that it was given indiscriminately to all and was not an award for heroism or bravery made it the subject of some sarcasm and criticism.

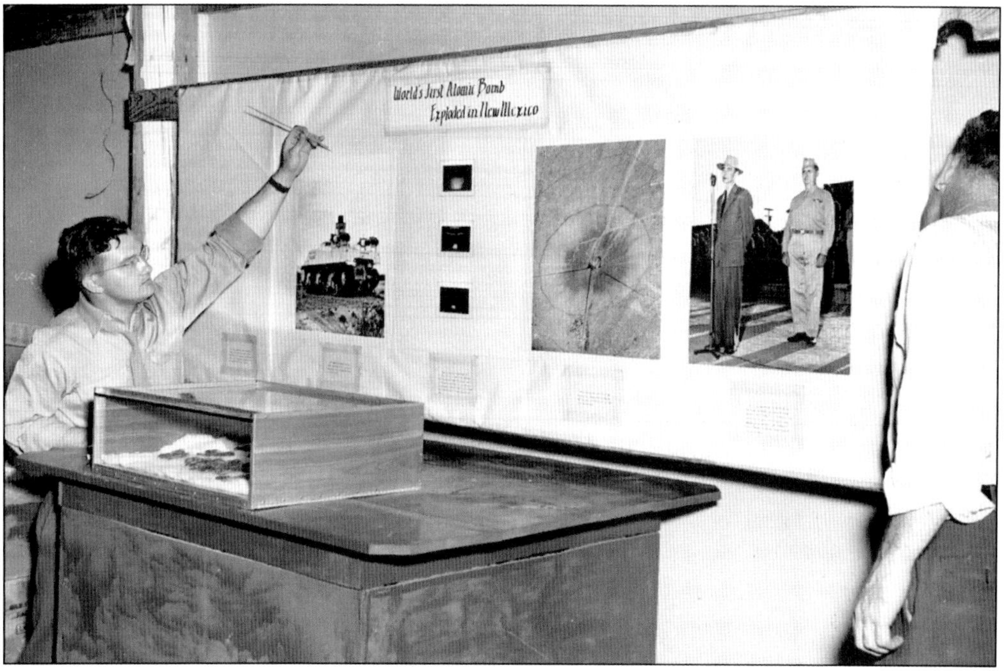

Only weeks had passed since the end of World War II and interest in the Manhattan Project was keen, so the photo lab staff was asked to present an atomic bomb display at the 1945 New Mexico State Fair in Albuquerque. Stan Zembaty and John Michnovicz organized the presentation, which included a Plexiglas box that held a sample of the mysterious trinitite. Photos showed the first atomic explosion and the crater that resulted at Trinity site.

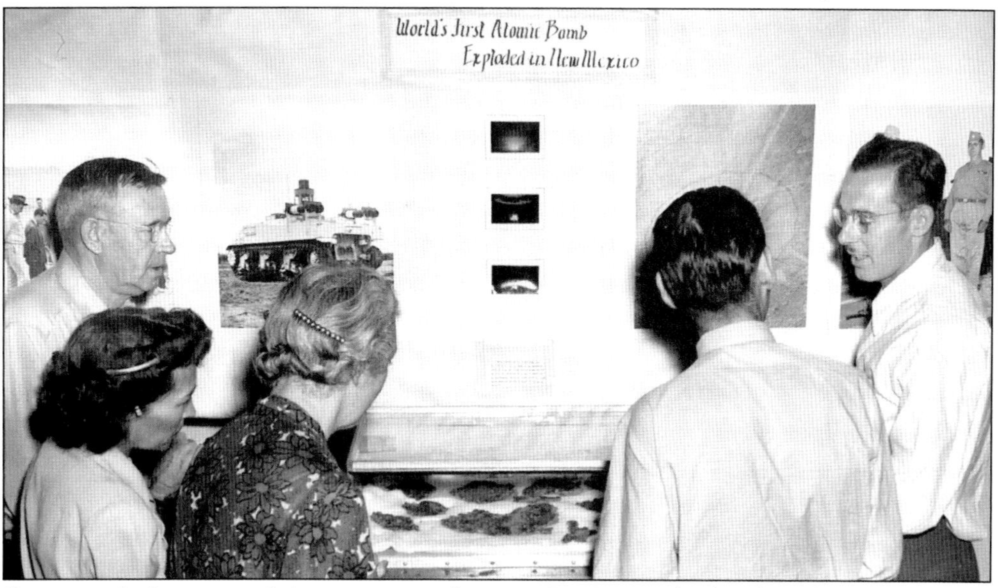

Curious onlookers viewed the trinitite at the state fair. It was the fused sand that looked like green glass and resulted from the heat of the Trinity test near Alamogordo, New Mexico. Those present at the Trinity test brought samples back to Los Alamos for souvenirs and jewelry. Although the amount of radiation that it emitted was considered low, proper handling of the substance was required, as it was able to cause a radiation burn if worn next to the skin.

PROGRAM OF PRESENTATION

MASTER OF CEREMONIES	COLONEL K. D. NICHO *Manhattan District Engine*
"AMERICA"	680TH ARMY AIR FORCES BAN *Clovis Army Air Fiel*
INVOCATION	MAJOR MATTHEW H. IMR *Post Chapla*
WELCOME ADDRESS	MASTER OF CEREMONI
PRESENTATION OF ARMY—NAVY "E" FLAG	MAJOR GENERAL LESLIE R. GROV *Officer in Charge, Atomic Bomb Proje*
RAISING OF ARMY—NAVY "E" FLAG	COLOR GUA *4817th S.C.U. Military Poli* *Detachment, Los Alam*
ACCEPTANCE OF ARMY—NAVY "E" FLAG	DR. ROBERT GORDON SPROU *President, University of Californ*
TOKEN PRESENTATION OF "E" PINS	COMMODORE W. S. PARSON *Senior Naval Officer* *Associate Director, Los Alamos Proje*
Pins Presented to	Charlotte Serber, Women Employe Hugh Bradner, Men Employees Carroll Gordon, Machinists A. E. Dyhre, Procurement
PRESENTATION OF WAR DEPARTMENT SCROLL	MAJOR GENERAL GROVE
ACCEPTANCE OF WAR DEPARTMENT SCROLL	DR. J. ROBERT OPPENHEIME *Director, Los Alamos Proje*
"THE STAR SPANGLED BANNER"	680TH ARMY AIR FORCES BAN
BENEDICTION	MAJOR MATTHEW H. IMR

This program was from the Army-Navy "E" ceremony that celebrated the successful conclusion of the Manhattan Project. The Army had initiated an award for contributions to war work in May 1942, and the Navy had a similar award that had been presented since 1906. In July 1942 it became a combined service award and was known as the Army-Navy "E" Production Award. This high honor was granted to the participants of the Manhattan Project on October 16, 1945. (Courtesy of the Los Alamos Historical Society.)

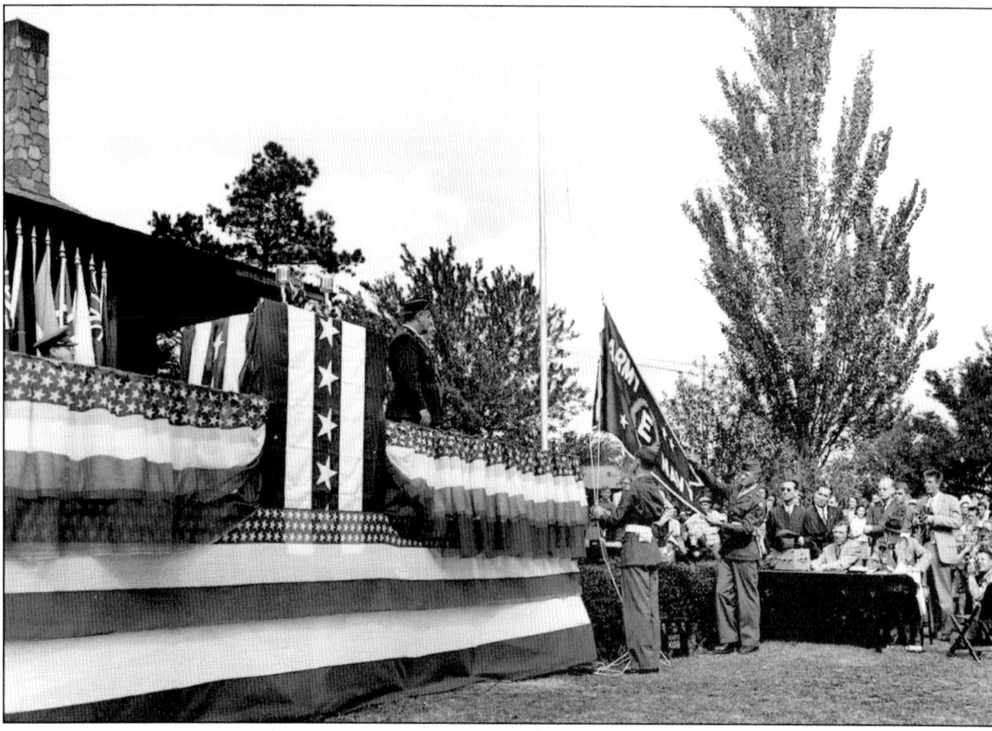

A patriotic stage was set beneath the blue sky, and the color guard made preparations to hoist the Army-Navy "E" flag before the ceremony began. Several men were seated to the right at the press table—a novel concept at this once-so-secret town—and Radio KOB's correspondent and microphone were ready to bring this occasion to the outside world.

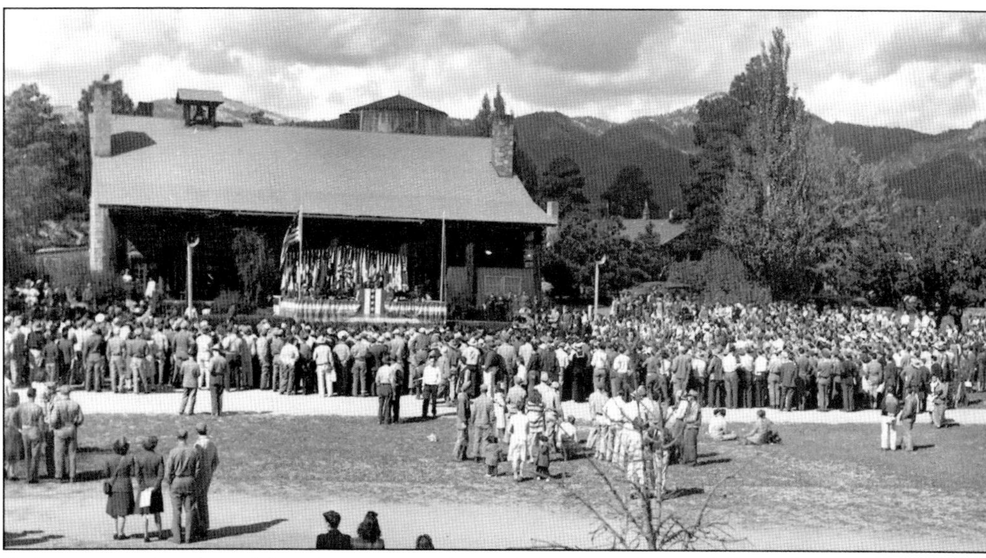

A large crowd gathered for the presentation of the Army-Navy "E" Production Award and War Department Scroll that fall day of 1945. Fuller Lodge was the staging area, with the tip of the water tower and top of the Jemez Mountains as the backdrop. Soldiers, WACs, moms, children, scientists, and civilians were present to witness the highest honors being given to the Manhattan Project in recognition of its contribution to war's end.

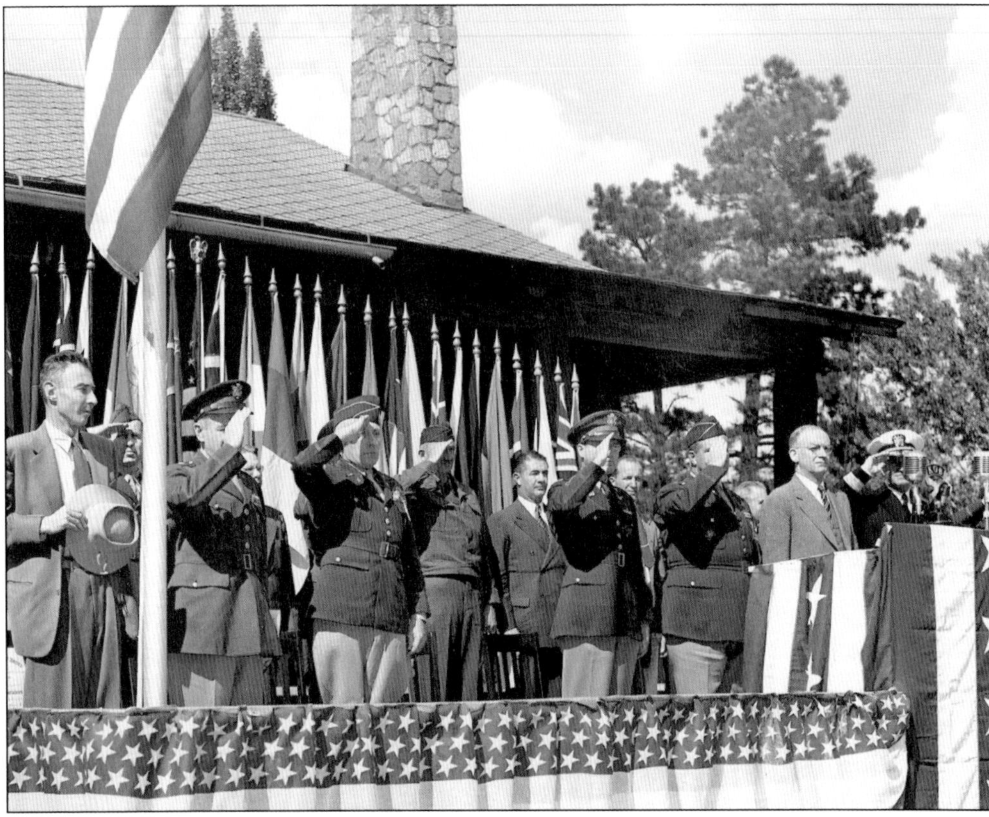

The program was presented with all the precision of military duty and care. The national anthem that opened the ceremony was played by the 680th Army Air Force Band from Clovis Army Air Field, and all rose in salute. On the far left is Robert Oppenheimer, and the civilian on the far right is Robert Sproul, president of the University of California. To the left of Sproul is Gen. Leslie Groves, and to the right is Comdr. William "Deke" Parsons.

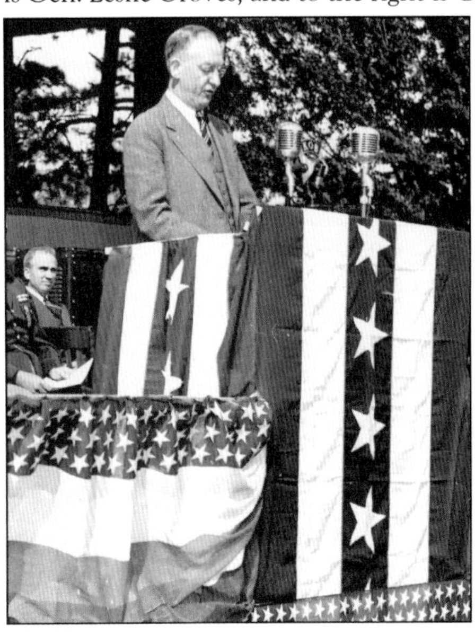

After an opening invocation, Dr. Robert Sproul received the "E" flag and thanked participants. The University of California was the institution charged with overseeing the lab and its employees. General Groves originally wanted all scientists involved with the Project to join the military service, but they could not be persuaded. So the lab was run under the auspices of the University of California, and Sproul was presented with the prestigious military award.

Comdr. William Parsons was the senior naval officer on site during the Manhattan Project. He called forward civilian representatives of various employees of the Project to receive the "E" pin. All Project employees received the small sterling pin stamped with "A-Bomb."

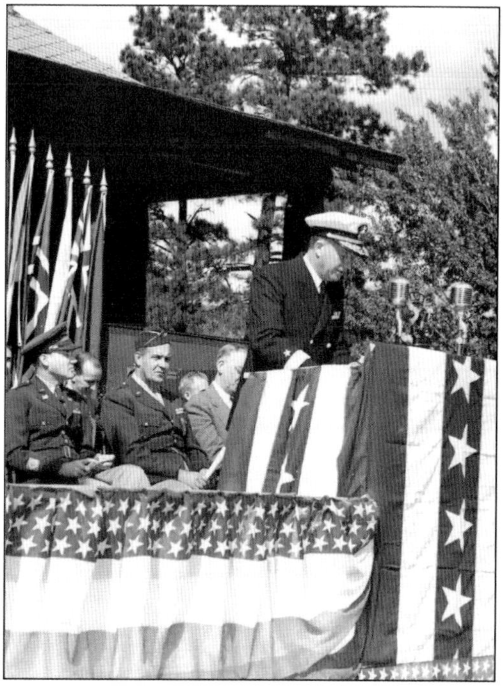

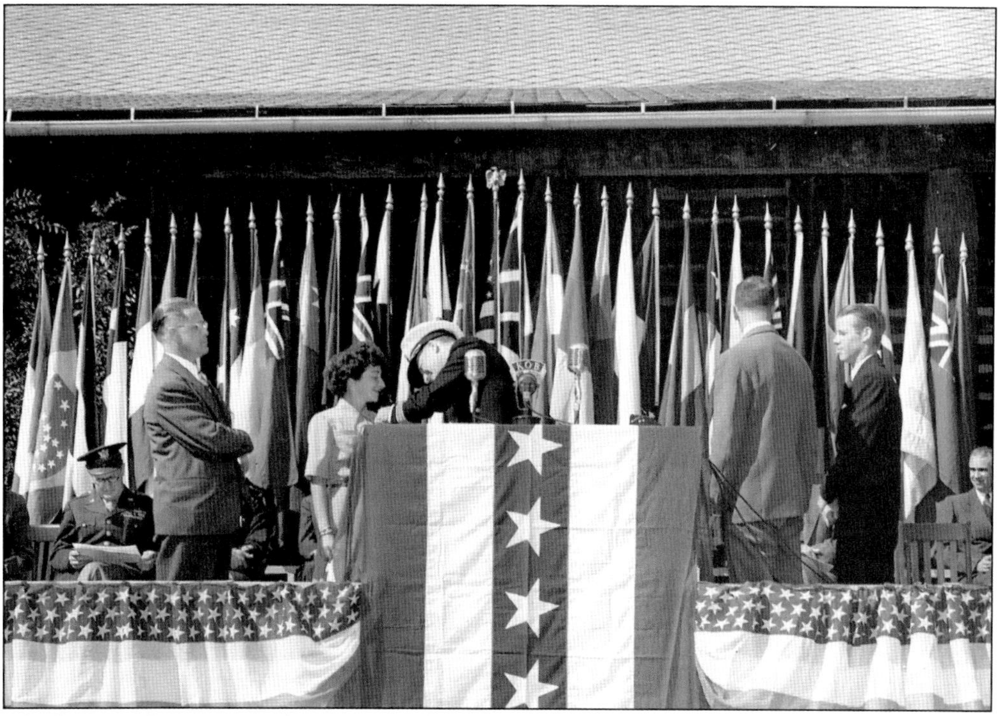

Charlotte Serber receives her "E" pin for contributions as head of the scientific library and document room and represented the women employees. A.E. Dyhre, who resided in Los Angeles as purchasing agent for the Project, stands behind her and represented the offices and employees in procurement. On the right are Hugh Bradner, standing for the men employees, and Carroll Gordon, the machinists' representative.

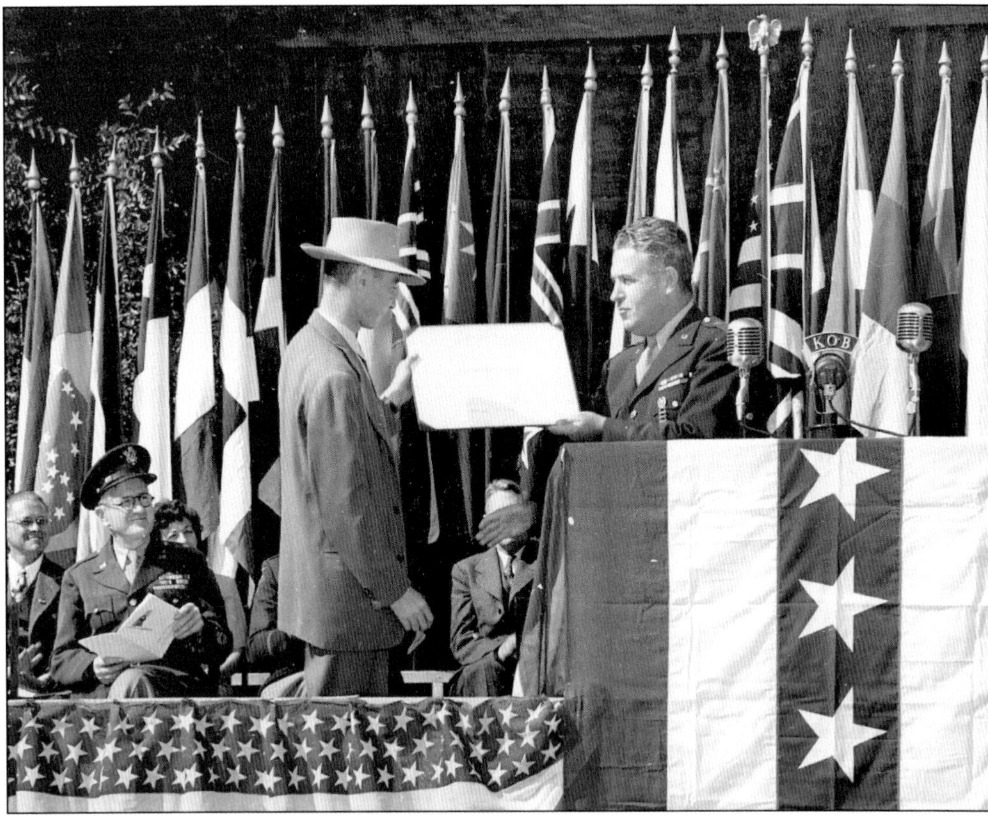

Robert Oppenheimer accepted the War Department Scroll on behalf of the Los Alamos Laboratories from General Groves. The citation on the award read, "This Certificate is awarded to Los Alamos Laboratories for valuable service rendered to the nation on work essential to the production of the Atomic Bomb, thereby contributing materially to the successful conclusion of World War II."

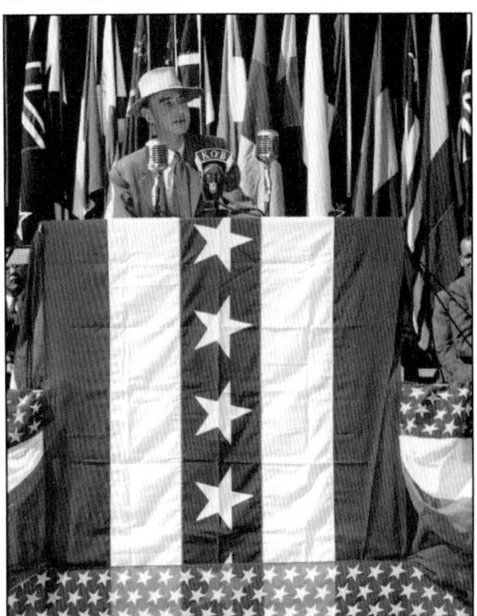

Robert Oppenheimer's remarks were brief and solemn. "It is our hope that in years to come we may look at this scroll, and all that it signifies, with pride. Today that pride must be tempered with a profound concern . . . The peoples of this world must unite, or they will perish. This war, that has ravaged so much of the earth, has written these words. The atomic bomb has spelled them out for all men to understand." It was Oppenheimer's last day as director of the Los Alamos Project.

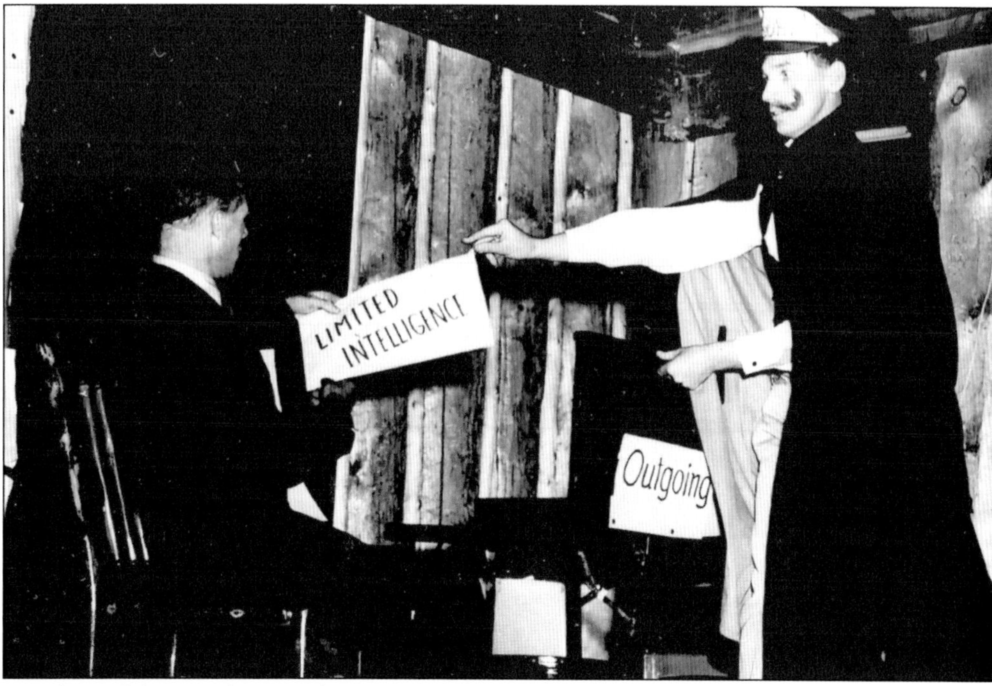

Members of the British scientific community began to arrive on the Hill to work on Project Y in 1943. At war's end, the British Mission thanked their hosts with a party celebrating "The Birth of the Atomic Era." In a skit, James Tuck (right) played the part of a devilish security officer. The story depicted the journey of Good Uncle Winnie's forces as they joined with Good Uncle Franklin's to undo the Bad Uncles Adolph and Benito.

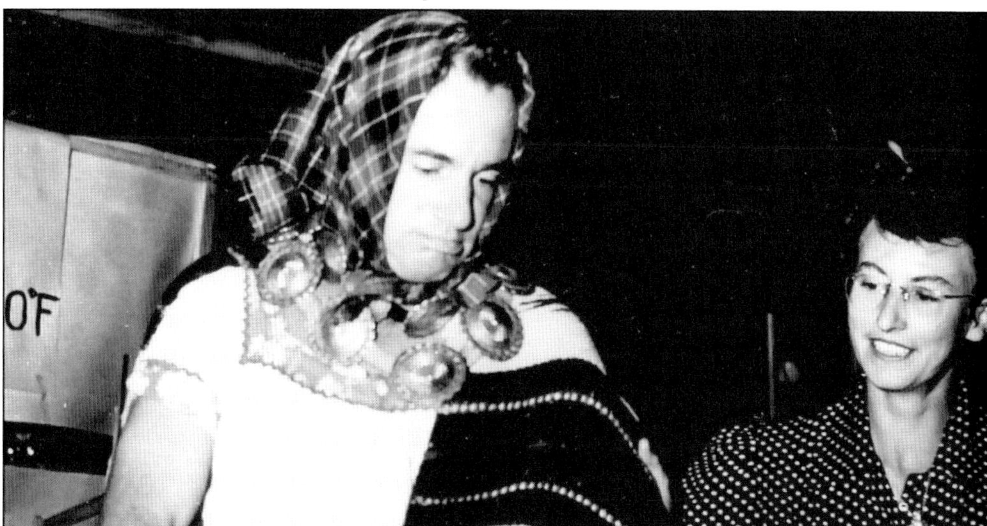

In the skit, physicist Otto Frisch was dressed as the Pueblo housekeeper for scientist's wife Elsie Tuck. He played up the part, wiping some dishes with window curtains and throwing others to the side without expression. Project wives depended on the help of the Pueblo women and found friendship with them as well. This exaggeration took to the point of hilarity the comparison between the regimented routines of the New England, Southern, or Midwestern transplants and the ageless, unhurried rhythms of the Indian natives.

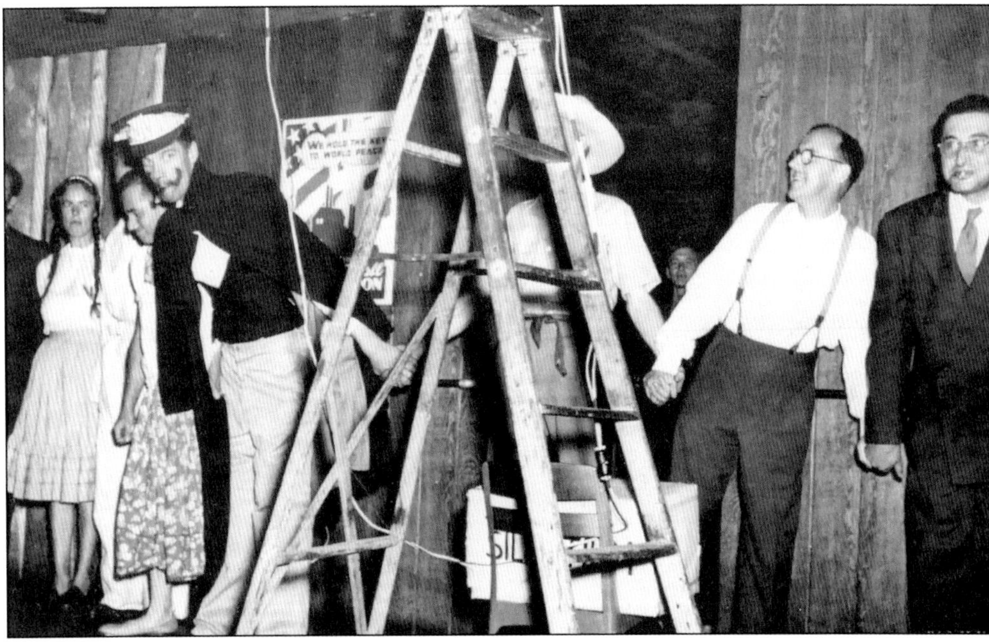

The finale of the skit at the British postwar party was a reenactment of the Trinity bomb test with lots of flashing and banging to accompany a drop from the towering ladder! Taking a bow after the final scene are cast members Winifred Moon (in braids), Otto Frisch (in flowered skirt), Jim Tuck, P.B. Moon (behind the ladder), Ernie Titterton (in the background), W.G. Marley, and G. Placzek.

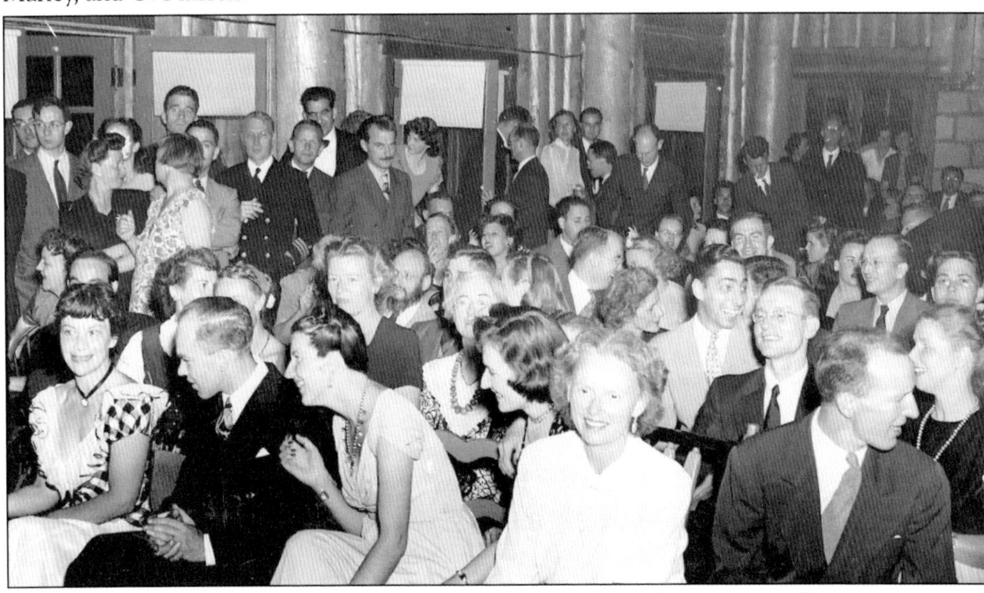

The British Mission celebration in September 1945 was a smashing success. Formal invitations had arrived in mailboxes, so unlike the mimeographed flyers that had been a Project necessity for so long. The British wives prepared a dinner of steak and kidney pie and trifle. Another British tradition—a toast with port wine was made to the king, the president, and the grand alliance. The evening's festivities were in Fuller Lodge, and naturally at the conclusion of the meal and skits, the Saturday night dance followed.

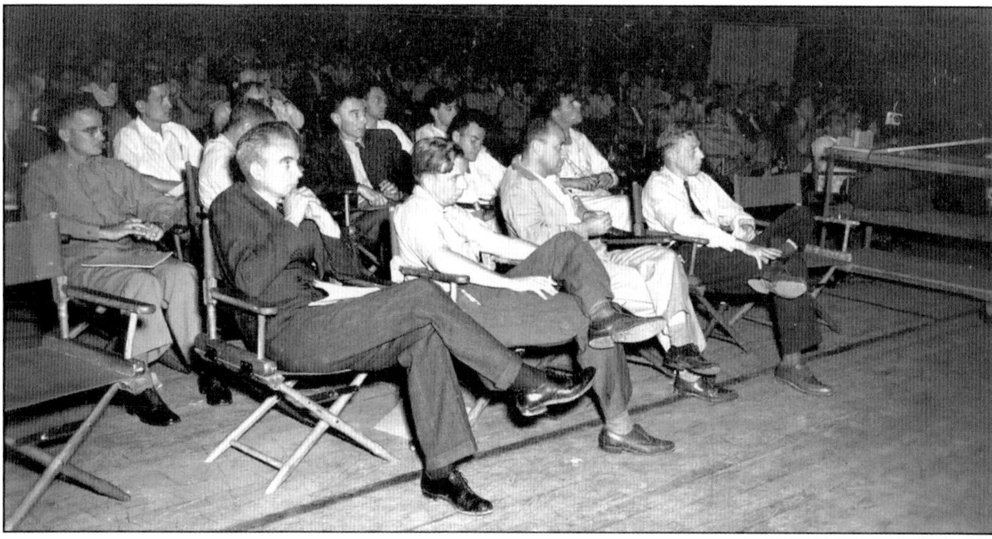

A weeklong physics conference was held in Los Alamos in August 1946, with more than 300 scientists from many universities across the country in attendance. Some of those included were, in the front row, from left to right, lab director Norris Bradbury and physicists John Manley, Enrico Fermi, and Jerome Kellogg. Robert Oppenheimer also returned to Los Alamos for the conference (second row in dark suit) and sat next to Richard Feynman.

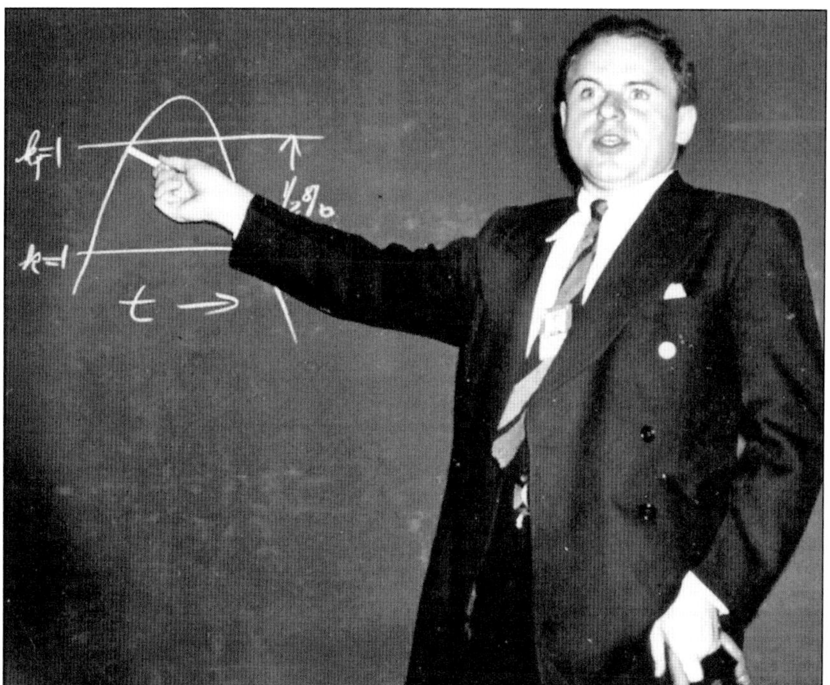

Dr. Philip Morrison had an impressive history of experience with nuclear science and was a conference speaker for the postwar physics gathering in 1946. He was present during the Trinity test near Alamogordo, New Mexico and was sent to Tinian Island to help assemble the bomb that was dropped on Hiroshima. In addition, he had observed the devastation of the blast firsthand when he went to Hiroshima to measure radioactivity and its effects on that city.

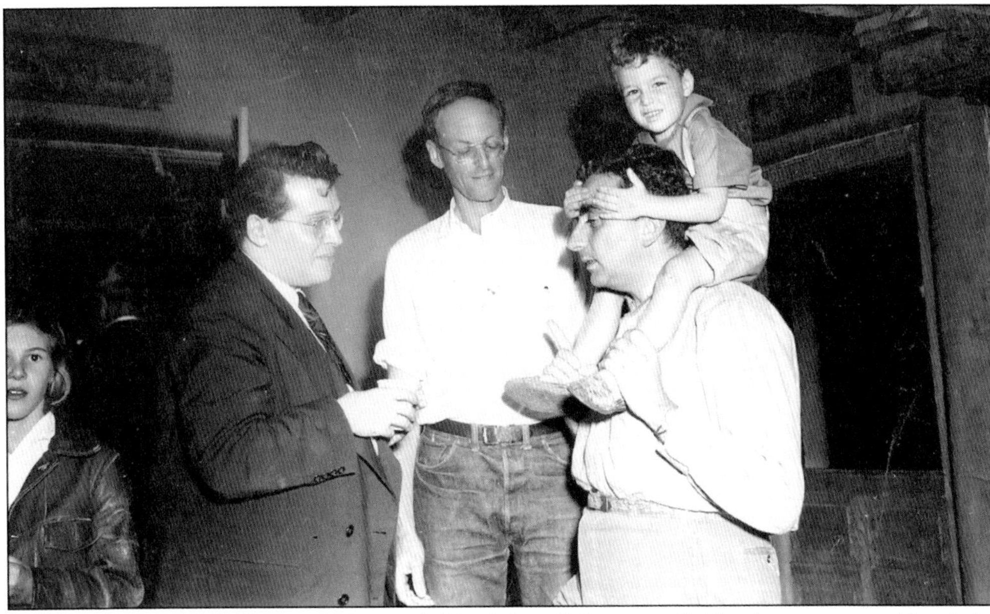

The 1946 physics conference was attended by Julian Schwinger (left) who some considered the "Mozart of Physics." David Inglis of Johns Hopkins University and Edward Teller, with son Paul on his shoulders, enjoy a light moment with Schwinger between presentations. Teller, a Project scientist who had recently chaired a secret conference in Los Alamos on the possibility of the hydrogen bomb, eventually became known as the "Father of the Hydrogen Bomb"—a device more powerful and destructive than the atomic bomb.

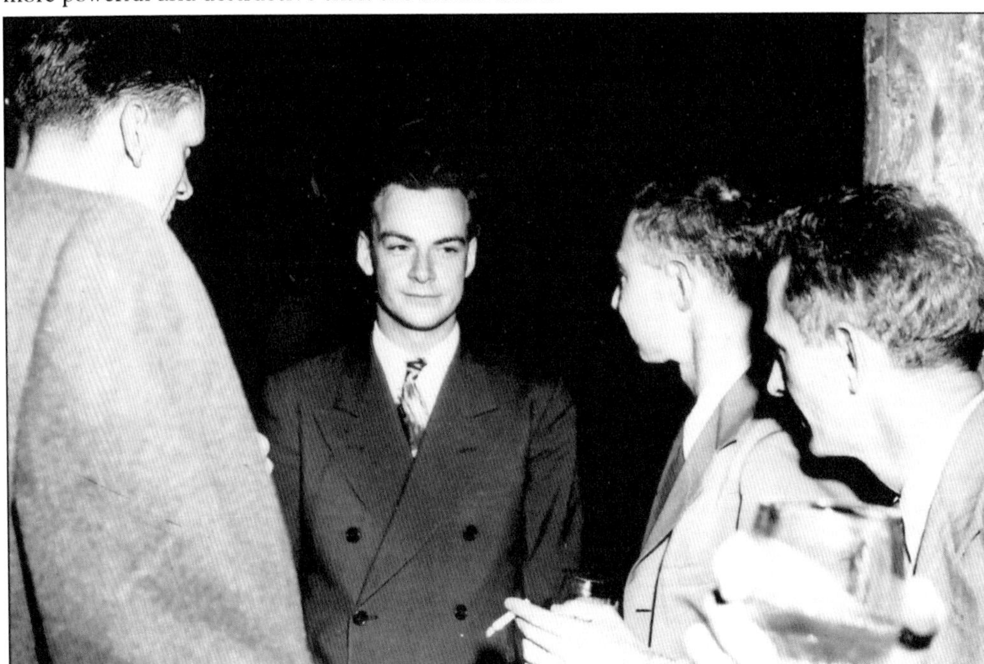

Richard Feynman (center) spent the years from 1943 to 1945 in Los Alamos as a young physicist and unorthodox thinker. In later years he was a well-respected teacher and winner of the Nobel Prize in physics. He assisted in the 1946 conference as one of the chairmen.

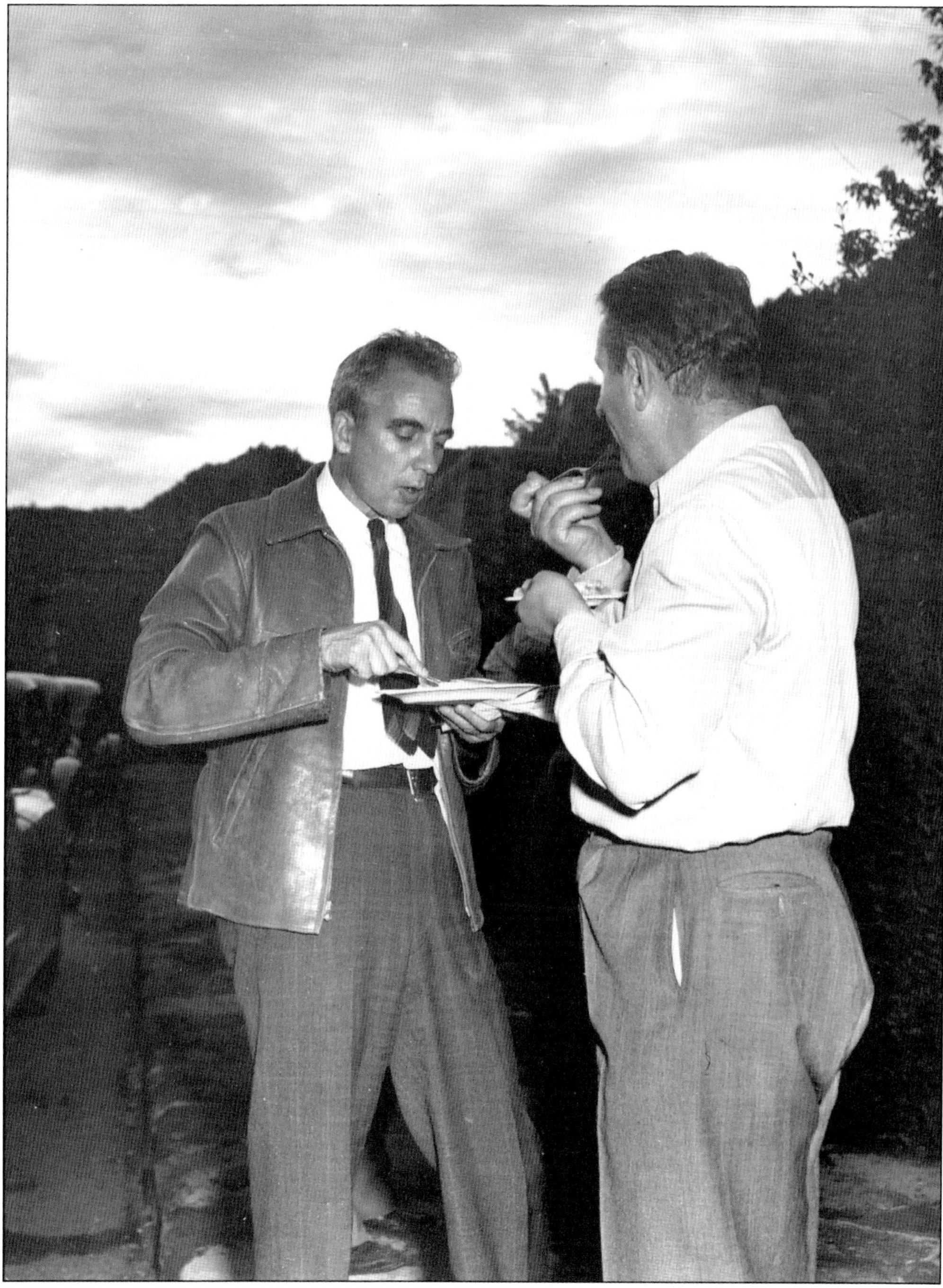

During the five-day physics conference in 1946, a number of social activities were planned for the participants. Time was spent in the surrounding scenic areas, and a mid-week picnic in Frijoles Canyon in Bandelier National Monument was organized. Here Norris Bradbury (left), Los Alamos Laboratory director, continues to enjoy the picnic while speaking to Jed Demson, assistant director of the laboratory.

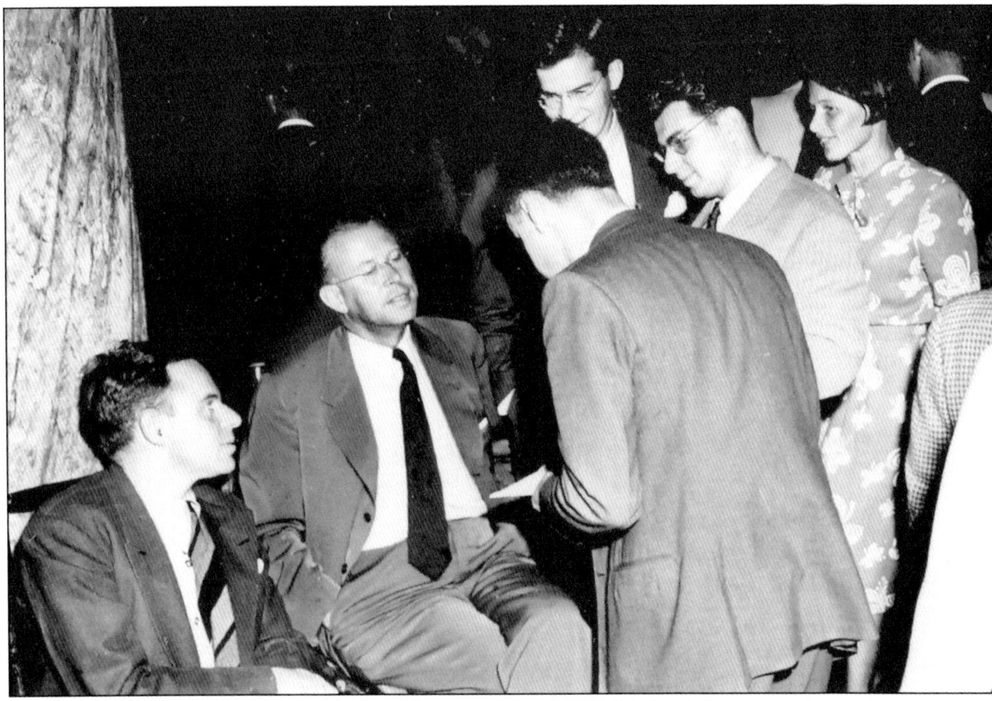

Physicist Ernest Lawrence, seated in the center next to Philip Morrison, drew the attention of some of the younger scientific attendees. Reports stated that the conference was a feast of information on tests, calculations, and information for younger scientists at the Los Alamos Lab. Lawrence was a scientific advisor to the Manhattan Project during the war.

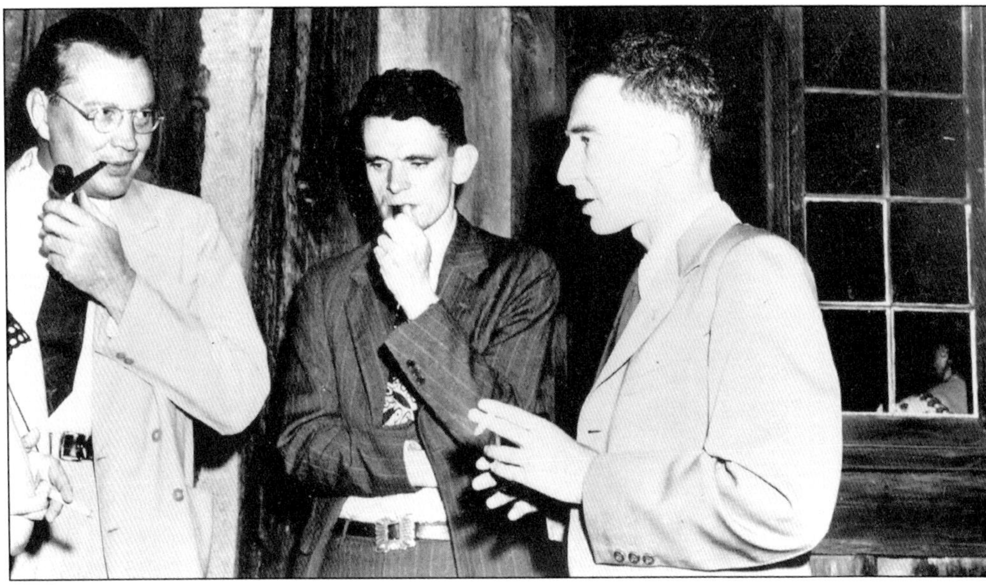

From left to right, original Project members Eric Jette, Charles Critchfield, and Robert Oppenheimer were reunited at the physics conference. At the time of the conference, Jette was the Los Alamos Lab's Chemistry-Metallurgy Research Division leader, and Critchfield was a physics professor at George Washington University. Oppenheimer, back at Berkeley and Caltech, consulted for the United Nations Atomic Energy Commission.

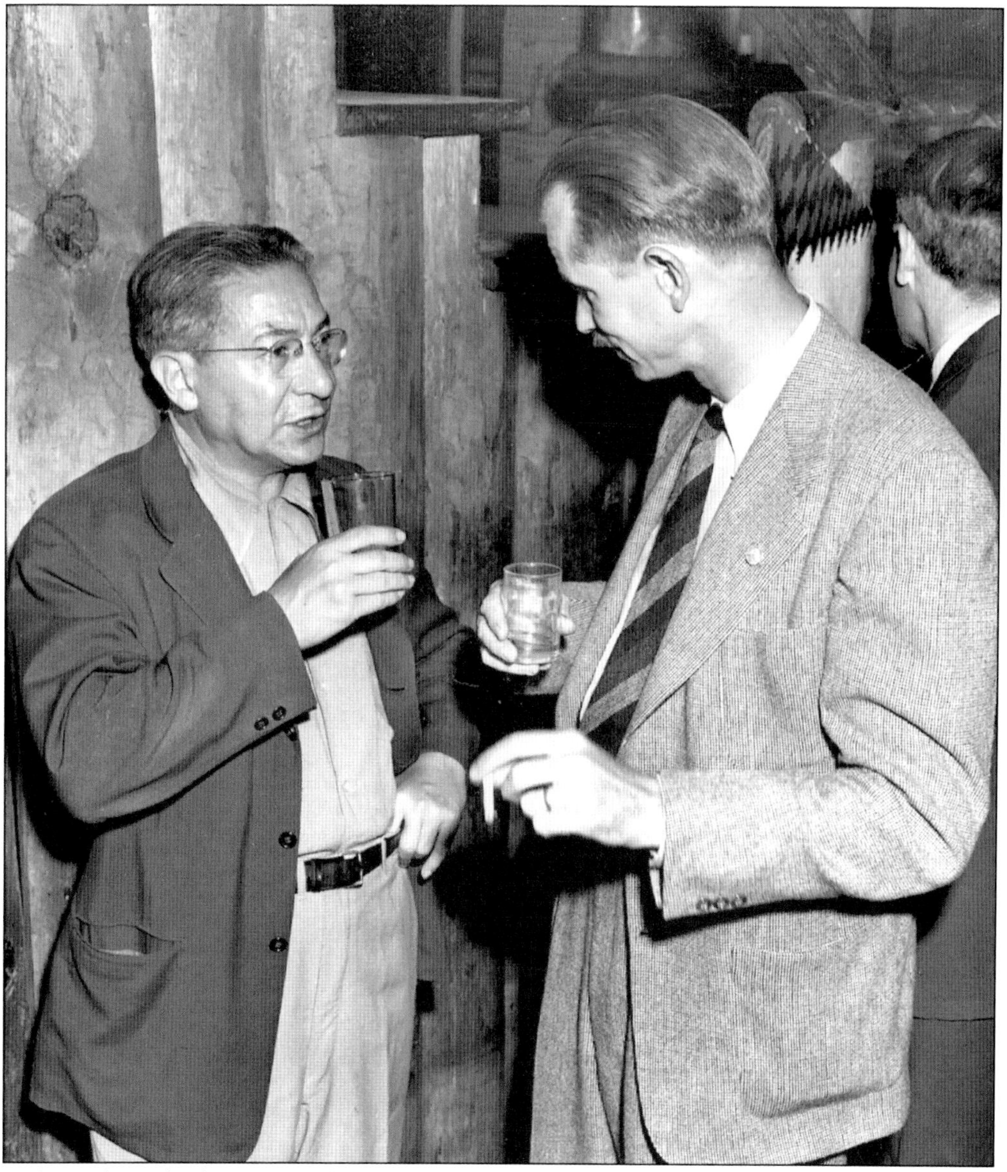

Isador Rabi and Edwin McMillan, two Manhattan Project veterans, enjoyed the conference's evening cocktail party at Fuller Lodge. In late 1942 McMillan and an Army entourage explored various New Mexico sites as possibilities for the secret bomb project. McMillan joined the Project, but Rabi, a Nobel laureate, remained at Columbia University as a professor and visited as a consultant.

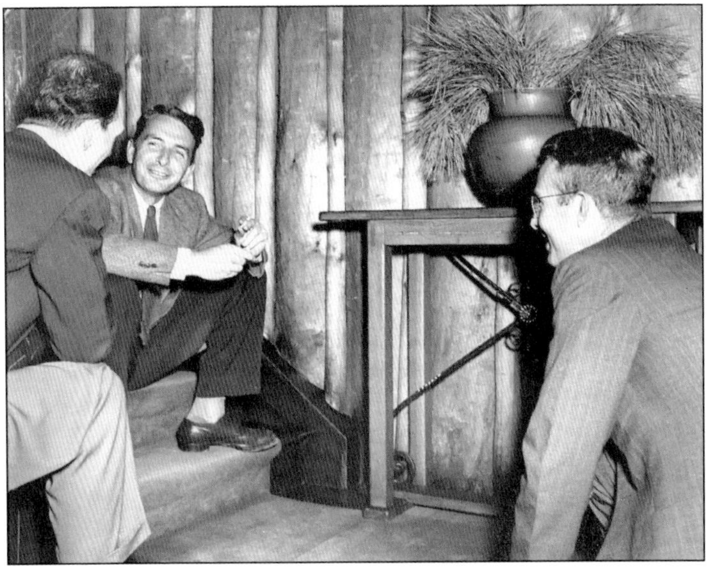

Physicist John Williams from the University of Minnesota relaxed on the stairs in Fuller Lodge at one of the parties during the physics conference. In the conference keynote address, lab director Norris Bradbury asked conferees for advice and consultation that could help determine the future of the Los Alamos Scientific Laboratory. But the past was also important as scientists renewed friendships and enjoyed memories.

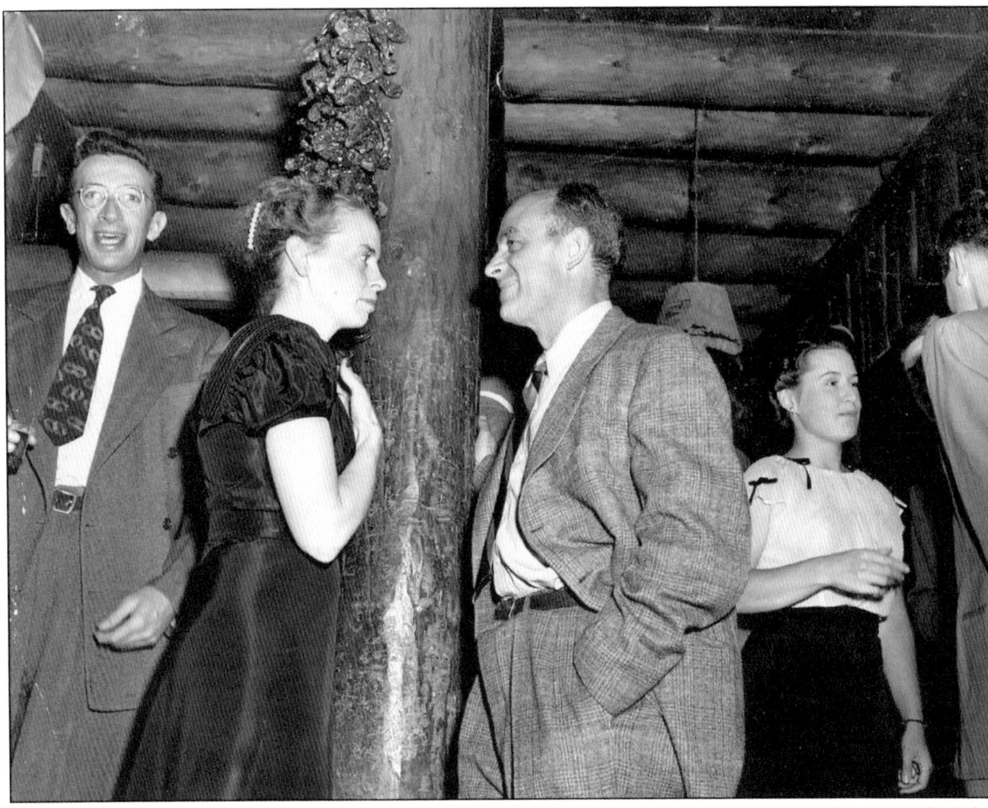

Enrico Fermi, gracious and relaxed, spoke to one of the wives of the scientists who attended the conference. Hanging from a vertical log in Fuller Lodge was an item unique to New Mexico—a ristra of red chiles. The chiles were grown locally, tied together with twine, and left to dry in the sun. The red chile sauce made from these peppers was a staple in New Mexican households and became a familiar food to many in the scientific community.

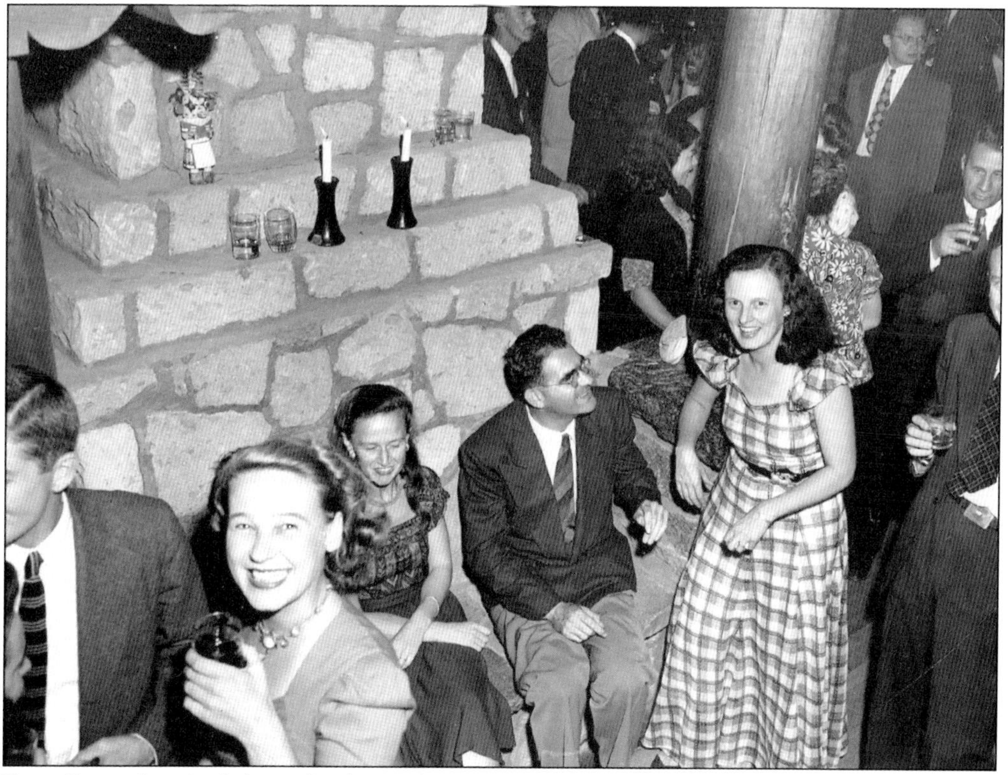

Betty Bryan (on the left, smiling) was the secretary to Norris Bradbury, lab director. While on vacation from *Fortune Magazine*, Bryan visited New Mexico and met physicists Enrico Fermi and Sam Allison. Their stories about the Hill prompted her to apply for a job. Victor Weisskopf from MIT is seated at the fireplace in Fuller Lodge during a physics conference cocktail party.

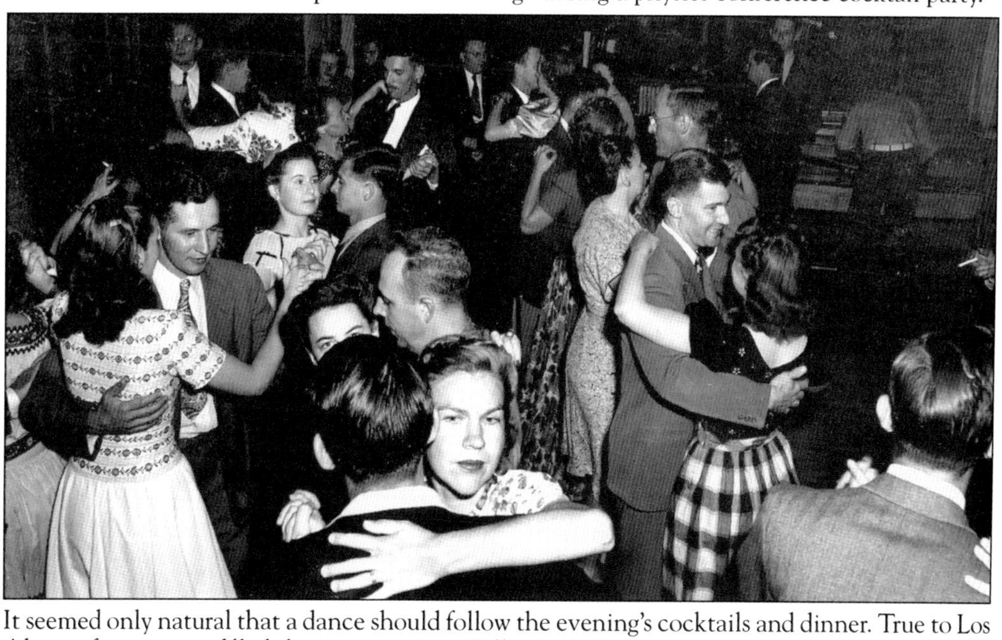

It seemed only natural that a dance should follow the evening's cocktails and dinner. True to Los Alamos form, music filled the main room at Fuller Lodge and the dancers took to the floor.

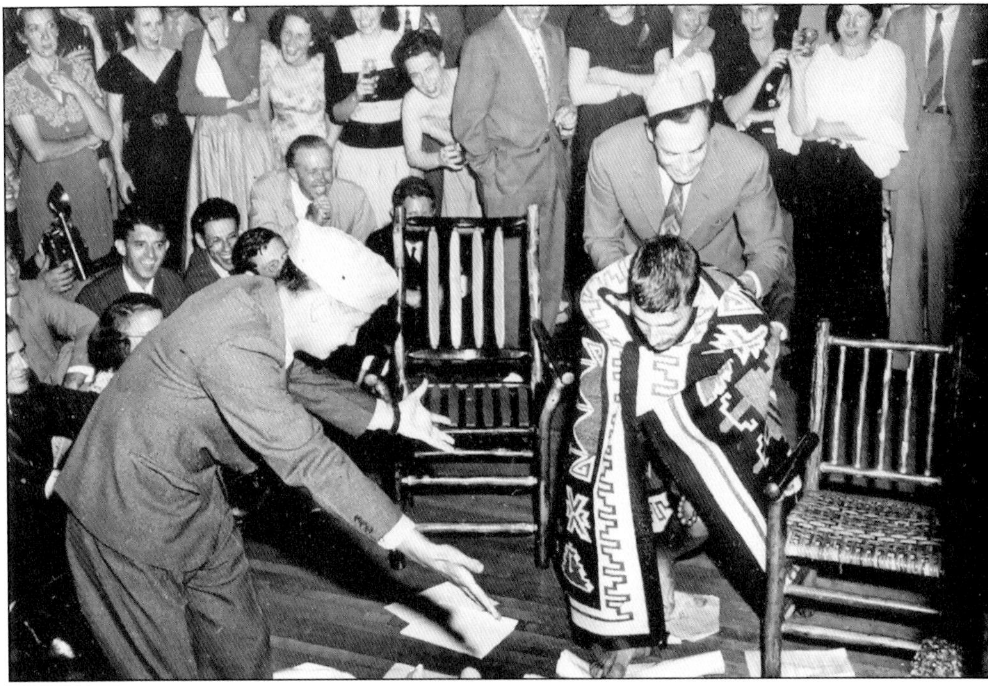

James Tuck and Ernie Titterton, British physicists, also attended the physics conference. Being duly remembered for successfully staging a spoof of the Project during the British Mission party several months earlier, they struck again. Titterton's papers at the feet of the blanket-clad Tuck were more shenanigans, much to the obvious enjoyment of the audience in Fuller Lodge. (Photo by Lab Photo Group.)

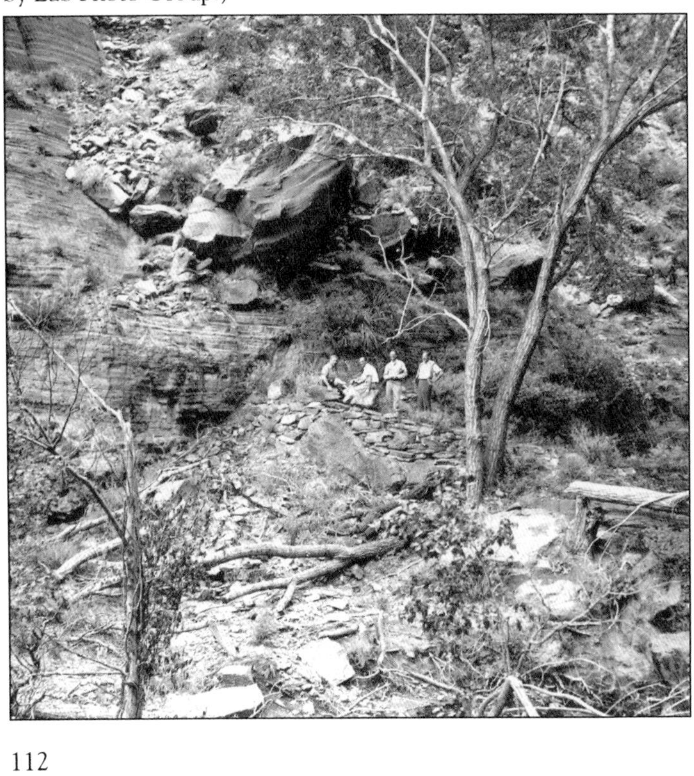

Hiking in the Frijoles Canyon at Bandelier National Monument was a familiar pastime for many of the scientists who returned to Los Alamos for the physics conference. The canyon size is evident in this perspective. In the midst of the questions and uncertainties raised at the conference about the future of the atomic bomb, the science of exploring the canyon and hiking the trails prevailed for the moment.

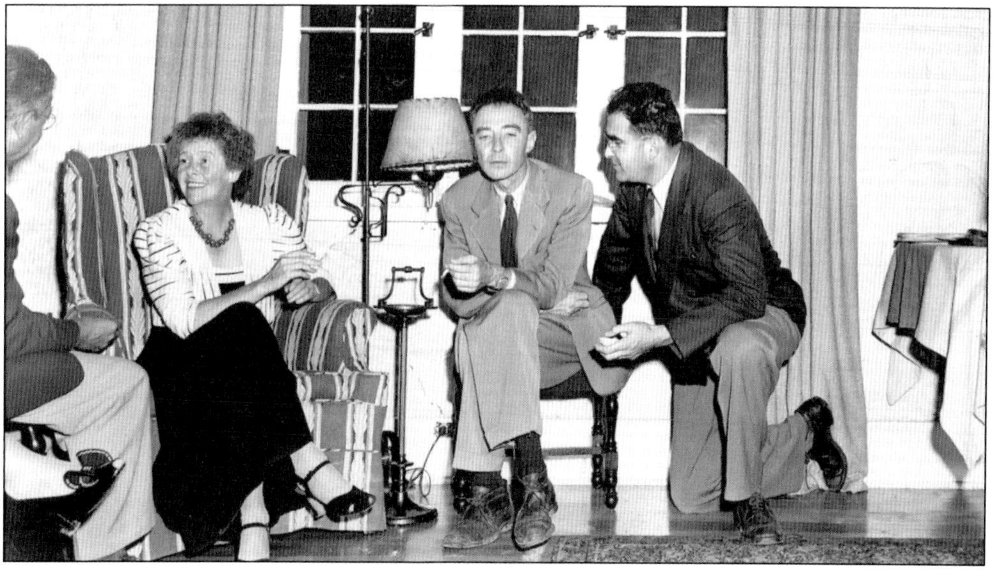

The 1946 conference was filled with a number of smaller social events as well. These included cocktail parties and dinners that were held in the homes of Norris Bradbury and others. At one of these gatherings, Isador Rabi, Robert Oppenheimer, and Victor Weisskopf chatted with Dorothy McKibbin, who from her office at 109 Palace Avenue in Santa Fe played an important role in greeting, directing, and comforting newcomers to Project Y. (Courtesy of the Los Alamos Historical Society.)

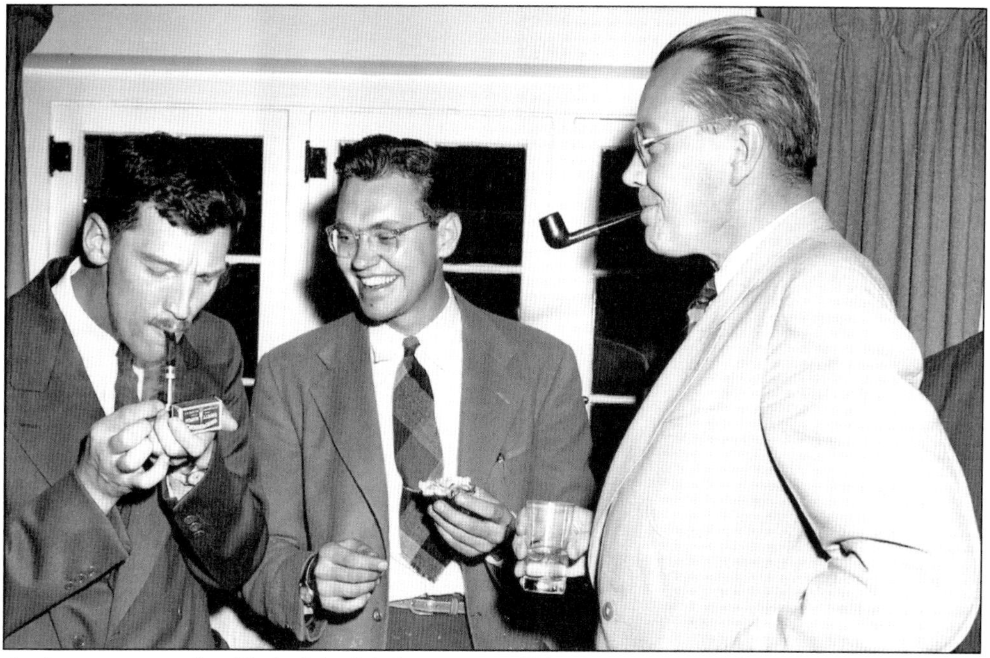

At the same party, Jim Tuck, John Michnovicz, and Eric Jette, pictured from left to right, joined in conversation and a smoke. After several years of postwar work in England, Tuck returned to the lab in Los Alamos and worked there into the 1970s. Jette's stay after the war was followed by a position at Union Carbide in New York, but he and his family returned to New Mexico in the early 1960s. (Photo by Joe Gluth.)

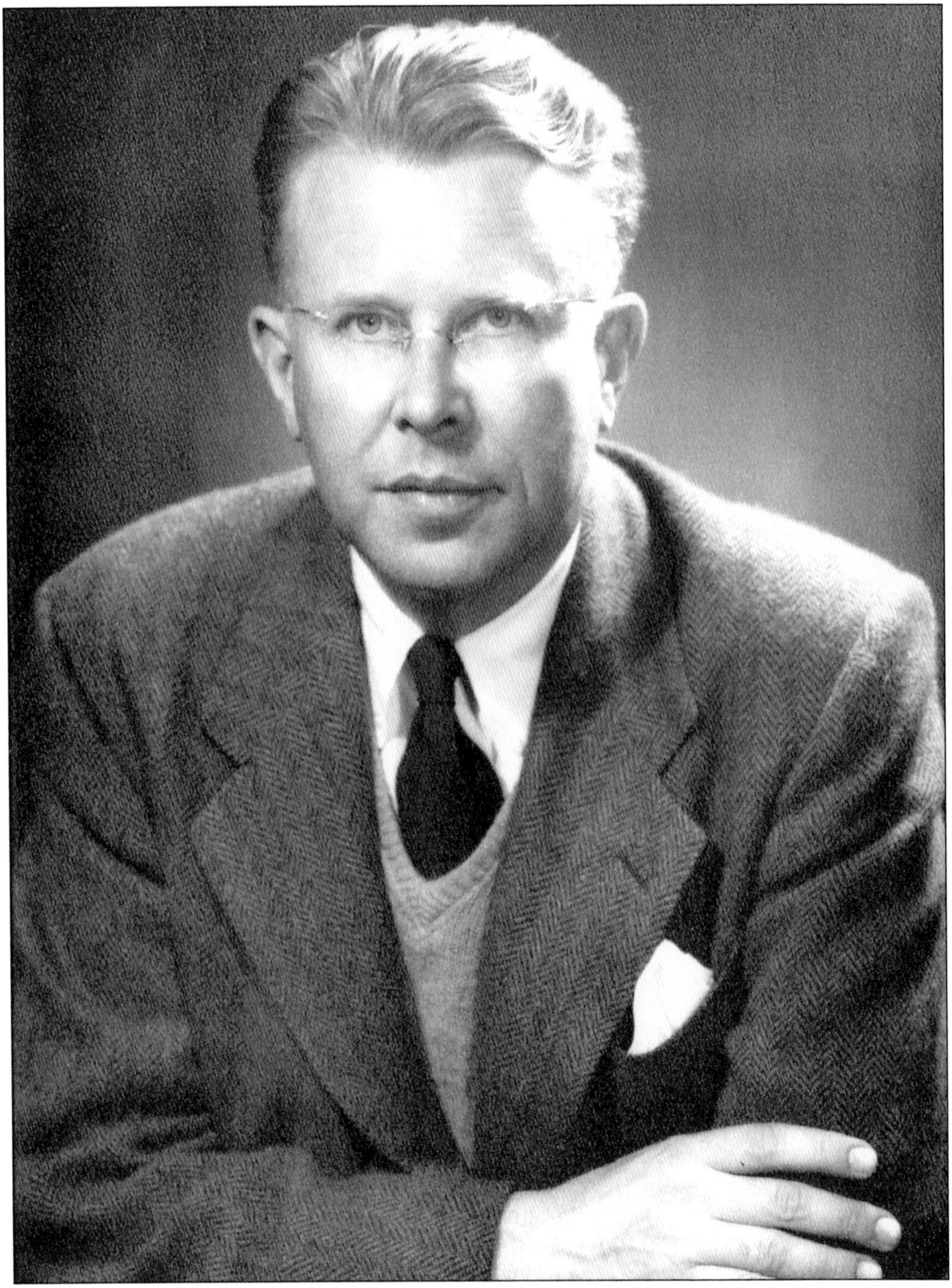

Ernest O. Lawrence, director of the Radiation Laboratory at Berkeley, was best known as the inventor of the cyclotron. He would have been Gen. Leslie Groves' first choice for lab director of the Manhattan Project except that his work in isotope separation was so crucial that he remained at Berkeley. Robert Oppenheimer and Ernest Lawrence became friends at Berkeley and spent time together at the Oppenheimer ranch in New Mexico. Lawrence's support of the hydrogen bomb left him at odds with Oppenheimer in later years. Lawrence won the Nobel Prize in physics in 1939.

Hans Bethe was a theoretical physicist in Germany when he was dismissed from his position in 1933 because of anti-Semitism. He accepted a professorship at Cornell University in 1934 and established his reputation as a solid theoretician. In 1942, Robert Oppenheimer invited him to the summer conference in Berkeley where atomic bomb theory was discussed. Bethe agreed to come to Los Alamos and became head of the Theoretical Division. He returned to Cornell after the war and received the Nobel Prize in physics in 1967.

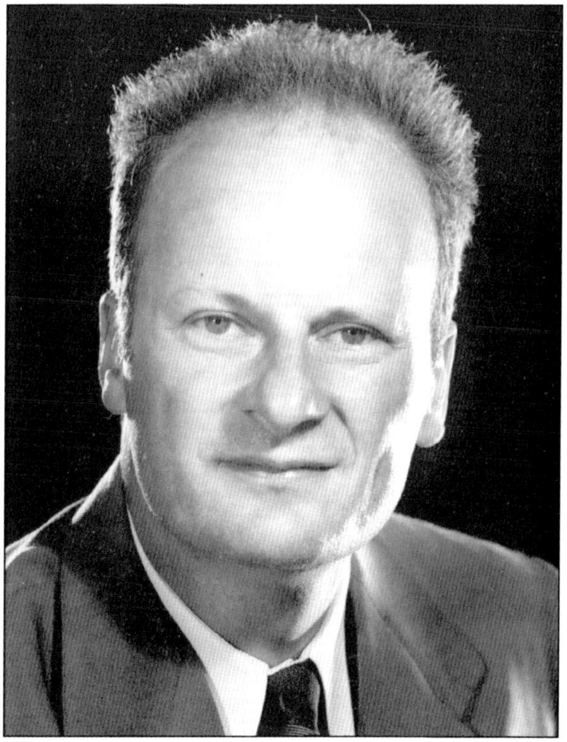

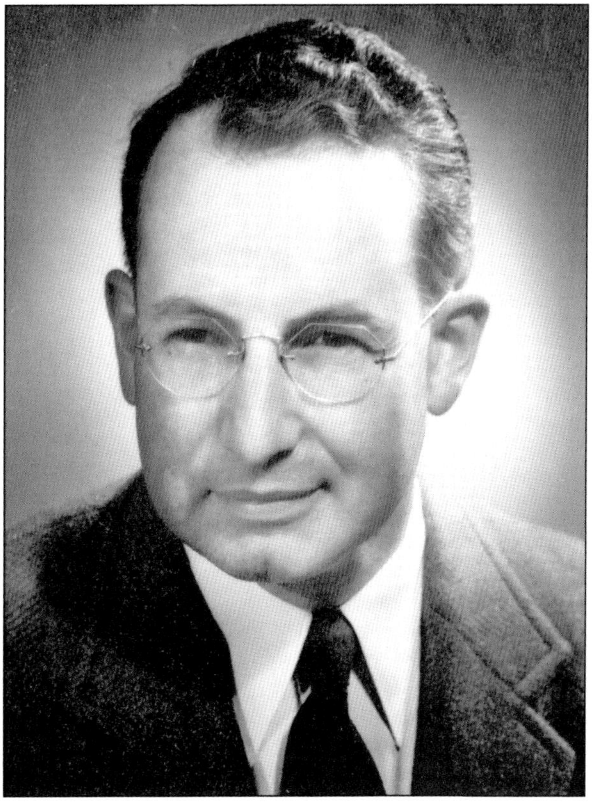

Robert Bacher was working at the Radiation Laboratory at the Massachusetts Institute of Technology when he joined the Manhattan Project. At first he headed the Experimental Physics Division, but his determined leadership was effective in convincing Robert Oppenheimer to pursue implosion even when the science seemed beyond reach. He eventually directed the "G" or Gadget Division that perfected the implosion bomb. Bacher returned to Caltech after the war and was one of the first members of the Atomic Energy Commission. He died in November 2004 at the age of 99.

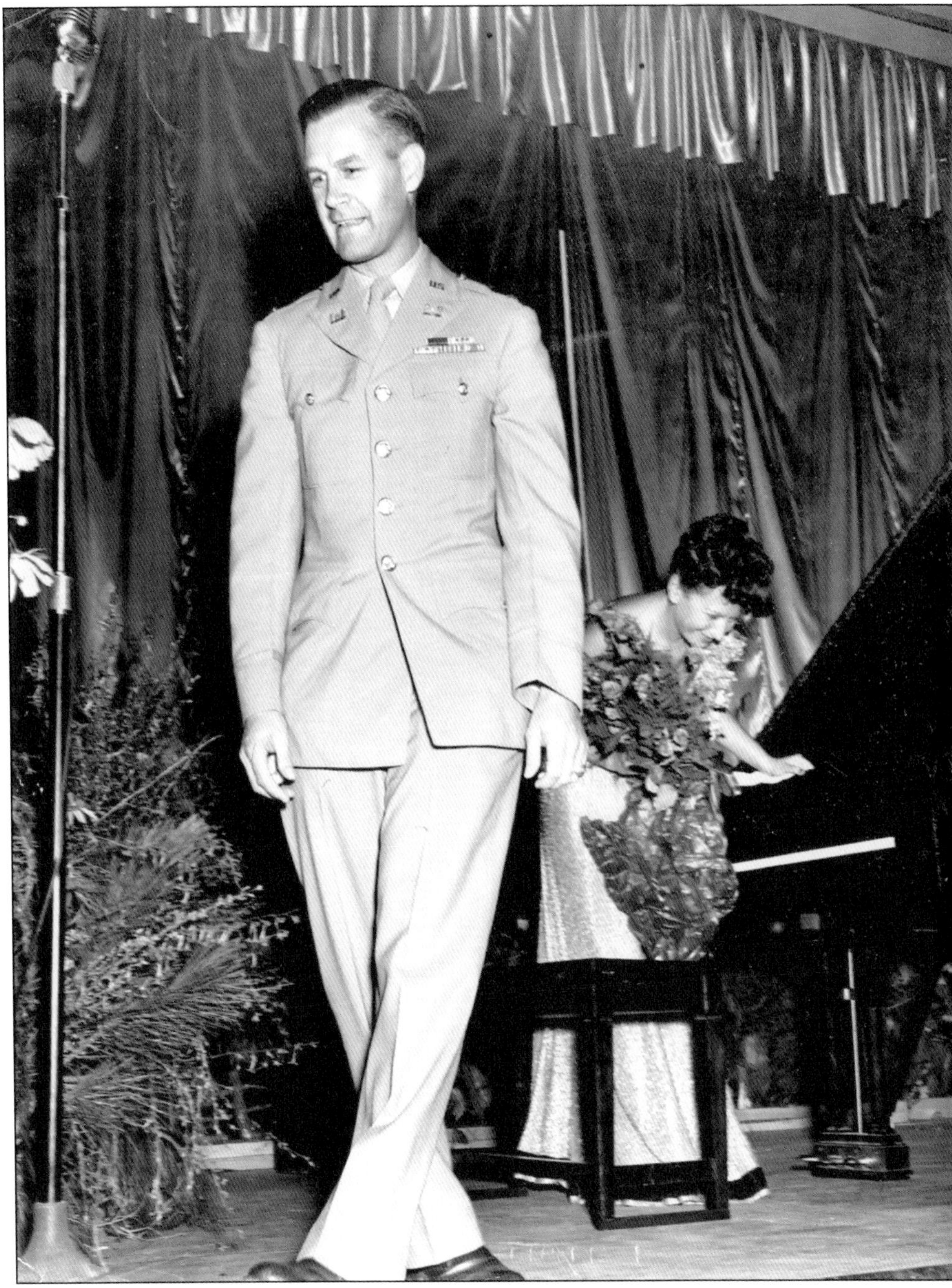

Col. Austin Betts, as deputy commander of the post in August 1946, had the privilege of thanking pianist Vitya Vronsky with a bouquet of flowers after her glowing performance. She and her pianist husband, Victor Babin, had performed in a live musical gala, the first in Los Alamos, which capped the week's physics conference. The husband-wife team were residents of Tesuque, New Mexico, and graciously performed for the Los Alamos audience in thanks for all that the Project employees had done to serve their country.

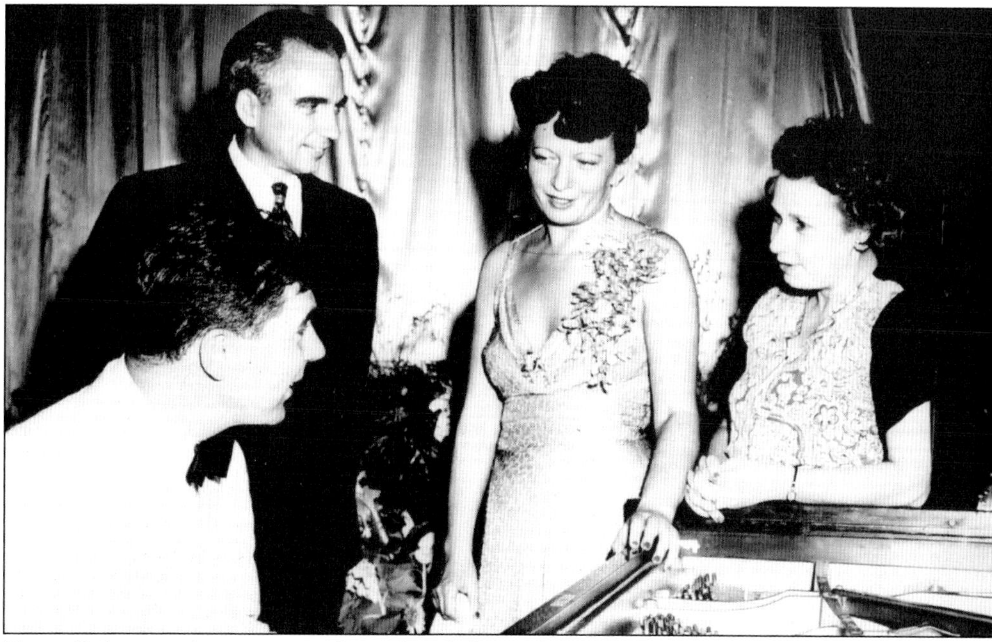

Victor Babin, at the piano, performed with his wife, Vitya Vronsky (center), after a two-year stint as a soldier with the Army Air Force Band. Babin and Vronsky were Russian born and met in a Berlin music studio. This concert marked their first return to the stage since 1944. Norris and Lois Bradbury were present to offer their congratulations.

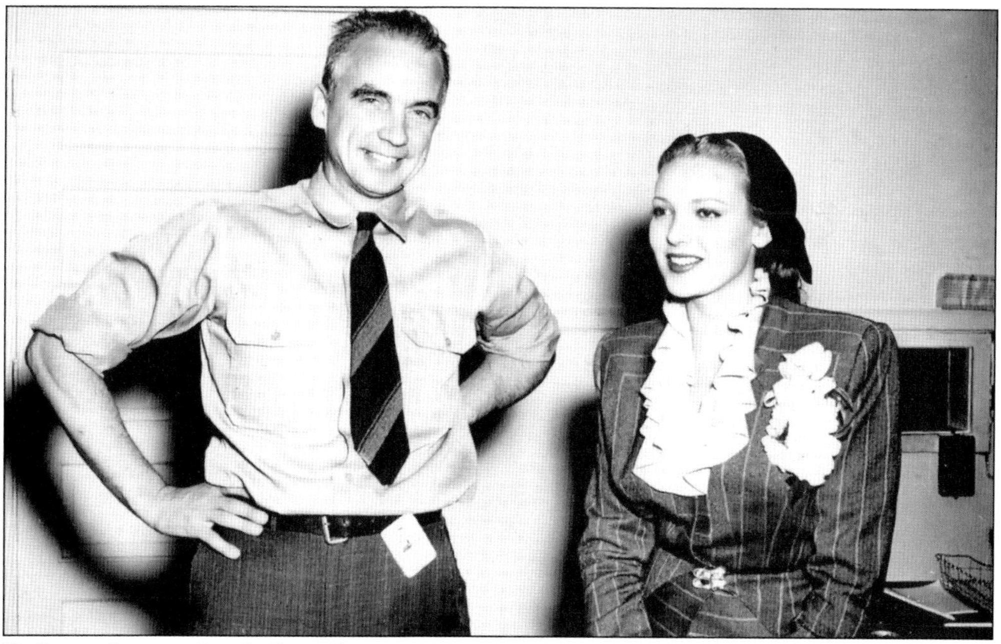

Hollywood actress Linda Darnell was a surprise visitor to Los Alamos in October 1946, and lab director Norris Bradbury seemed most pleased to welcome the special guest. The actress had just filmed *Forever Amber* and was vacationing in Santa Fe incognito when, by chance, she was recognized by a young admirer. The lovely lady impressed the soldiers, and in reply Darnell was heard to say that Los Alamos "reminded her of a Hollywood film studio."

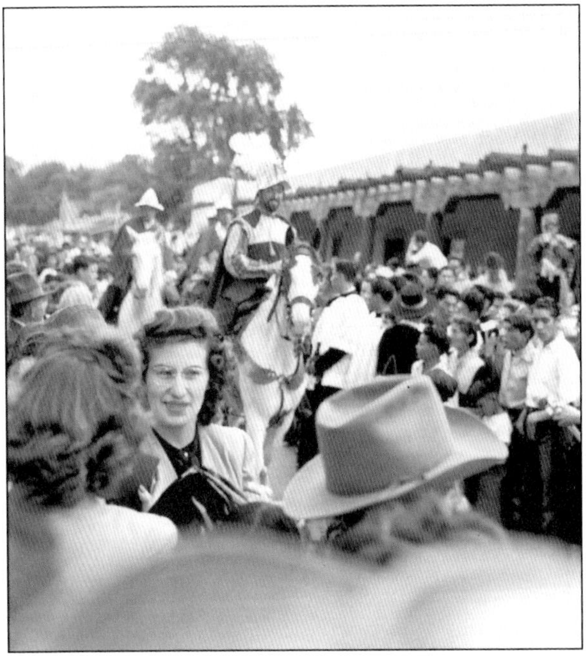

In honor of the 1692 Spanish reconquest of Santa Fe after the Pueblo Revolt of 1680, a processional was instituted to honor the Blessed Virgin as "Our Lady of Victory." The reentry into Santa Fe of Don Diego de Vargas was portrayed each year, and to further commemorate the occasion, an annual fiesta was proclaimed in 1712. The 235th observance of the Santa Fe Fiesta was celebrated in 1947, and the crowds watched the reenactment of De Vargas and his soldiers by the New Mexico National Guard as they entered the city.

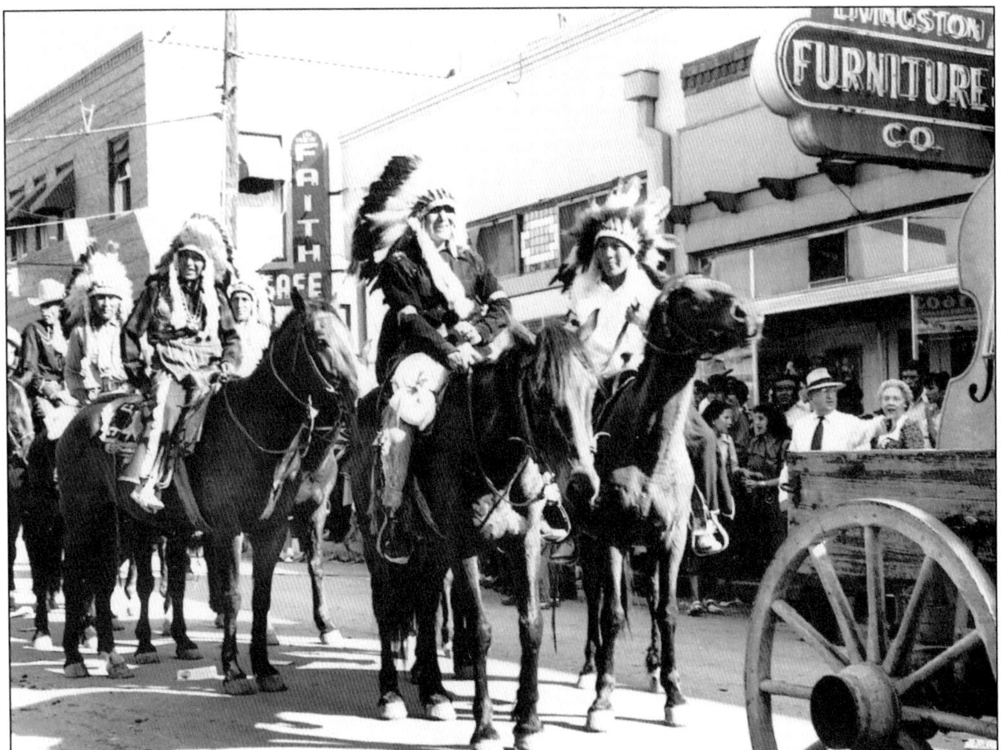

Indians participated in the Santa Fe Fiesta parade, and with the mariachi band, it was a festive time. It was the Spaniards' injustices that led to the Pueblo Revolt, but the Santa Fe Fiesta had become a great day of celebration for all parties by 1947, and the noble riders with feathered headdresses added grandeur.

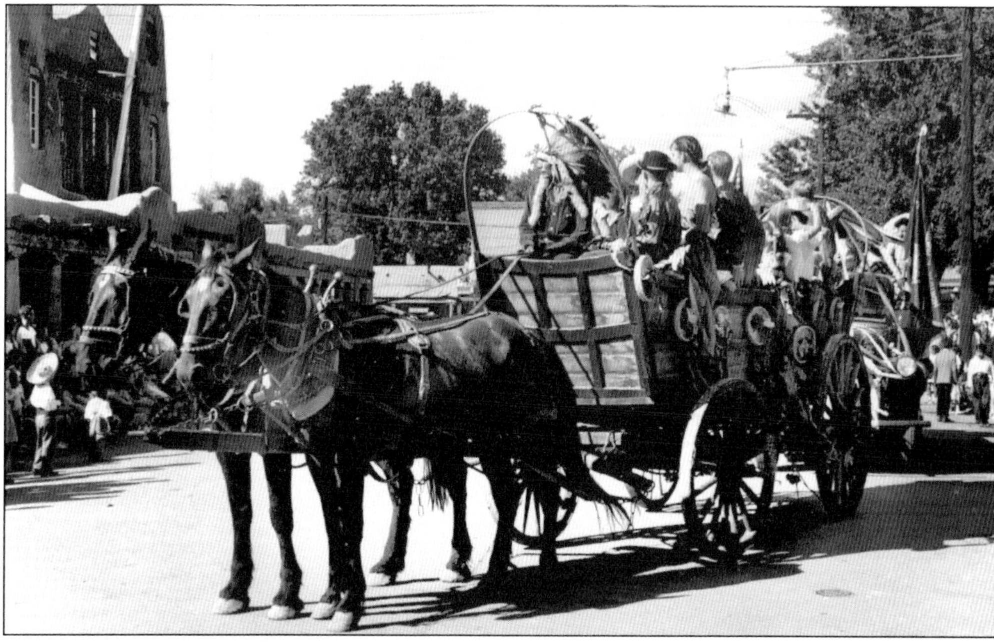

There were several parades during the four-day fiesta, and this one included a group that called itself the Kansas City Saddle and Sirloin Club. It represented the traders from the earlier days and entered the town in horse drawn wagons that circled the plaza and the downtown area.

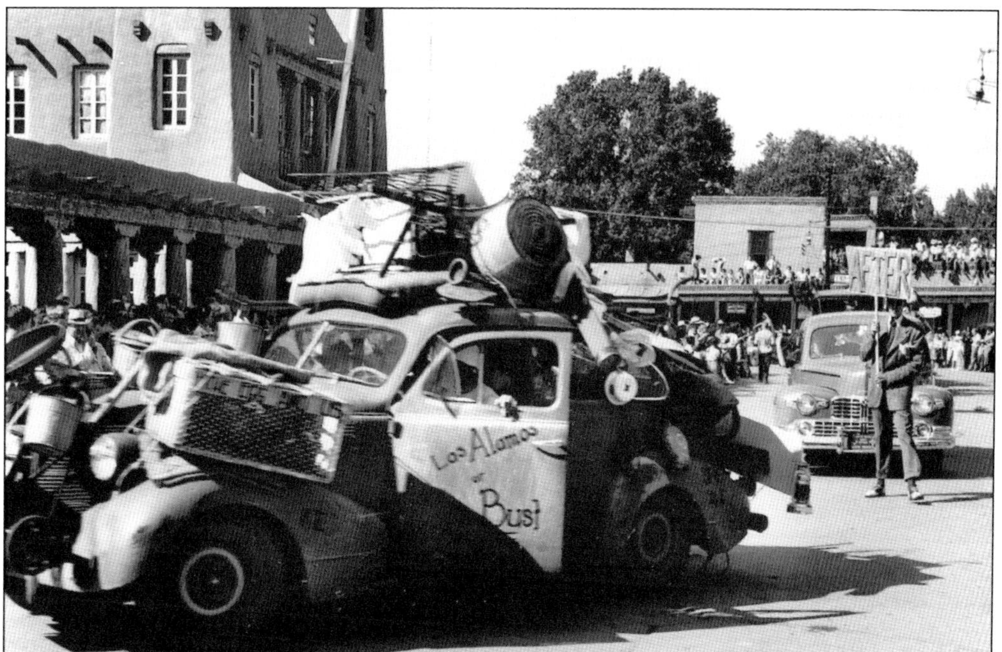

The Hysterical Parade featured floats and stunts that caricatured individuals and current issues. On the side of this old jalopy was "Los Alamos or Bust," and what a heap it carried. It was an all-too-true reminder of a slow climb up a hill of curves and switchbacks. The jalopy was followed by a brand-new car escorted by a dandy carrying the AFTER sign, a dramatic difference in living conditions during postwar times.

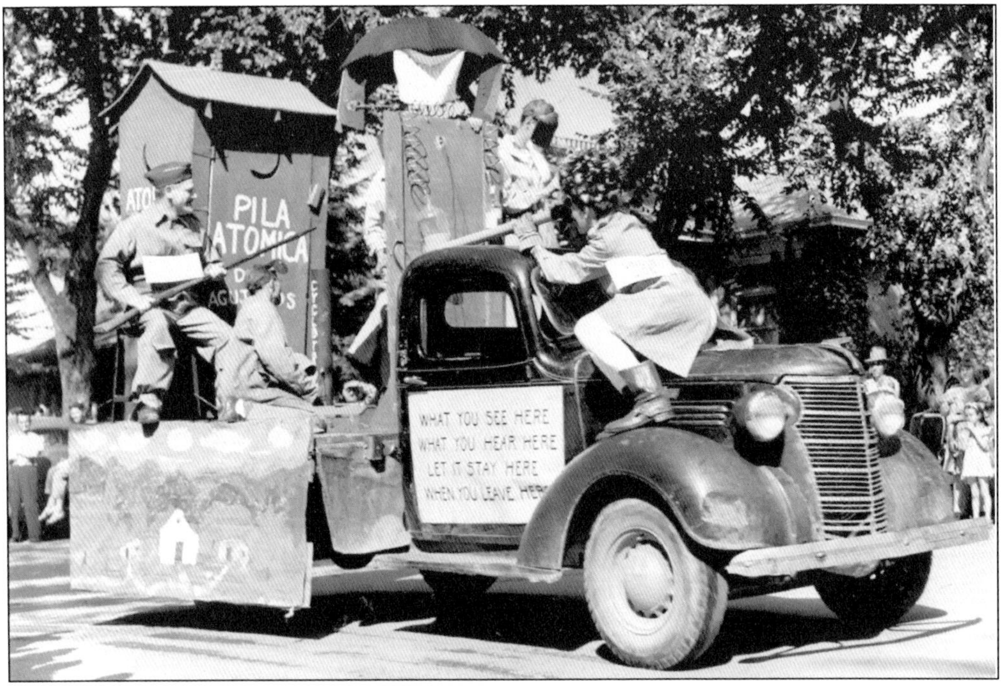

An atomic pile was the original name of the nuclear reactor, and in this spoof, General Trees (not Groves) guards the outhouse-shaped Pila Atomica. The masked man in the center stands next to the umbrella-shaped (not mushroom-shaped) atomic cloud, and Uncle Joe spies on all of them. A real warning from Project days was mounted on the side of the truck. This float in the Hysterical Parade gave an especially good laugh to those who had lived through the Manhattan Project. (Courtesy of the Los Alamos Historical Society.)

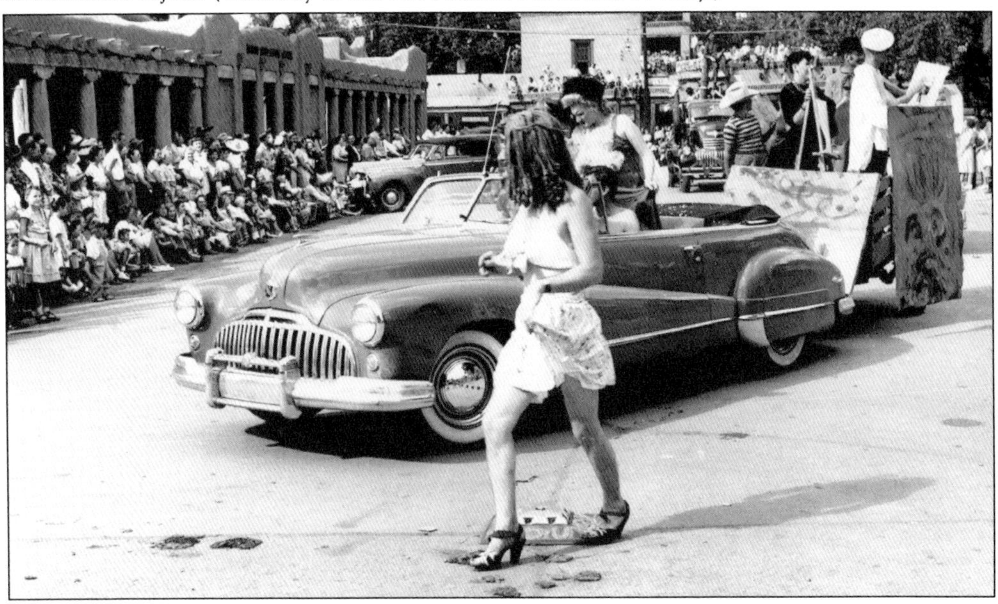

It appears that the jokes are being tossed at the art community in this float. Artistic interpretations adorned the wagon behind this car. And the beauties alongside? Well, they were stunning to say the least. The Hysterical Parade could be a little risqué!

Thumbing their way south are a couple of soldiers on their way to El Paso from Los Alamos. Since travel was no longer restricted after the war, John Michnovicz and his friends headed out. They made it down to Texas and back but posed for Michnovicz just to prove that they did.

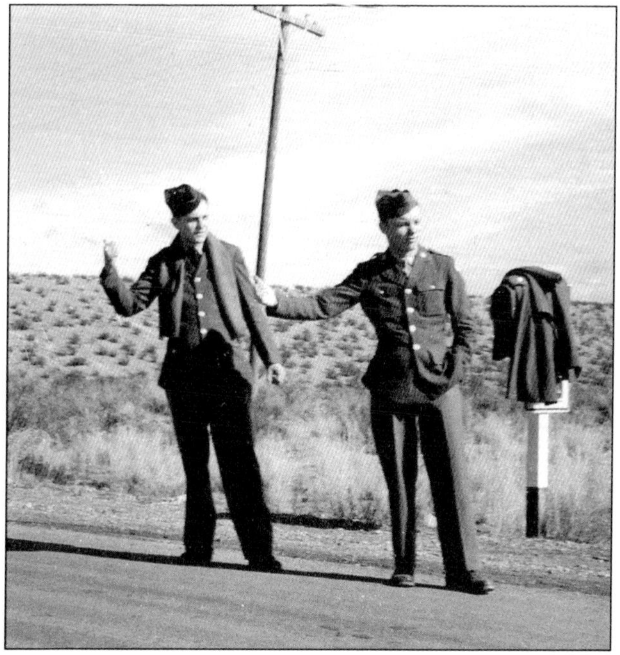

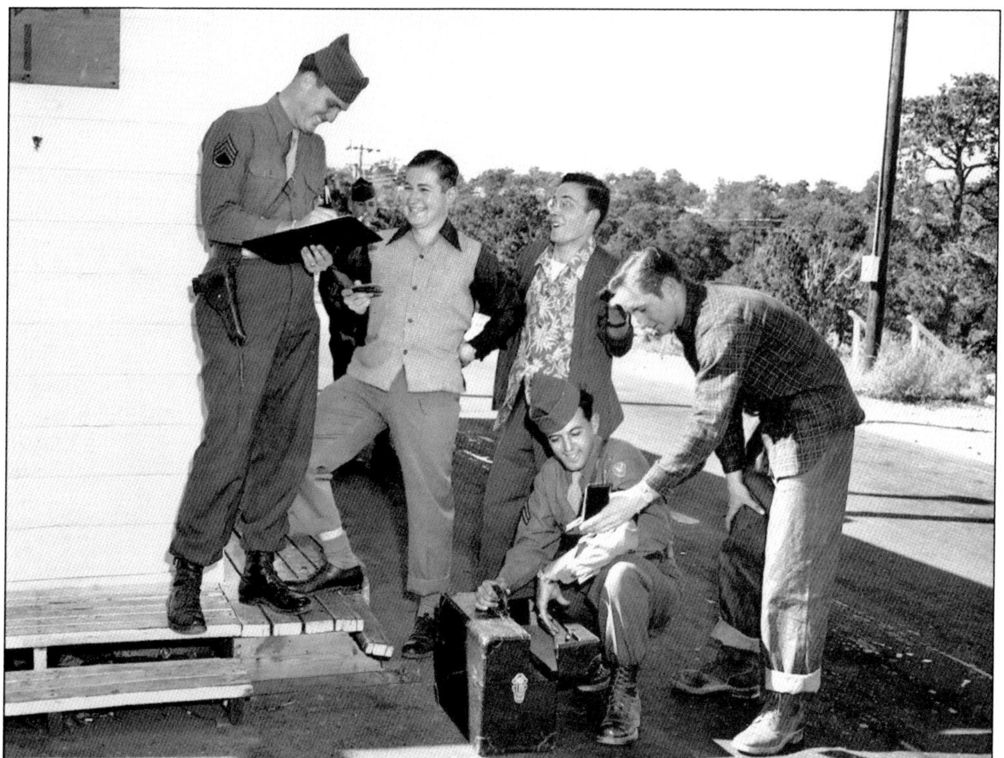

The door was opened for many servicemen and women to be discharged from active duty and return to civilian life in the months after the war. This shot was set up to show the military police checking the ID cards of the new releases, all smiles, free to go. However, there was a revolving door for many in the military as they chose to return to their post assignment as civilians.

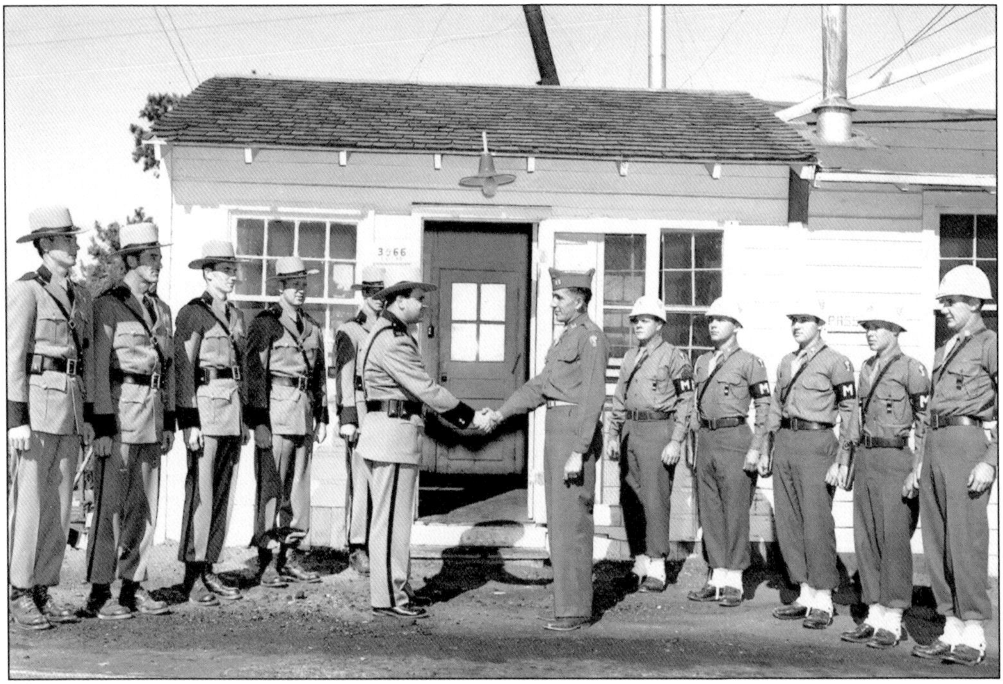

This picture was posed to show the symbolic transfer of base security operations from the Army to a new civilian authority sometime in 1947. At the main gate's pass office, an Army Corps of Engineers' post operations lieutenant, on the right, shakes the hand of his civilian counterpart from the U.S. Marshall's office while the men of the force stand in review.

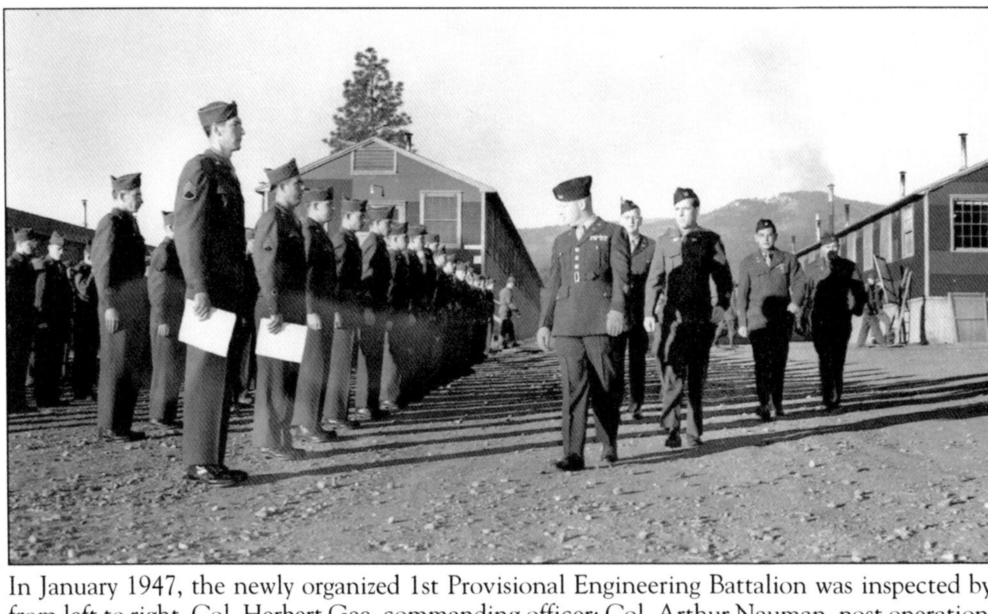

In January 1947, the newly organized 1st Provisional Engineering Battalion was inspected by, from left to right, Col. Herbert Gee, commanding officer; Col. Arthur Nauman, post operations officer; Capt. George McMaughan, executive officer; Maj. Richard Newcomb, commander of troops, and Lt. Harvey Kohl, S-4. At this time improvements were made in the barracks so that the men of the detachment would have indoor latrines and showers and would not have to brave the cold to shower and shave!

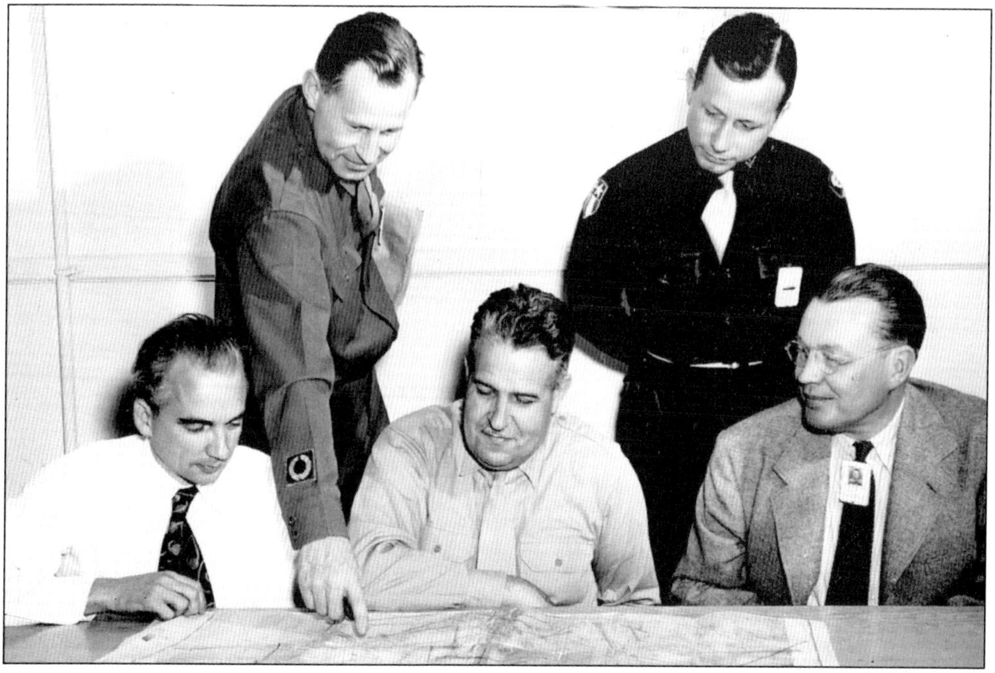

Gen. Leslie Groves flew from Washington to attend a meeting of scientists and officials of the Los Alamos Project to discuss plans for permanent housing. From left to right are Dr. Norris Bradbury, Col. L.E. Seeman, General Groves, Lt. Col. E.E. Wilhoyt, and Dr. Eric Jette. The men examined blueprints, and their agreement signaled the first permanent housing, called the Western Housing Area, built between 1946 and 1947.

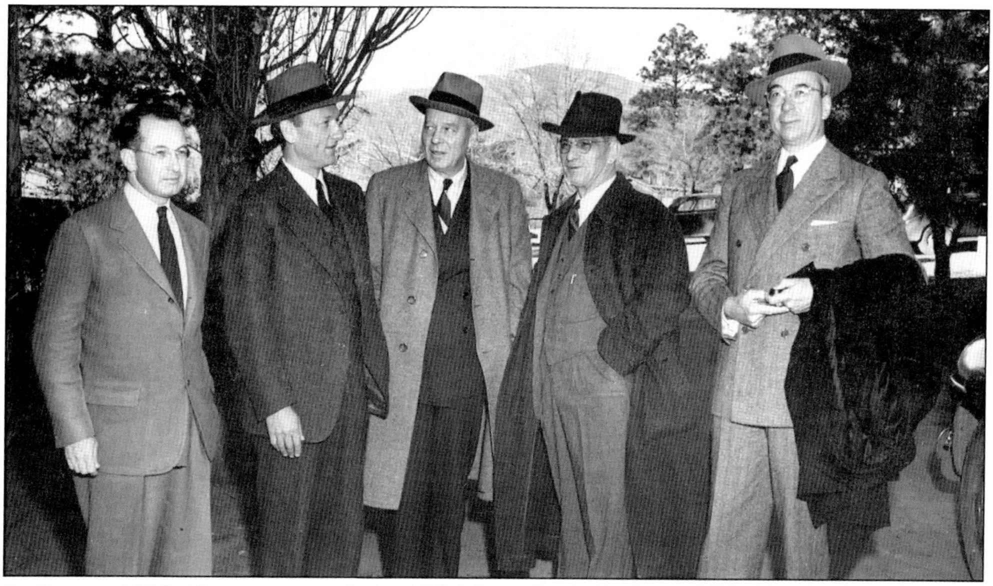

In August 1946, Congress passed the McMahon Act, which established the Atomic Energy Commission (AEC). The men appointed by President Truman to head the first Atomic Energy Commission included, from left to right, Robert Bacher, David Lilienthal, Sumner Pike, William Waymack, and Lewis Strauss. Military control of Los Alamos ended when the AEC assumed leadership of the site. (Photo by Elmer Donor.)

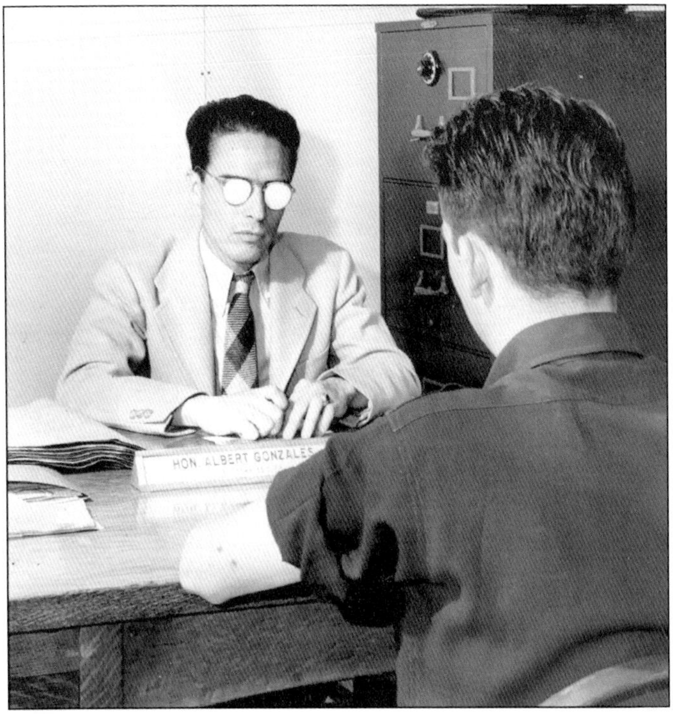

By mid-1946, U.S. Commissioner Albert Gonzales was appointed by the federal district judge to oversee the trials of Los Alamos residents who had committed petty offenses. A town council had been the only governing body in Los Alamos before this appointment, and its duties were advisory and not judicial. Gonzales, blind since age 19 and a graduate of Georgetown University Law School, heard cases involving speeding, parking violations, intoxication, and disorderly conduct. Fines ranged from $2 to $15.

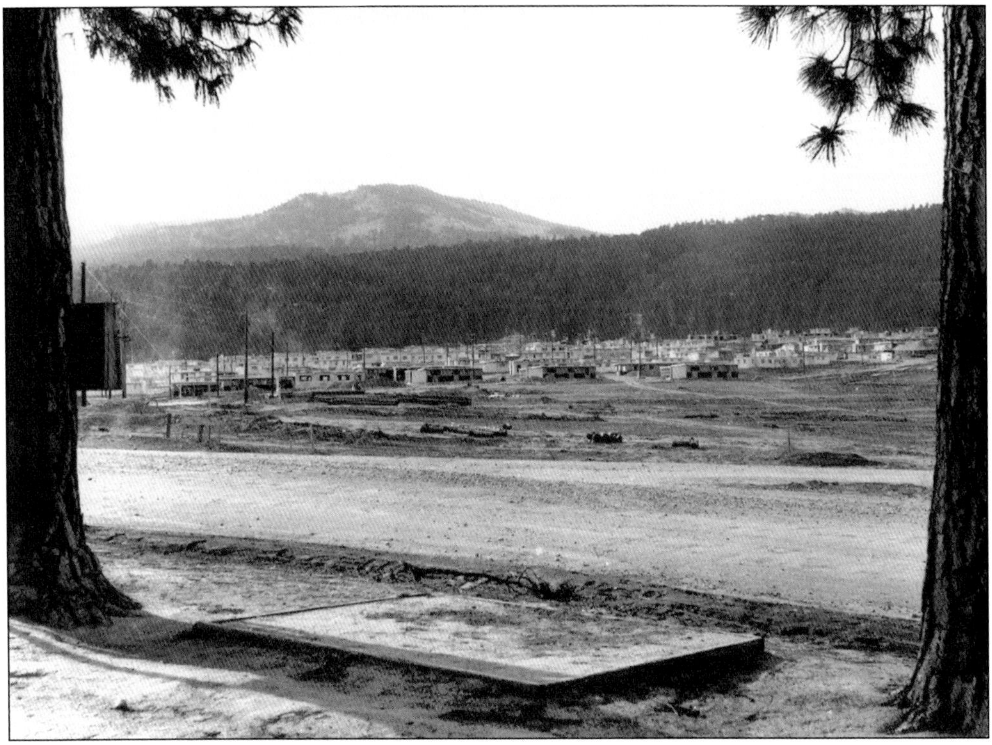

Homes that were once a dream were now a reality in Western Area. The little square sandbox in the foreground was once the spot where golfers teed off for their golf game. There would be no more golf at this location because development and progress were on their way.

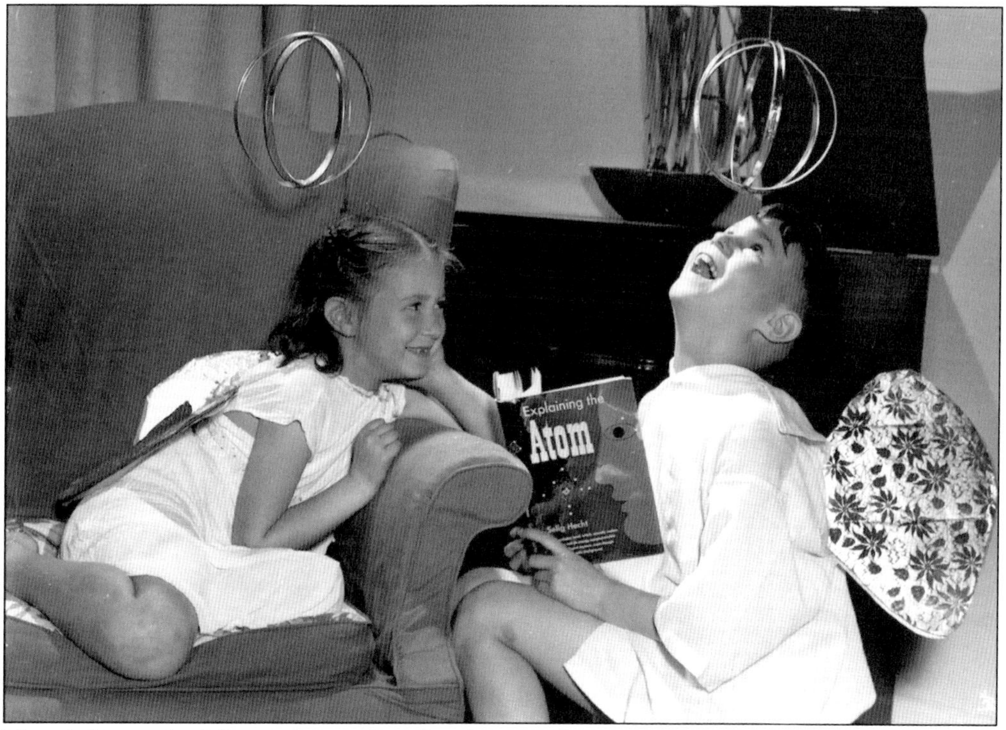

The children playfully used an embroidery hoop collection to create their own model of the atom. These photos were taken as family portraits and even for these youngsters, life was never to be the same. Classroom science classes would now include a lesson on the smashing of the atom. Oh, how simple it seems when one looks at the title of the book: *Explaining the Atom.*

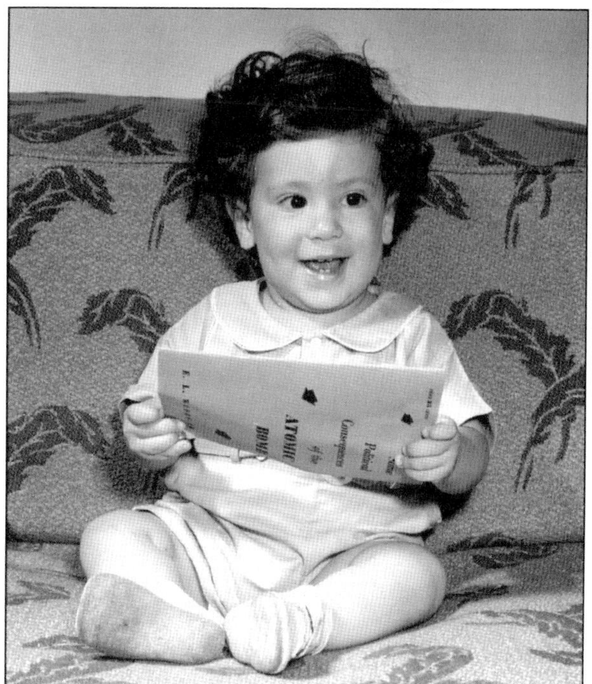

A little child sits for his portrait. Settled quietly on the couch, he holds in his little fingers a booklet that found its way to Los Alamos, where the Atomic Age had opened. The book's title—*Some Political Consequences of the Atomic Bomb*. It was a copy of a lecture that had been delivered in November of 1945 by Professor E.L. Woodward of Oxford University. Words of fear and pessimism about the discovery of the atomic bomb filled the pages. The child still smiled as the picture was taken.

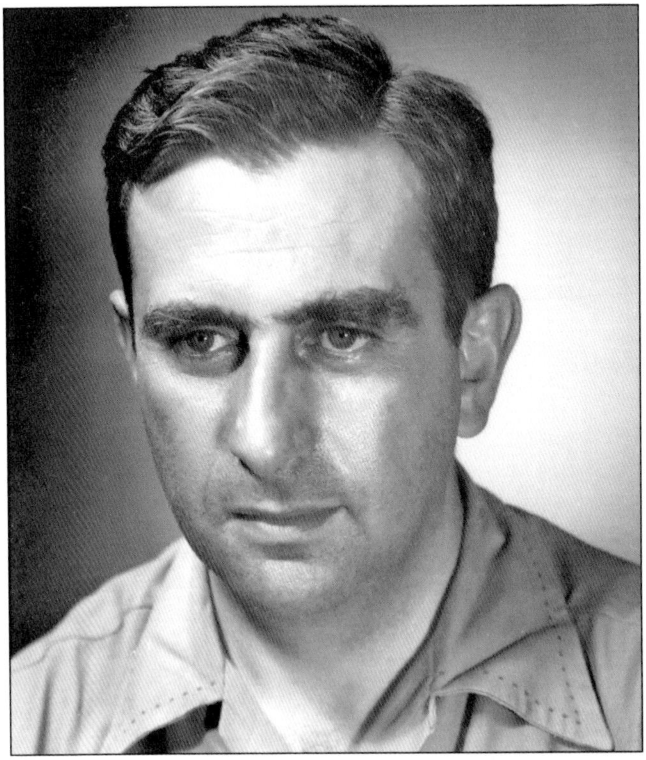

Edward Teller brought his piano and washing machine with him to Los Alamos. He was known to play his piano late into the night and arrive late for work in the Tech Area. Teller was a leading proponent of the hydrogen bomb and in this he disagreed with Robert Oppenheimer, who called it "the plague of Thebes." Teller continued his work on the H-bomb in Los Alamos but then joined a second weapons lab in Livermore, California, in 1952. Subsequently, the first H-bomb test occurred at Eniwetok (an atoll in the Marshall Islands) in November 1952.

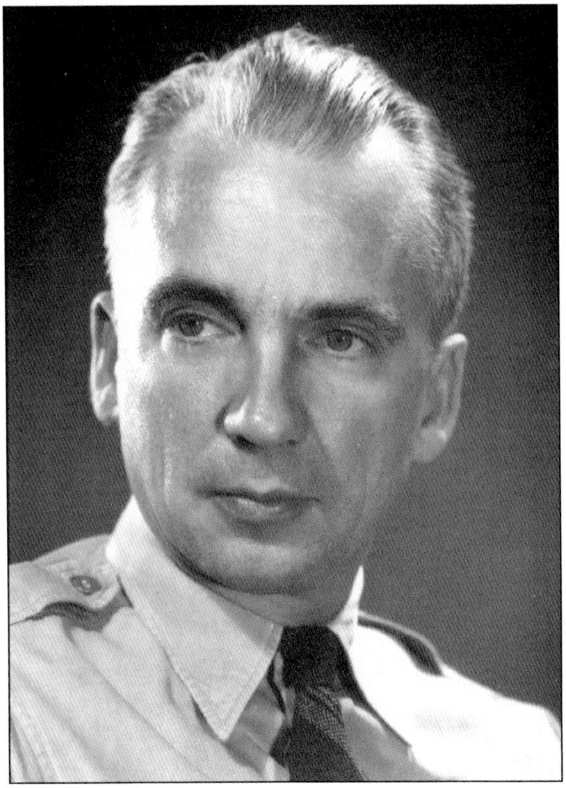

Norris Bradbury was appointed as the director of the Los Alamos Scientific Laboratory late in 1945 when Robert Oppenheimer stepped down. Bradbury arrived in Los Alamos as a naval officer after a career as professor of physics at MIT, Stanford, and the University of California. In the aftermath of war, the Los Alamos Lab struggled with its identity and vision, but under Bradbury's skillful leadership, its direction was expanded to include peacetime applications of nuclear energy. He remained as director until 1970.

P. O. BOX 1663
SANTA FE, NEW MEXICO

October 1, 1945

T/4 John J. Michnovicz

Dear Mr. Michnovicz:

This letter is to acknowledge your contribution to the development of the atomic bomb.

The striking success of this project was only made possible by the work and sacrifices of the military members. According to your group leader, you are to be commended for eleven months spent in the project photographic service engaged there as a photographic technician, and as such performing work which was essential to the development of the atomic bomb.

You and your colleagues have consistently turned out high quality work, and throughout the long period of high pressure effort you have cheerfully cooperated in meeting the most urgent demands of the project.

Very truly yours,

J. Robert Oppenheimer, Director

Robert Oppenheimer sent this letter to John Michnovicz as a commendation for the photographic work done during the Manhattan Project. Thank you for a job well done!

Bibliography

Barkham, Barbara and Peter Sinclaire. *From Santa Fe to O'keefe Country*. Santa Fe: Ocean Tree Books, 1996.

Brode, Bernice. *Tales of Los Alamos: Life on the Mesa 1943–1945*. Los Alamos: Los Alamos Historical Society, 1997.

Church, Fermor S. and Peggy P. Church. *When Los Alamos Was a Ranch School*. Los Alamos: Los Alamos Historical Society, 1998.

Evans, Jacob and Fern Lyon, eds. *Los Alamos: The First Forty Years*. Los Alamos: Los Alamos Historical Society, 1984.

Fermi, Rachel and Esther Samra. *Picturing the Bomb: Photographs from the Secret World of the Manhattan Project*. New York: Harry N. Abrams, 1995.

Ferris, Timothy, ed. *The World Treasury of Physics, Astronomy, and Mathematics*. New York: Little, Brown and Co., 1991.

Hoard, Dorothy. *A Guide to Bandelier National Monument*. 3rd ed. Los Alamos: Los Alamos Historical Society, 1989.

Jette, Eleanor. *Inside Box 1663*. Los Alamos: Los Alamos Historical Society, 1977.

Kirby, Deanna Morgan. *Just Crazy to Ski: A Fifty-Year History of Skiing at Los Alamos*. Los Alamos, New Mexico: Los Alamos Historical Society, 2003.

Los Alamos Times, 22 March 1946–29 August 1947.

Martin, Craig. *Quads, Shoeboxes and Sunken Living Rooms: A History of Los Alamos Housing*. Los Alamos: Los Alamos Historical Society, 2000.

Rhodes, Richard. *The Making of the Atomic Bomb*. New York: Simon & Schuster, 1986.

Roensch, Eleanor S. *Life Within Limits*. Los Alamos: Los Alamos Historical Society, 1993.

Serber, Charlotte and Jane S. Wilson, eds. *Standing By and Making Do: Women of Wartime Los Alamos*. Los Alamos: Los Alamos Historical Society, 1997.

Smith, Alice K. and Charles Weiner, eds. *Robert Oppenheimer: Letters and Recollections*. Cambridge, MA: Harvard University Press, 1980.

Thayer, Kasha V. and Edith C. Truslow. *Manhattan District History: Nonscientific Aspects of Los Alamos Project Y 1942 through 1946*. Los Alamos: Los Alamos Historical Society, 1997.

Woodward, E.L. *Some Political Consequences of the Atomic Bomb*. London: Oxford University Press, 1945.